Social Skills, Emotional Growth

and Drama Therapy

Lee R. Chasen

Social Skills, Emotional Growth and Drama Therapy

Inspiring Connection on the Autism Spectrum

Foreword by Robert J. Landy, Ph.D., RDT-BCT, LCAT

Jessica Kingsley *Publishers*
London and Philadelphia

First published in 2011
by Jessica Kingsley Publishers
116 Pentonville Road
London N1 9JB, UK
and
400 Market Street, Suite 400
Philadelphia, PA 19106, USA

www.jkp.com

Library of Congress Cataloging in Publication Data
Chasen, Lee R.
  Social skills, emotional growth, and drama therapy : inspiring connection on
the autism spectrum / Lee R. Chasen ; foreword by Robert J. Landy.
      p. ; cm.
  Includes bibliographical references and index.
  ISBN 978-1-84905-840-7 (alk. paper)
  1. Autistic children--Rehabilitation. 2. Autism spectrum disorders--Patients--Rehabilitation.
3. Drama--Therapeutic use. 4. Social skills in children. 5. Child psychotherapy. I. Title.
  [DNLM: 1. Child Development Disorders, Pervasive--therapy.
2. Psychodrama--methods. 3. Socialization. WS 350.6]

  RJ506.A9C437 2011
  618.92'891523--dc22

                           2010039524

British Library Cataloguing in Publication Data
A CIP catalogue record for this book is available from the British Library

ISBN 978 1 84905 840 7

Printed and bound in the United States

For Marianne,
who persisted for years that we create a
social-skills group to meet the specific
needs of high-functioning autistic children,
and my four peer model ambassadors to
the world, Emma, Lili, Sage and Mary.

Acknowledgements

I want to thank all of the parents, relentless in seeking support and acceptance for their children, who bring their families to our center. We are honored to perform this service for your shiny happy people.

I have such gratitude for Kid Esteem group leaders Doreen Montefusco, Jenny Shore, Krista Granieri and Stefanie Schaller. I love playing with you! I so appreciate all of our interns and volunteers, Theresa Henderson, Christine Sofia, Samantha Brennan, Rachel Calloway, Elizabeth Edwards, Maggie Robbins, Jennifer Richards, Nicole Hudson, Brian Hicks, Mary Chasen and Lili Chasen, who helped with co-leadership, notes and observations during the writing of this book. Thank you to Rachel Menzies and Helen Ibbotson of Jessica Kingsley Publishers for being so gracious and supportive of this project. I send a great big thank you to Robert J. Landy for 30 years of guidance and support!

I offer deep and heartfelt gratitude to my friends and family, mother, father, sister, aunts, uncles, nieces, nephews, cousins, mother-in-law, brothers and sisters-in-law. Finally, to my soul mate co-creator, Marianne, and our four children, thanks for reflecting back my dreams with such light and love!

Contents

Foreword: Mirrors and Bridges   11

Introduction: Mirror, Mirror on the Wall   17

Part I—Behind the Scenes: Theoretical Constructs   25

1. Dramatic Encounters   27
   Matthew   27
   Jason   29
   Kenny   33
   James   35
   David   38
   Janet   39

2. Engaging the Pervasive Developmental Disorders   43
   The diagnoses   43
   Possible causes   44
   Treatment approaches   45
   Developmental considerations   49
   Positive intervention   53
   Back through the looking glass   57

3. Drama: Mirroring the Neurological Soul   63
   Reflection for the ages   63
   Drama is therapy   66
   Process Reflective Enactment   70
   Theatre, drama and PDD children   97

Part II—Center Stage: Theory in Action 103

4. Constructing a Drama-Therapy Approach to
   Social Skills   105
   Space and materials   105
   Roles of leadership   108
   Group protocols and interventions   110
   Process-oriented social skills: Three layers of engagement 115
   Revisiting Aristotle   123

5. Recognition: Establishing Roles   127
   Orientation   127
   Session 1: Naming Names   132
   Session 2: Greeting Others/Saying Hello   138
   Session 3: Listening and Responding to Greetings   142

6. Unity: Building Ensemble   147
   Session 4: Finding Myself   147
   Session 5: Noticing Others   152

7. Character: Reflecting Goodness and
   Appropriateness   157
   Session 6: Sharing My World   157
   Session 7: Finding Matches   161

8. Plot: Organizing Events   167
   Session 8: Working and Playing Together   167
   Session 9: Lights! Camera! Action! Putting It All Together 170
   Session 10: Movie Day   174

9. Diction and Reasoning: Social Scripting,
   Facial Cues and Body Language   177
   Session 11: Reunion and Reconnection   177
   Session 12: Interpreting and Responding to Nonverbal Cues 182
   Session 13: On the Right Track—Building Conversation   187

10. Complication and Resolution: Interactive
    Language Skills   193
    Session 14: The Right Words in the Right Place at
    the Right Time   193
    Session 15: Stay to Play or Walk Away?   197
    Sessions 16 and 17: Director's Chair—Asserting
    Social Language and Solving Problems   202

11. Comedy and Plot: Broadening Perspectives and
    Constructing Solutions   213
    Session 18: What's So Funny?   213
    Session 19: Lights! Camera! Action! Putting It All
    Together Again   216
    Session 20: Movie Day, The Sequel   219

12. Actions and Life: Simulating Events   223
    Session 21: My Story   223
    Session 22: How to Be a Real Winner   228
    Session 23: Calling All Friends!   233
    Session 24: Out to Lunch   237
    Session 25: Roll with It   240

13. Reversal: Individualized Scripting   245
    Sessions 26–28: Power Videos   245

14. Episodic Outline: Tools for Reflection
    and Celebration   253
    Session 29: Yearbooks   253
    Session 30: Sharing Memories   256

15. Reflections: I See You   259

    References   265

    Subject Index   269

    Author Index   272

Foreword: Mirrors and Bridges

By Robert J. Landy, Ph.D., RDT-BCT, LCAT

I first began working with young people with emotional, developmental and physical disabilities in 1967. I was hired as a teacher of English in a private special-education school, grades K-12. I was ill-prepared, as a graduate-school dropout in English literature and an aspiring actor. My only psychological preparation was an undergraduate course in Introduction to Psychology, where I learned about behaviorism—all the rage in the early 1960s. In fact, B.F. Skinner appeared in class one day as a guest lecturer. I was very impressed and eager to read him, but it was 1963 and his major work was yet to be published, and so I settled on reading his novel, Walden Two. The utopian book about a world engineered on behavioral principles turned out to be a more satisfying experience than reading his later works on operant conditioning. After all, I was a student of arts and humanities, not science.

In 1967, special education as a field was growing up. New legislation was passed under John F. Kennedy's leadership, especially in the area of mental retardation. Learning disabilities were added as a category deserving special education, and families of young people with special needs raised their voices to demand more services. This was a time of profound change in the United States, when so many marginalized, oppressed and neglected groups of citizens stood up for attention and representation.

The mid '60s was also a time of experimentation in the arts, in science, and in the cultural lives of young people and ordinary citizens. With no background in special education, I was hired at 22 years old to teach special-needs young people. My training included an undergraduate degree in English, one year of graduate school, numerous acting classes and a few scattered lectures, the week before my first classes began, on neurological impairments and emotional disturbances.

As I soon discovered, some of my students were as old as I, with less formal education but more street knowledge. The highest functioning students were openly experimenting with the drugs and alternative lifestyles that were so attractive to many of my generation. I often had to consciously remind myself that I was a professional whose job was to contain the excesses of my students. The lower functioning, however, included a dizzying mix of disturbances and disabilities. In my early days as a teacher, many students of mixed levels of disability and ability were placed in the same classrooms. As told to me the week before my first day in the classroom, some were brain damaged, others had cerebral palsy and related forms of physical disability, and still others had unspecified forms of mental illness. I was unaware of the existence of the *Diagnostic and Statistical Manual of Mental Disorders* (DSM), which was first published in 1952 with a listing of 66 disorders. The second, expanded edition was not due out until 1968 with a listing of just over 100 disorders. By then, in my third year of teaching, I was slightly less ignorant, as I enrolled in a Master's degree program in special education.

When I began teaching, I was unaware of the term "autism." For me and many of my colleagues, some of our students were simply odd—noted by hand-flapping, reciting obscure dates and numerals, isolating themselves from their peers and teachers, speaking in gibberish or non-sequiturs. Only when I began my special-education studies did I realize that some of the most difficult, baffling and fascinating students were autistic to varying degrees.

In the 1960s, I learned that autism was caused by psychogenic factors such as having distant mothers, who at the time were called "refrigerator mothers." Further, the psychotherapeutic treatment of choice at the time was psychoanalysis. This approach was promulgated by Bruno Bettleheim, whose book, *The Empty Fortress* (1972), presented a chilling image of autism as a form of childhood schizophrenia caused by brutal family dynamics, somewhat akin to the treatment of concentration-camp victims in Nazi Germany.

In fact, Bettleheim, in his book *Surviving and Other Essays* (1981), refers to Paul Celan's poem, *Todesfuge* (Death Fugue). In the poem, Celan presents the metaphor of black milk to represent the distortion of nurturance which existed in the extermination camps.

Bettleheim's interpretation of these lines is even more shocking than Celan's metaphor of the Nazi death camps:

> When one is forced to drink black milk from dawn to dusk, whether in the death camps of Nazi Germany or while lying in a possibly luxurious crib, but there subjected to the unconscious death wishes of what overtly may be a conscientious mother—in either situation a living soul has death for a master. (1981, pp.110–111)

Thirty years later, Bettleheim's research on autism has been firmly discredited. Those he claimed to have successfully treated were not autistic at all. We now know that autism is not a single condition but exists on a spectrum. We know that it is not caused by psychogenetic factors but by a combination of neurobiological and environmental conditions. And we now know that treatment is most responsive to behavioral approaches and that outcome studies focus primarily on measuring the effects of these forms of treatment.

However, the condition known as Autism Spectrum Disorder (ASD) remains somewhat baffling in its etiology, complexity of manifestations and treatment strategies. As such, the condition raises old issues about effective treatments for ASD and related developmental disorders. The issues arise especially with the latest research in neuroscience, which has revealed the brain to be even more complex than was ever imagined in the 1960s and even 1980s.

In research by Damasio, for example, we learn that the mind and body are linked in unexpected neurological ways, and that treatment for various neurological disorders requires not only cognitive approaches but also approaches through the body and the emotions. We learn from Damasio that Descartes might have been wrong in suggesting that the mind and the body are separate, an idea that has typified the training of physicians and the delivery of medical services for hundreds of years.

And from Gallese and his colleagues who discovered and researched the phenomenon of mirror neurons, we learn that there is a profound connection between moments of observation and moments of action. We learn that vicarious experience, typified in the theatrical experience of audience members and ordinary observers, has a deep effect on the development of cognition and emotional intelligence.

With these new discoveries as a backdrop, we come to Lee Chasen's exciting new book about teaching social skills to children on the autism spectrum. Chasen is a drama educator and drama therapist whose methods are creative and playful. As such, he and his partner, Marianne Franzese, founders of Kid Esteem, have devoted their professional careers to demonstrating how children on the autism spectrum respond and change through play and drama. Chasen's approach challenges the primacy of cognitive-behavioral therapies. He does so not by denying the gains of those who painstakingly work through applied behavioral analysis and related forms of treatment, but by laying out his own unique methodology and grounding it firmly within a process orientation that is in itself fully grounded in neuroscience.

This book is an exhilarating journey as we get to know several of Chasen's young clients and see precisely how their social skills deepen through their immersion in this unique approach. The common wisdom among scholars and practitioners in the field of developmental disabilities is that autism is characterized by an impairment of the mirror-neuron system. This view implies that children on the spectrum are unable to link observation and action. It also implies that autistic children are not able to comprehend a dramatic experience in which an actor plays a fictional role and a viewer vicariously participates with the dilemma of a protagonist. Given this state of affairs, such children would be unaffected by play and drama—which, by nature, concerns an ability to negotiate the dual realities of the imagination and everyday life, of reality and representation.

And yet, in each chapter, Chasen refutes this common wisdom with his own uncommon practice. Using the image of the mirror throughout, Chasen makes the case that all children are capable of learning social skills through acts of play, wherein the world of the imagination mirrors the world of reality. Like other children, these special children are capable of observing and acting based upon their observations. I began reading Chasen's book with the question of how best to foster this mirror integration. I ended it with an answer: through a creative methodology and imagery that is deeply about facilitating integrations—mirrors, doubles, mirror neurons.

All children, even the most autistic, have the capacity to build bridges that link polarities in their nervous systems and in their social systems. Because of their neurological challenges, autistic children have a very hard time doing so. Lee Chasen, teacher and drama therapist, does not offer a quick fix or promise a transformation of a deeply troubling condition. But he does offer an alternative to Bettleheim's misguided, cynical efforts, as well as to the effective and promising efforts of scores of applied behavioral analysts who have brought new hope to many families of autistic children. The alternative is a playful one that relies on the exercise of the imagination as a way to regenerate neurological pathways.

Chasen writes in his Introduction about his discovery of his workspace in an old dilapidated basement, lined wall to wall with mirrors. As I conclude this Foreword, I end with the image of the bridge across an expansive space, as I see Chasen as one who is able to hold and support many polarities. As a guide for autistic children, he is able to help them negotiate the difficult antipodes of self and other, of thought and feeling, of seeing and doing, of the mirror and its double, the natural, social world. The bridges that Chasen, Franzese and all their colleagues and students in drama therapy build are hopeful ones that stretch inward to the wiring of the brain and outward to people whose symbolic actions have meaning that invites response.

Introduction: Mirror, Mirror on the Wall

Upon incorporating Kid Esteem, the emotional-intelligence and social-learning center for children and families we founded in 1997, my wife Marianne and I began our search for a space that could embrace and contain the different groups and programs we had been creating and experimenting with. After an initial stint in a cavernous cement church cellar, and then crammed into two small rooms shared with a psychologist friend, we were relieved and delighted to find a suite of rooms, then used for storage, that had once housed a now-defunct beauty school in the basement of a building one block away from our home.

As the landlord escorted us through our initial encounter with the space, he assured us that the junk piled in the rooms would be cleared out, and the lime green wallpaper with hot pink swirlies left over from the school's heyday in the '60s and '70s would be painted over. When we entered what would eventually become our primary group room, he explained how he would remove the catwalk, a seven-by-twenty-foot (two-by-six-meter) raised stage running the length of the room that the models-in-training had used to practice runway walking, along with the floor-to-ceiling mirror covering an adjacent wall. Discreetly ogling the large costume closet that was also in the room, I coolly explained that he wouldn't need to remove those items, as they would be useful in our work, which I vaguely described as counseling for children and families. He shrugged his shoulders and the deal was made.

Being young drama therapists anxiously embarking on a new untried venture with four young children, a mortgage and no safety net, we were ecstatic at the luck, or synchronicity, of finding an affordable place with potential to provide such a "furnished" home for our vision. Not that there weren't any problems with the space… It was essentially a 2000-square-foot basement in an old building. The air was musty and damp. Fuse boxes constantly needed resetting. And while Marianne mused that our work of guiding children toward a sense of internal beauty and personal strength would eventually purify the rooms of the otherwise stale, remnant energy of glamour, vanity and all the accompanying heaviness and abuse of the superficial world of beauty-school training, the process was a bit messy. After one especially rainy season flooded our space, my assistant Doreen and I laughed until we cried from fantasies of vengeful, make-up smeared zombie models emerging from the buckling floorboards, a la *Poltergeist*, as we saved the puppets from the rising waters, hoisting them to higher ground.

Doreen and I fixed the floor as best we could and carried on with our mission to empower the emotional and social vitality of children and families in a culture seemingly structured to achieve the opposite. As our program grew, with offerings like *The Kid Power Hour, Making Friends* and *If You're Angry and You Know It…*, we noticed more and more children with symptoms associated with Pervasive Developmental Disorder (PDD), particularly high-functioning autism, Asperger's Syndrome and Pervasive Developmental Disorder Not Otherwise Specified (PDD-NOS), attending our groups. These were, for the most part, children from regular classroom settings, many of them undiagnosed due to their verbal skills and cognitive ability to function successfully in a typical classroom. But the telltale and often subtle signs of social isolation, difficulty with interaction, repetitive patterns of behavior and communication, and an unusual, quirky or eccentric obsession with certain mechanical or science-related interests, told us that there was more to the story than their frustrated teachers and parents were aware of.

The children we assumed to be affected by ASD did fairly well in these groups meant for neurotypical children—certainly better than in most other social and structured settings, according to their parents— but it was often difficult to keep them engaged. Probably the biggest contributor to this difficulty was the floor-to-ceiling mirror I was so excited to have. Once the ASD children entered the space, it was nearly impossible to pull them away from that mirror. It was a novelty for everyone at first, but while the neurotypical children easily made the transition into the other spaces and activities of the program, the ASD children did not.

It was really something to see: the small bunch of kids in the group who were apparently ASD, ranging in effect from flat to overly animated (either way behaving in a generally disconnected manner), suddenly become perfectly contained, making eye contact (with themselves), faces lit up and highly engaged with beaming smiles when facing the mirror. They studied their reflections intently as they tried out different facial expressions. They delighted in following the movements of their hands. They were riveted by their own body images staring back at them.

I tried different ways to cover the mirror when we weren't using it—curtains, butcher-block paper, bed sheets—so the children would focus on other aspects of the program, but they always managed to find a small window, a sliver of reflection through which they could resume the task of finding themselves. As I watched their heightened engagement with their own reflections, it occurred to me that alongside their difficulty with perceiving, connecting with and modeling the social behavior of others, maybe they had a hard time perceiving, connecting with and modeling pragmatic images of an interactive self as well. While it was often difficult to deal with what was, in that context, a distraction, this mirror provided these children with something, apparently something essential, and we often joked that preoccupation with the mirror served as an informal diagnostic tool for determining which children in the program were likely to be on the autism spectrum.

I thought about my own ongoing meta-awareness of how I see and present my self, my persona, to the world, based on the role I am functioning in at any given moment in my life. Even now, sitting here at the computer completely immersed in this writing, I'm aware of how I lean forward in my chair as I type excitedly with my two index fingers, eager to share this information. It's as if a surveillance camera in the back of my head constantly monitors my actions and provides me with a steady stream of information on how I move through and respond to the world, a sort of third-person perspective of self. Sometimes I become overly caught up in it and sometimes I don't think about it at all, but I know its always running, continuously juxtaposing my sense of self and other in each act of being, providing me with images and context to refer back to as I adjust to circumstances around me.

It occurred to us that these children were perhaps lacking this surveillance equipment—or that maybe the equipment exists but the wires are a little mixed up or not optimally connected, causing static on channels programmed for smooth reception of images associated with meaningful, pragmatic self-reflection, inadvertently keeping a vision of self from coming through clearly and consistently. The mirror seemed to provide the ASD children with an alternative network, another source through which they were able to access and explore an intact, pragmatic sense of self that was otherwise unavailable to them.

As this dynamic became clearer to us, we felt increasingly conflicted about steering the ASD children away from the mirror, which was perhaps what they needed the most, in order to support their mainstream participation in our neurotypical programs. It was a frustrating dilemma and I could see how teachers in their typical classrooms, as well as their parents, were frustrated and angry with these children. It became apparent though that many of the co-morbid difficulties these children were having at school and at home, such as opposition, avoidance and disruptive behavior, were instigated and amplified as a result of not receiving the proper understanding, structure, opportunity and guidance that their conditions called for. This dilemma inspired us to develop a social-skills program geared specifically for children on the autism spectrum who were essentially caught in an unintended trap: high-functioning enough to participate in typical settings, but floundering socially (and often academically) because those settings were not structured to meet their pragmatic needs.

As we brainstormed for what would eventually become the *Systematic Social Skills* program for high-functioning children on the autism spectrum, encounters with the mirror served as one of our guiding principles. We sought to create tools and experiences that would provide participants with concrete prompts and feedback for developing skills and processes associated with self-awareness, self-modeling and social interaction.

Along with helping participants define, develop, focus on and successfully play a role of "self as social being" through the drama therapy techniques, it made sense to us that the activities of the program incorporate a pragmatic structure, reflective of what normally happens in a successful social encounter: people meet and greet each other, they exchange names and share ideas, they notice things about each other, they make inquiries to initiate and maintain contact, they purposefully communicate emotion and affect, they express and perceive relevant information through language, they find common interests, they play and interact with each other, they deal with problems that occur in the encounter, and eventually they bid farewell. We outlined our approach to follow this pragmatic model.

Finally, we felt very strongly about establishing the element of fun as a cornerstone of our program. Children are more likely to connect with an activity and its participants if it's fun. The joyous, exhilarating, intriguing and liberating feeling of fun prompts a desire to engage in and sustain play, the foundation of human development, beckoning us to explore and interact with objects and concepts that project, reflect and expand the essence of who we are. Socialization, especially from a child's perspective, makes a more positive impact if the encounter is fun and playful. We noticed, in spite of their disconnected behavior and lack of interaction, that the ASD children in our program were certainly capable of experiencing fun and demonstrating typically joyful and playful affects, although this usually occurred in isolation from others and was often buried under layers of idiosyncratic and stereotypical modes of expression.

Moreover, we saw how otherwise well-intentioned teachers with exclusively behavioral orientations all too often thwarted the joyful play of ASD children in other settings, citing their somewhat atypical modes of expression as inappropriate. Behavioral considerations certainly have their place in educating and socializing ASD children, but, after observing social skills and behavior management programs in public-school settings and talking to teachers who run them, it does seem as though many behavioral interventions end up squashing joyful expression and censoring critical operations related to play and development. For these and a myriad of other neurological, behavioral, environmental and emotional reasons, it's often difficult for the ASD child to maintain a sense of joy and playfulness while attempting to function within a neurotypical group process.

We set out to create a program that could access and sustain joyous expression as a means for integrating self-awareness, self-modeling, pragmatic skills of socialization and interactive play experiences. Through the tools and techniques of drama therapy, we sought to harness the universal penchant for fun and bring it to a shared stage where individual experiences are mirrored and perceived within the ensemble, where it was hoped to jumpstart an inherent yet dormant desire to connect and interact socially.

Fast-forward to the summer of 2009. The six-week summer session of *Systematic Social Skills* is usually reserved for children who have completed the 30-week clinical program between September and June. It's comprised of recreational activities like talent shows, game days and team-building events for the children to apply the skills they learned from their participation during the year. Following our pragmatic model, we felt that by allowing a child to begin in the summer, their ability to acclimate and connect would be that much more difficult. The summer's activities do not walk through the specific skill sets of meeting and greeting, exchanging names, sharing ideas and all the other steps toward building connection that are facilitated during the year. A new group member starting in the summer would basically be dropped into the interactive play phase of the program without any much-needed context or skill building, potentially setting him or her up for failure.

In spite of these concerns, we recently began making exceptions and allowing children to start in the summer due to growing interest and logistical necessity. Billy was one of those exceptions. As the summer session wore on, I began to feel as though my initial misgivings about making these exceptions were well founded. Eight-year-old Billy seemed to be lost in a dynamic that had become, during the year, relatively cohesive. The rest of the group knew our routines and protocols; they had a reasonably attuned sense of each other and their own place in the group. Billy, however, was non-responsive and disconnected. He made no eye contact and spoke, when he did speak, in difficult-to-understand non-sequiturs and utterances that had no meaningful connection to anything that was going on. Purposeful participation was non-existent. Other children became irritated with his invasive, dissociative behaviors. I felt sure that this was going to be a case where his parents would deem the experience unsuccessful and he would not continue when the fall session began.

Billy did continue in the fall, though, and we have since adjusted the summer program to incorporate some of the skills facilitated in earlier activities. As Billy's participation in the activities of the fall session progressed, he provided me, in this era of rigid, evidence-based research that allegedly determines a program's scientific value, with one of the most satisfying examples of what I'll call circumstantial evidence of our program's effectiveness. He found me in the hallway on the way to group one day toward the end of the fall session. He approached me, took both my hands in his, looked straight into my eyes and with a broad, engaged smile, said, "I'm so proud of you, Dr. Lee!" The language, although choppy, stilted and idiosyncratic, was bursting with enthusiasm.

I chuckled at his exuberance and, thinking he meant to communicate that he was proud of himself, sought to prompt clarification of the possible pronoun/subject switch common with autistic children. I asked, "You're so proud of *me*, Billy? Why are you so proud of Dr. Lee?" He held my hands and his gaze, and without missing a beat, emphatically exclaimed, "Because I'm so happy!" I don't know if Billy was mixing up words and was sharing that he was proud of himself for something that had occurred earlier; maybe he was reiterating something his parents had said or echoing something he saw on television. Maybe he really was proud of me for providing him with the space and opportunity to be happy. What I do know is that his desire and excitement to reach out, connect and share something positive, was authentic and meaningful. The freedom of expression and opportunity for cognitive organization prompted by drama therapy sparks a liberation of the same joyful soul that exists in all children, autistic as well as neurotypical.

This book celebrates the individuality of children diagnosed on the autism spectrum and their potential for social connection through drama therapy. Part I begins with a narrative chapter depicting scenarios of ASD children encountering some of the tools and techniques of drama therapy that we employ and the impact it has on their ability to connect with others. Chapter 2 looks at the clinical conditions, possible causes and various treatments of PDD with an emphasis on recent neurological research. A theoretical orientation of the field of drama therapy is explored in Chapter 3, along with a discussion of concepts, techniques and developmental considerations pertinent to the treatment of children with PDD. Chapter 4 in Part II explores the logistics of developing a program, including space, materials and related concepts, and suggests a model for a more process-oriented approach to facilitating social skills. Chapters 5 through 14 describe the program in detail and offer specific protocols for implementing the program for children ages 5–11 in other settings and agencies, providing a new lens through which the typically joyous affect of ASD children may be seen and celebrated as part of a comprehensive clinical strategy. Chapter 15 offers some concluding thoughts.

Part I—Behind the Scenes: Theoretical Constructs

Chapter 1

Dramatic Encounters

Matthew

Matthew receives a kiss from his mother and steps tentatively into the group playroom. At six years old, his face portrays a combination of suspicion and confusion as he looks around, taking in everything or nothing in particular. He cautiously walks the perimeter of the room with an uneven gait. As we greet and address him, he responds with words and fragments of sentences that are at first inaudible and ultimately unintelligible. He stands at a distance from the ten other five- and six-year-old boys who are busying themselves with the play objects in the room. Some of the boys play with each other; some play alone with the objects; others are content to amuse and lose themselves, for the moment, in their own thoughts. Matthew, it seems, does not know what to make of this scene. Matthew is one of the many children, a large majority of them boys, recently diagnosed with some form of autism.

Specifically, Matthew's diagnosis is PDD-NOS. While Matthew displays many of the characteristics that would warrant a diagnosis of Autistic Disorder, which is also in the PDD category, he does not meet some of the symptomatic criteria listed in the *Diagnostic and Statistical Manual of Mental Disorders* (4th edition), or *DSM-IV-TR* (American Psychiatric Association 2000).

Matthew's social interaction is impaired in the same way that a child with Autistic Disorder is. He makes little eye contact. His facial expressions, body posture and gestures are somewhat rigid, awkward and difficult to understand. He appears to have very little if any spontaneity with regard to sharing interests and enjoyments that eventually lead to the development of peer relationships. He has tremendous difficulty reciprocating any type of social or emotional communication. His spoken language is delayed and, initially, he demonstrates no interest in make-believe or interactive play.

While Matthew meets these criteria for Autistic Disorder, he shows no signs of the behavioral symptoms listed in the final category, according to the *DSM-IV-TR*. Matthew does not appear to be intensely preoccupied with repetitive or stereotypical patterns of restricted behavior related to a particular interest or focus. He shows no adherence to specific, nonfunctional routines or rituals. He has no motor mannerisms or tics, such as hand or finger flapping, or body movements such as repetitive twisting. Matthew does not display any persistent preoccupation with parts of objects. Barring any of these symptoms, Matthew's diagnosis is relegated to PDD-NOS.

During the first few sessions of our weekly Saturday morning social and emotional skills development program for children diagnosed on the autism spectrum, Matthew is compliant and cooperative. He parallel plays quietly and uneventfully with the various objects and does not initiate interaction with the other children. He responds to the demands of basic group protocol, follows procedures, manages transitions, helps clean up toys and sits in our meeting place when we begin structured activities and discussion time. Yet he is quiet and almost non-responsive with regard to expressive language, and he barely involves himself in the general flow of group process. He participates in the activities in a mechanical manner with rigid body posture, flat affect and, except for what is required by the activity, minimal interaction with the other children and staff.

One morning, though, Matthew wanders over to the baskets of costumes. After shuffling through the various pieces, he takes hold of two cheerleader pompoms and begins shaking them in front of his body, looking at them quizzically. After a few minutes, he raises the pompoms up above his head, stretches out his arms and shakes them in a rhythmic motion that is soon accompanied by bold strides around the room and a broadening smile across his face. As we encourage him, he walks up to some of the other children, smiling with excitement at this activity he has created. Some of them smile back. Some of them join him. Soon, Matthew adds a loud and relatively clear "Rah-rah!" and "Go, team, go!" to his routine.

As the sessions progress, Matthew spontaneously experiments with other costumes—a cape, a clown nose, mouse ears—always positioning himself in relation to another child after his wardrobe is complete. He applies language to this self-initiated activity, standing in front of his audience with his broad smile, as if to say, "See me, so we can share and enjoy together what I have created!" This significantly more animated and connected affect acquired through his encounters with the costumes soon finds its way into his participation in the activities of the program, prompting him to be generally more responsive, humorous and interactive with the other children and staff. Matthew's experience with the costumes allows us to see and cultivate a different and perhaps newly activated neurobehavioral pattern related to these otherwise pervasive developmental delays.

Jason

Five-year-old Jason, a strikingly handsome boy from the same group, with dark curly hair and big brown eyes, walks into the room with a vacant stare and no visible or audible acknowledgement of any of the people or objects that greet him as he enters the space. His father, with a resigned smile, waves after him and calls, "Bye, Jason... Have fun..." in a manner that expresses sincerity and resignation, at the same time knowing that he will get no response from his son and wondering if his words of encouragement register at all in Jason's world. After standing a few feet from the entrance for a couple of minutes, Jason eventually finds some nearby crayons and settles on a spot on the floor. He begins lining up the crayons in patterns known only to him and continues this activity for the duration of the initial ten-minute open-play period of the session.

Occasionally, he utters what sounds like gibberish syllables in quiet, high-pitch tones. At the same time, he grasps his hands together, bends back and wiggles his fingers in ritualistic fashion while stretching his arms over his shoulder. He does not acknowledge the staff members who sit next to him on the floor and start playing with the unused crayons in attempts to interact with him. His mother claims he has Asperger's Syndrome, a significantly higher functioning form of PDD also listed in the *DSM-IV-TR* that will be discussed later. Jason's teenage brother has Asperger's Syndrome, and his father, who brings him to the program on Saturdays, feels that Jason's symptoms go beyond Asperger's. It is clear that Jason has Autistic Disorder.

Jason's eye contact at this point is non-existent. While Matthew's furrowed brow and suspicious facial expressions awkwardly respond to his environment, Jason's facial expressions appear to have no connection to what is going on around him. He will suddenly smile and twist and flitter his fingers, stimulated and amused by something that occurred only in his mind. His posture is not as rigid as Matthew's, but his sudden tics and body twists are unpredictable and pronounced. There is no sharing of interests or enjoyment, and no emotional or social reciprocity, even when a staff member pursues the most basic connection by paralleling his crayon play, gently interacting next to him on the floor.

Jason's language is restricted to gibberish syllables and "TV talk," repeating words and short phrases from television shows that are not relevant to the social situation at hand. He will occasionally respond with simple one- or two-word answers—mostly "yes" and "no"— to basic questions such a desire to sit in a certain spot or need to use the bathroom. Sometimes he will repeat, or echo, a sentence or phrase prompted by a leader to say within the context of an activity. Any make-believe play is restricted to repetitive and stereotypical patterns of behavior related to a particular focus, illustrated by his preoccupation with lining up the crayons.

Luckily, Jason shows some flexibility and does not adhere to these routines to the degree that it becomes impossible for him to function in group. He is receptive and responsive to language from staff members that prompt transitions and group procedures. When he hears that it is time to clean up, he throws the crayons in the bucket and moves quickly to the specific spot he likes to sit in. If he were not able to respond to our directions, that combined with his lack of expressive language would preclude him from participating in our group, which is geared for higher functioning children. He follows our basic protocol, which is certainly beneficial to his socialization; but he does not, at this point in time, respond to any of the more sophisticated, language-based concepts presented during the activities.

Later on in the season, the children use videos to work on specific social, emotional or daily life situations from actual life experiences that are challenging to them. The children choose which scenario they want to work with, or their parents suggest one, prompted by a notice handed out a week earlier. Children and parents come up with specific situations, such as joining in with a group of cousins at a family function, managing frustration when it's time to leave a playground, dealing with videogame defeats or accepting a family's decision on which restaurant to go to. Jason is not able to tell us what situation he wants to work with. His father writes down that he would like Jason to work on simply greeting others and responding to greetings when he enters a room or space.

The children prepare for this activity by taking turns sitting in the director's chair and telling their stories, sharing what is difficult for them and brainstorming approaches and solutions with the group that might improve their situation based on skills learned from previous sessions. They then cast their shows, choosing members of the group to play different roles from their stories. The children telling the stories play themselves. We do a quick run-through and then use a video camera to film their "movies," reflecting the more empowered responses to the situation suggested by the group. After we complete three or four, the amount allowed by session time limitations, we watch the movies together, placing the protagonist of each show in the director's chair, close to the television set. We then hand out a "Certificate of Success" with much pomp and circumstance, indicating what the child "was able to get better at."

At this point later in the season, Jason has warmed up to the program and the process. Vacant looks have been replaced with occasional smiles, and he has some limited interaction with certain staff members who have been able to enter his world over the past couple of months. This video activity usually takes three sessions to complete all the children's stories. We wanted to wait until the second or third week to do Jason's show, so he could watch the other children and become more comfortable with the procedure. But when the session ends after the first week of the video activity and Jason doesn't get his certificate, he is beside himself (to use a phrase which speaks in another context to a key goal of the activity that will be discussed later). He cries and fusses, calling out, "My paper! My paper!" He is not consoled when we explain to him that he will have a turn next week, indicating all the other children who did not get a paper this week. His father tries to reassure him as he spills out into the waiting room, angry tears still dripping out of his big brown eyes. He does not calm down until we give him a blank certificate to take home.

Jason comes to group the next week and enters the room with a big smile. It is his turn to tell his story. He hops onto the director's chair and smiles at the group sitting in front of him on the floor. I ask him what his show is going to be about. He says, "Show!" and continues to smile at the group. As I help to narrate his challenge, he calls out, "Show! Kids!" and then, "Hello!" in a singsong voice, as if he is rehearsing for the upcoming event. He is able to pick, on his own, two children from the group to play the parts of friends that he will greet. As we set up the scenario, placing the other two children on the stage and getting the camera ready, Jason walks up to them, saying, "Hello!" before we are ready. We are inspired by his enthusiasm and guide him to repeat his performance with the cameras rolling.

Jason waits patiently for his turn to watch his show on the television toward the end of the session. He glows with excitement as he climbs into the director chair. He sits, literally on the edge of his seat, body tilted toward the screen, eyes wide, connected and framed by a radiant smile, seeming to absorb every moment. He proudly accepts his certificate and joyfully waves it at his father after we dismiss the children. His father informs us that he made copies of the blank certificate we gave him last week and now uses them to reinforce and reward other desirable behaviors that he looks to cultivate in Jason. Jason's positive response to this activity reflects a general comfort level with the program that took him a number of months to develop. The activities and approaches of the program seem to have accessed and engaged a perhaps dormant aspect of Jason's functioning, empowering him to connect to the process in a clinically meaningful manner.

As the season progresses, Jason is able to invest in his emerging ability to reciprocate socially and emotionally. He consistently seeks out certain staff members to play and laugh with and will plop himself in their laps. He is more attentive, communicative and responsive during structured activities, speaking to staff and other children with more extended phrasing. Some days he greets us with a happy "hello" as he enters the room; some days he does not. But, even on the days he does not greet us verbally, he makes contact with a quick glance toward our eyes and a huge smile that appears to say, "I'm excited to be here, and I'm happy that you are here, too!" Jason's perception of his presence on the screen seems to have supported him toward a more functional presence in the group.

Kenny

We hear six-year-old Kenny talking as he makes his way down the hall toward the group playroom. His speech, although highly idiosyncratic, is appropriately loud, clear and articulate, but he is alone, and his words are lifted verbatim from a television show or some other media source that he has encountered. He enters the room and gives me a big hug—a habit his mother is trying to break—and says, "Oh, hello, Dr. Lee! How are you doing?" in his exaggerated singsong voice. We remind him about the hugs and he separates himself, extends his hand and repeats the same phrase in exactly the same tone. He doesn't wait for my answer, and moves toward his favorite section of the room as I bend down to make eye contact and respond to his question. I call him back and he returns, but his thoughts are already somewhere else as I try to engage him. As he breaks away to find his spot by the cushions, he tosses me, in his attempt to satisfy my desire to connect with him, some gratuitous acknowledgement of my response.

Like Jason, Kenny has Autistic Disorder, even though he is clearly more verbal. Eye contact is infrequent and on his terms. He might look right at you if you comment on the dinosaur he has brought to group while telling you that it is a *Brachiosaurus* from the Jurassic period, but he'll likely shift and look past you, and then break away completely if you ask him a question, even about the dinosaur, that is not part of his prescribed agenda. He will probably continue to recite other facts about the dinosaur he was prepared to list in his singsong voice as he wanders away.

At this point, Kenny demonstrates no interest for symbolic, make-believe or interactive play. He focuses on and interacts with parts of materials, objects or toys, rather than approaching and using them as a whole. His onset of language was markedly delayed as a toddler, and while he has come a long way in his articulation, vocabulary, syntax and comprehension, he has a significantly difficult time using his language skills for pragmatic social communication. He functions fairly well within the dynamic of our group protocol, although he may need numerous prompts when the group transitions, as he remains fixated within his own fantastical thoughts. He may offer a comment during our group discussions, but it is more often than not a rendition of where his thought process is at the moment, a non-sequitur rarely relevant to the topic at hand.

Kenny begins most sessions by rolling and twisting his body around the cushions, isolated from the other children, echoing lines and dialogue he has absorbed from television or other forms of media. Occasionally he will reach out to staff members and children in the group and attempt to engage us with his ideas and thoughts, but he will only maintain contact if we function within his agenda as passive mechanical aids, responding in some intended manner known only to Kenny. He will detach and continue his conversation with himself if our nudge toward social reciprocity, the response to the input of another, is too much for him. We strive to hit the "sweet spot" of meaningful and reciprocal interaction when talking with Kenny, straddling the line between playing the part he needs us to play, while gently maneuvering so that he will perceive and respond to our input.

We notice one morning that Kenny has begun to invite puppets into his world during the open-play period. Before he goes to his spot, he retrieves one or two or three puppets and takes them back to the cushions. He rolls around with them and speaks to them individually or as a group. Sometimes he seems to wait for their response. Every now and then, we see him glancing, for a few seconds, toward the more typically raucous scene on the other side of the room where a group of children enthusiastically play together with their puppets at the puppet stage.

In a few weeks, Kenny begins moving around the room, puppet on his hand, talking sometimes to himself, sometimes to other people, through the puppet. One morning, as he approaches another child with the cow puppet, we notice a shift in how he is communicating. Instead of speaking from his pre-existing set of ideas that have no bearing on the social encounter, Kenny says, "Look! I have a bell!" referring to the bell around the cow's neck. His speech is still highly idiosyncratic and not very age appropriate, but the content is relative to the situation he is creating; he is speaking, or the cow is speaking, in a spontaneous and functional manner to another person.

As he becomes more adept with his puppeteering, he occasionally wanders over to the puppet stage if it's not too crowded, and successfully interacts for a moment, speaking about a shared topic through his puppet, hearing others' responses and then responding to them appropriately. The puppet functions as a concrete object that facilitates a shared and meaningful encounter, a symbolic vehicle for social interaction that Kenny is both inspired by and able to control. Two worlds, for those moments, are bridged.

As with Matthew and Jason, Kenny's participation and functioning level in a group is enhanced after discovering and interacting with the puppets. Besides the clinical significance that Kenny's pursuit of this symbolic, imaginative activity that prompts spontaneous, functional interaction is self-directed, we notice that Kenny is more "tuned-in" during group discussions and his responses are more appropriate. He is still isolated and echoes irrelevant dialogue, but his interest in and interaction with the puppets has provided us with a small opening through which we are able to expand his ability to reciprocate socially and emotionally.

James

James enters the room of nine-to-eleven-year-old children and immediately seeks out an adult staff member to participate in a detailed conversation on the history of the sousaphone. At ten years old, James seems to have the intellect of a college professor, able to speak in depth on a number of science-related topics. He is enthusiastic and engaging, clear and articulate, and appears, on the surface, to be appropriately responsive to the input of others. Although he seems to be a typical, pleasant and obviously gifted child, James has Asperger's Syndrome, a high-functioning form of PDD that has only recently (1994) been included as part of the autism spectrum in the *DSM-IV-TR*.

At first glance, James presents as entirely appropriate and even eloquent when greeting and communicating with other staff and children, and it may seem, initially, like he is not a good fit for the group. He has fairly consistent eye contact. His facial expressions, body posture and gestures, aside from a few hardly noticeable tics of eye rolling and throat clearing, are within the realm of normal functioning. It soon becomes apparent, though, that he interacts with the same disconnect, albeit on a much more subtle level, that has been described for Matthew, Jason and Kenny, hindering his ability in social and emotional reciprocity and blocking his development of peer relationships.

While James is highly motivated to share his enjoyments with other people, his interests are limited to certain topics, and his desire to engage with others is more about his compulsion to recite facts and ideas rather than participating in a true sharing of ideas. He exudes an urgency to speak about things such as the Earth's composition, how Jedis calibrate their light sabers, or the history of World War II. While James can respond to the input of others, it is difficult for him to switch gears as the flow of conversation naturally leads to other topics. He may give a conciliatory word or two toward the other topic that emerges, but he'll work hard to pull the focus back to the original topic of his choice. The motivation to do this is neurologically driven, not a product of emotionally driven immaturity, insecurity or self-absorption.

The surprisingly rigid perspective and one-sided willfulness that belies James' easy-going nature becomes clear one morning during Director's Chair, an applied theatre activity in which the children, as in the video activity, are asked to come up with a situation that is challenging to them. During this session, we look more specifically at emotional challenges, a particular time from their real lives when the children may have felt especially mad, sad, frustrated or scared. We do not video the enactment. The child sits in the director's chair and tells his or her story while the group leader prompts, "Where were you when the story happened? … Who else was there? … What did you say? … How did it end? …" The director, the child sharing the story, then casts the roles but instead of getting on stage, chooses someone else in the group to play his or her role while remaining in the director's chair to watch the live performance.

James tells us, in a matter-of-fact voice that expresses clear understanding but no sense of social embarrassment, how he had a tantrum during his little league game when he hit into a force play and got so angry because he wanted the coaches to change the rule and let him stay at second base. He adds almost as an afterthought that two adults had to carry him off the field and it took him 20 minutes to calm down. We are surprised, even in the context of the Asperger's, at the intensity of the reaction that this otherwise peaceful and cheerful boy describes to us. We focus on the part when the umpire calls him "out."

He casts his show and we watch it together, calling "Cut!" just before the tantrum takes hold. I ask the group, the actors and the children in the audience, to offer words that might describe what it was like for James in that moment, or, what they think it's like to be James in that situation. They respond intently with words like "Mad! ... Sad! ... Frustrated!" We ask James to choose and complete a phrase from our "Power Lines" poster hanging on the wall above the stage so he can redirect Ryan, the boy playing him in the scene, with new lines. He picks five of them and tells Ryan to say, "I am SO MAD! I don't want to have a force play rule! I want to get to second base!" and then a calmer "I can hit again" and "I know I like to play baseball." The troupe plays the scene to his satisfaction and we prepare for the next show.

James' parents report that his latest fixation is using the power words to integrate his intellect with his otherwise unchecked tendency for intense emotional reaction. They place the certificate we provide for the children after they complete their shows—an image of a scene marker clapperboard with the child's title of the show and chosen power words printed inside—in a prominent place in their house. Besides documenting a prideful celebration of his work, the certificate serves as a visual prompt that keeps James on track, using his cognitively intact rational side to ease the split of his emotional divide.

A diagnosis of Asperger's syndrome is also indicated, in spite of James' relatively typical demeanor, by his comfort level with being in a group with some children who function on a noticeably lower level. Typical children would quickly recognize and likely react to the differences between themselves and children on the spectrum. Unless they have had exposure to PDD children, they would likely feel uncomfortable with being placed in such a group, or at least, with no other explanation, question the placement. Even with all his intellect and perception regarding objective topics, James does not have the equipment, or has not yet accessed the neural connection, that can perceive self, interpret cues presented by another, and filter through the subtleties of social judgment that would register differences and cause discomfort. He might look at a child who is rocking, nonverbal and drooling, and determine, "He's shy."

David

David, an 11-year-old boy who attends the group, enters the room and walks right up to the new intern. In one breath he says, "Oh, you're new. How old are you? Is your grandmother alive because you look like you're old enough for her to be dead but young enough for her to still be alive." The intern is, understandably, a bit taken aback. David is similar to James with regard to intellect, verbal ability, pleasant affect and lack of social judgment; but instead of fixating on science-related topics, David persistently asks inappropriate personal questions, usually having to do with comparisons of time frames, especially if he is meeting that person for the first time.

David's Asperger's Syndrome is accentuated with *savant* characteristics, a condition that prompts him to instantly calculate and relate events to specific years, months and days of the week. He will know how many days it rained during a particular week in a summer from years ago, or what date and day a television show from his childhood debuted. David seems to explore and satisfy the savant nature of his neurological makeup by asking provocative questions, filing and organizing the information he obtains within the regions of the brain that help him to make sense of the world.

After participating in our groups for years, he catches himself before the intern answers, looks at me and says, "That was too personal." The smile on his face and twinkle in his eye indicate the degree to which these kinds of exchanges have become something of a game for him. He has become aware, if only from a cognitive standpoint, how his questions can make others feel uncomfortable and why they might not want to answer. Ironically, David bristles at any question directed toward him that might reveal any personal information. A moment later, when I ask him where he went on vacation the previous week, the usually gleeful and verbose David pulls back and offers a terse "I'm not comfortable answering that."

He is extremely uncomfortable with any type of overlap or mixing of people and environments to which he is accustomed that challenge his rigid understanding of how the world works. If he sees classmates at a mall or his parents at a school function, he becomes highly agitated and runs the other way. His reaction transcends embarrassment as he adamantly declares, "They don't belong there!" This has precluded the otherwise outgoing David from developing any peer relationships, as he cannot fathom the thought of interacting with an acquaintance from school in any other environment.

Through various role-play activities, David has become more successful in navigating his rigidity when encountering these types of social interactions. When participating in a role-play exercise, David initially chooses the most inappropriate and atypical response he can muster up. He does this consistently and on purpose, offering the loudest voice, most contorted body or most ridiculous language—any exaggerated response that is opposite to what the situation calls for. After a good and sustained laugh, he will then create a response that is entirely appropriate and balanced.

It's as if the highly stereotypical negative response he expresses within the safe confines of the role-play activity is able to counteract his highly stereotypical and rigid response to the world, clearing the way to explore more appropriate and functional responses. More important, according to parents and teachers, he applies these more functional responses in a methodical manner to his everyday interactions. David has begun to initiate contact and interact with classmates outside of school; he "allows" his parents to attend school functions; and he recently had a successful pool party at his home attended by children from his school as well as members of the group.

Janet

Janet, a 12-year-old girl who attends the group, doesn't come in the room right away. She waits just outside the door, fingers in her ears, rocking and muttering to herself under her breath. We gently approach her to offer support. In a polite yet frantic whisper she tells us to stay away. We give her space and wait until she is ready to come in. When she does eventually enter, she is constantly moving, separate from the others, rocking back and forth while pacing and circling the perimeter of the room, until it is time to sit together as a group. She sits apart from the rest of the children, head and eyes cast down toward her lap, fingers in her ears, still rocking and whispering anxiously in what seems to be an attempt to reassure herself.

Different practitioners have diagnosed Janet at different times with PDD-NOS or Asperger's Syndrome. It is not an exact science.

Symptoms often overlap and children develop over time, sometimes changing the manifestation of the condition. One thing is clear, though: Janet is bombarded by a sensory overload, a common characteristic of people on the autism spectrum that causes or adds to her high level of anxiety, which in turn heightens her sensitivity. The manner in which she perceives visual, auditory and tactile stimuli is overwhelming to her, imposing a very dense obstacle to communication and social interaction.

As we move through the season, Janet slowly becomes more comfortable with participating in group activities as well as her own skin. Painstaking attempts to finally get her to take turns on stage with activities after everyone else has gone have turned into frequent volunteering, sometimes to go first, so she can "get it out of the way." Her voice is idiosyncratic and strained; sometimes sounding like she's being asphyxiated. But Janet's ability for sophisticated levels of humor and insight are becoming an increasingly visible component of her enactments. She pushes through the wall of sensory distortion and the anxiety it instigates, contributing to group discussions and offering empathy and supportive advice to other group members.

During the spring session of this group, the members create movies, videos that encompass all the voice, body and dialogue training they have received during the fall and winter sessions. They develop a short film about their future, projecting an image of how they would like to see themselves ten to twenty years from the present. Unlike the previous video activity discussed, the teens have four to eight weeks to create and develop their vision, focusing on their own character, establishing the setting, plot and script; casting other group members as supporting characters; directing the production; and gathering any necessary costumes, props, scenery, sound and special effects.

At the end of the program we have our Film Festival, when we view the films and vote in various categories for the next and final week's "Oscar" party. Categories and nominations listed on the ballot handed out to the children after viewing the films include the usual *Best Actor, Best Director, Best Playwright* and such, along with *Most Realistic Vision, Best Use of Voice, Most Expressive, Ensemble Player Award, Best All-around Social Skills Presentation* and other pertinent categories. Everyone, of course, gets an award.

Janet reacts in her usual anxious way when we announce the inception of the filmmaking project, prematurely expressing worry that she doesn't have an idea for her movie. But after some abbreviated pacing and rocking, she approaches us, face alight, and says, "I just figured out what I can do for the movie, and it's what I just realized I want to do for a job. I want to be a therapist." Six weeks later, the premiere of *Getting Help at Dr. Janet's Office* is a great success.

The movie activity allows Janet to create and objectively perceive a controlled image of herself that can embody any quality she chooses to highlight. She is able to direct and control the environment and energy around her as she develops the project, providing her with an experiential model through which she can feel more grounded and confident for managing and modulating the overwhelming sensory stimulation she experiences.

These "dramatic encounters" seem to awaken, ignite and empower an aspect of functioning that has the potential to be developmentally profound for these children. The tools, techniques, structures, materials and support systems that naturally occur in drama seem to spark a desire and ability to access and express subjective information regarding the individual's state of being, while meaningfully integrating that experience within the shared collective space of the drama. As the drama coordinates and reconstructs otherwise fragmented aspects of development, rifts between perception and expression, impulse and language, emotion and behavior and other neurological and operational divides, the children become better at formulating and expressing understandings and connections in ways that they hadn't yet demonstrated. Attention is captured and held. Ability to envision, cognitively as well as affectively, is empowered and integrated, as dormant developmental systems seem to be jumpstarted and synchronized.

As I look back at what I have written about these children, I am struck by how they might seem, as their stories begin, almost inhuman, with their disconnected and distorted affects. Toward the end of each narrative, though, I am happy to see how the person emerges from their dramatic encounters as a sympathetic character, a fully functioning soul struggling to make sense of a chaotic and caustic world with equipment that operates on a different frequency. How and why this occurs remains, for the most part, a mystery.

Chapter 2

Engaging the Pervasive Developmental Disorders

The diagnoses

The Pervasive Developmental Disorders (PDD) or Autism Spectrum Disorders (ASD), as illustrated by the children described in the previous chapter, present neurodevelopmental conditions, usually by three years of age, affecting speech, cognitive functioning, learning, attention, sensory processing, and behaviors associated with social connection, communication and interaction. The signs and symptoms of PDD can be as subtle as they are blatant. From the classic hand flapping and non-responsive vacant stares of Autistic Disorder to the more nuanced, disconnected verbosity of Asperger's Syndrome, behaviors attributable to autism cover a wide range, as indicated by its identification and categorization as a "spectrum" disorder.

An expanded definition and understanding of ASD was published in the *Diagnostic and Statistical Manual of Mental Disorders IV* in 1994, when Asperger's Syndrome and PDD-NOS debuted as separate conditions within the PDD spectrum. In addition to Autistic Disorder, Asperger's Syndrome and PDD-NOS, PDD also includes the less prevalent and more severe Rett's Disorder and Childhood Disintegrative Disorder. Changes are presently being considered for once again re-categorizing aspects of the autism spectrum in the upcoming publication of the *DSM-V* in 2012.

At this point in time, scientists, clinicians and interested participants in the field are not sure what causes autism, although theories abound. What is clear is that the number of children diagnosed with PDD is increasing at an alarming rate. Presently, according to the Centers for Disease Control and Prevention (CDC) (2009), 1 of every 110 children born today—including 1 of every 70 boys—will be diagnosed with some form of autism. This was revised upward from a previous CDC report of 1 in every 166 children (2007), representing a 57 percent increase in the period between 2002 and 2006, and a 600 percent increase over the past 20 years. The National Children's Health Survey Report found a rate of 1 in every 91 children (Yavorcik 2009). The cause for the increased rate of autism diagnoses is also unknown, although theories promoted by impassioned individuals abound as well.

Possible causes

One of the more hotly debated theories involves the claim that the mercury-based preservative thimerosal used in vaccines and immunizations causes a reaction in children that leads to the development of autism. While various studies and court rulings assert evidence supporting either side of the debate (Obradovic 2010), countless anecdotes of infants and toddlers suddenly showing signs and symptoms of autism after receiving their shots have been a source of concern for decades. In 2009, The Center for Modeling Optimal Outcomes found that glycine, a stabilizer used in measles, mumps rubella (MMR) and other vaccines, can cause a disruption in homeostasis, triggering a cascade of hormones and an imbalance among neurotransmitters that inform mind and body responses, causing conditions associated with autism (The Medical News 2009).

Related theories for a biomedical cause of autism as well as the increased diagnosis rate cite the deluge of other toxins that have found their way into our environment and our bodies over the past 50 years. In 2005, the Environmental Working Group detected 297 substances, including mercury, flame retardants, PFCs, Scotchguard, Teflon and rocket fuel, in the umbilical cord blood from ten randomly selected newborns. All of the toxic substances were found in each of the babies tested. Mitochondrial dysfunction leading to symptoms observed in autism have been linked to environmental triggers, including aluminum, pesticides and other sources of pollution (Bradstreet and Rossingol 2008). Research suggests that environmental toxins have turned what was a relatively rare condition decades ago into a frequently occurring one (Kristof 2010).

Connections recently established between environmental toxicity and autism due to advances in neurobiological research likely tell part of the story. There is increasing consensus around the notion that a potent interaction between a genetic predisposition and exposure to environmental toxins is a major cause of autism. Sudhir Gupta, MD, PhD, Chief of the Division of Basic and Clinical Immunology at the University of California at Irvine, perhaps stated it most succinctly when he said, "Genes load the gun and environment pulls the trigger" (Belli 2010).

An exclusively genetic explanation for the rapid increase referred to as "Geek Syndrome" (Silberman 2001) emerged from the phenomena of exceptionally high autism rates found in Silicon Valley. The scenario suggests that math and engineering professionals concentrated in the area combine genetic tendencies and produce children with "turbocharged" affinities for mechanical and mathematical concepts and activities, characteristics prevalent in autism. Over the years at our center we have observed genetic, cognitive and neurological similarities within some families that have one or more autistic children, but this is not always the case.

Aside from environmental toxins and genetics, some see the increased rates resulting from better diagnostic tools, a more inclusive definition of what autism encompasses and a generally more educated and aware professional field that is more capable of making accurate diagnoses. It seems reasonable to assume that some causes of autism and increasing rates of diagnosis are a result of certain genetic combinations that occur more readily in the global village, some a result of more interaction with environmental toxicity, some a result of increased awareness and some a combination of many yet-to-be-discovered factors.

Treatment approaches

Various approaches to treatments of autistic symptoms are an even greater source for debate and controversy. On the biomedical front, many of these treatments are costly and, according to some, a waste of time and potentially dangerous, while others swear by them.

Chelation, involving the removal of excess heavy metals from the body, is administered orally or intravenously. Calcium bentonite, also used for removing heavy metals, is taken internally or as a clay bath. Hyperbaric oxygen therapy (HBOT) places participants in a chamber with a pressurized source of oxygen that can then be transported at increased capacity in the blood. Doctors affiliated with the Defeat Autism Now (DAN!) movement often administer these treatments.

There are presently no medications designed specifically for the treatment of autism, although autistic children are often prescribed medication for hyperactivity, anxiety, obsessive compulsion, disruptive behavior and related symptoms. I am not a medical practitioner, but I can say with confidence and experience that medication often does little to alleviate these symptoms in autistic children, and I have seen it backfire, especially with the use of psycho-stimulants. Autistic children who are hyperactive and distracted, when given these medications, can become extremely agitated and emotionally distraught, with manic-like behavior. Moreover, much has been written in general about the over-medication of children with psycho-pharmaceuticals and psycho-stimulants, many of which have not been approved for use in children by the Food and Drug Administration (FDA) (2010).

While many parents and professionals attest to the benefits of these medications with autistic children, others steer clear and choose an alternative path, using vitamins and supplements such as fish oil with Omega 3 fatty acids along with various herbal and homeopathic remedies to elicit calmness, focus and balance within the system. Oxytocin, a hormone fostering love and emotional connection, has recently gained attention as a possible treatment that can generate more sustained social connection for high-functioning children with autism (Warner 2010). These alternative and supplemental courses of treatment must also, of course, be administered with professional care and guidance.

Nambudripad Allergy Elimination Techniques (NAET) is an alternative holistic approach that identifies allergies and irritants that often "fly under the radar" of traditional Western methods. The air we breathe, the water we drink and the food we eat, as discussed in the previous paragraphs, are fraught with toxins and poisons that we, as a culture, have knowingly placed there. The dyes, preservatives, chemical additives and processing meant to make our food more attractive and manageable from a corporate perspective underscore the self-destructive manner in which we approach nutrition and health. Autistic children, because of their sensitivities, are especially susceptible to these potentially mood-altering, immune-suppressing irritants that provide no nutritional value.

Along with cosmetic additives, the actual foods we consume also pose a problem that is magnified for autistic children. Our increasing reliance on corn syrup and processed wheat products within the food chain is aided and abetted by commercial promotion and subsidizing of these agribusiness crops. Meanwhile, the rate of celiac disease, a digestive autoimmune condition caused by consuming wheat and other grains that damages the small intestine and disables the absorption of nutrients, has dramatically increased, according to the Mayo Clinic, and more people have become intolerant to corn, wheat and dairy products (Toman 2010). Fifty percent of autistic children have gastrointestinal symptoms, food allergies, poor digestion and absorption issues to begin with (Horvath *et al.* 1999). These types of foods that make up the bulk of our collective diet only exacerbate their situation.

Our society suffers from excessive yeast, inflammation and digestion issues that cause a general sense of discomfort, irritation and sensitivity. Just ask any family a day or two after a typically indulgent holiday celebration, when all the sugars, salts and fats start moving through the system. Autistic children, already dealing with more pronounced gastrointestinal disturbances and sensitivities, are particularly affected by these unhealthy and addictive eating habits. An increasing number of families with and without autistic children are responding to these imbalances by getting rid of sugary snacks laden with chemicals, preservatives and dyes, and are adopting gluten-free casein-free (GFCF) diets as a strategy for lessening some of the symptomatic behavioral and sensory issues intensified by poor food choices.

There is passion and controversy on all sides of the biomedical treatment debate. Some people claim that their autistic children have been cured by one or more of the approaches, while others take issue with what they say is a misleading characterization of the extent of a treatment's impact. The likely bottom line is that all treatments, services and practices have the potential to improve functioning for various symptoms and conditions within different individuals.

Whole food nutrition and supporting a toxin-free environment are obviously approaches that benefit everyone. We have a very odd and even pathological mindset in our culture that can be exemplified by our consumption of white napkins. We buy white napkins because their whiteness makes them seem clean and pure, a quality we want in napkins. The napkins are white, however, because they are bleached with carcinogenic dioxins, making them, in reality, dirty and poisonous. Unbleached napkins, with their natural tan or brown color that perhaps suggests impurity, are the truly more "clean and pure" napkin. The appearance and illusion of cleanliness and purity has a stronger hold on our collective psyches, at this point in time, than the actual danger cultivated by the blatant festering of dirt and poison that we perpetuate. This is one small example of how our culturally affected thinking and subsequent actions create an effect that is in opposition to what we profess to value. If we are truly interested in promoting health and well-being as a way of life, this mindset needs to change.

Social skills, behavior management and emotional development approaches to treatment have also emerged with the increase in autism diagnoses. Applied Behavioral Analysis (ABA) follows a methodology that seeks to improve social behavior by teaching relevant skills and altering undesirable behavior (Healing Thresholds 2009). While ABA is presently the most widely used treatment approach in schools and supporting agencies, its local interpretation and application can cause problems discussed in the introduction, whereby critical developmental operations associated with play and expression are often thwarted in the name of "appropriateness."

Development, Individual Difference, Relationship-based (DIR) Floortime, a more child-centered approach (Greenspan and Wieder 2001), focuses on emotional development by establishing an interactive relationship with the individual in the home, educational and/or clinical setting. Relationship Development Intervention (RDI) teaches parents and practitioners how to engage autistic children in a manner that generates more flexibility, creative problem-solving, emotional self-awareness and dynamic interaction (Gutstein 2009). The Son-Rise Program (Kaufman 1995) trains parents to maximize empathetic nurturing and join the autistic child's ritualistic behavior as a means for engaging interactive play and building relationship capabilities.

These child-based approaches reflect the importance of developmental play, emotional intelligence and relationship building in the treatment of autistic children, similar to strategies used in drama therapy. While DIR/Floortime, RDI and Son-Rise are mainly applied with individuals, a drama-therapy approach can use these strategies with individuals in the context of a larger shared group process. The clinical power of group process as a healing and socializing mechanism, a key factor of a drama-therapy approach, will be discussed in later chapters.

Developmental considerations

When dealing with social and emotional reciprocity, sensory input and responsive communication, it seems as though people with autism are working with a manual transmission system that they haven't been trained to use—likely operating with some pretty significant glitches—to embark upon a journey more adapted for vehicles with automatic transmission. Anybody who has driven a stick shift knows that changing gears is tough at first, with a lot of grinding, jolting around and sudden stops and starts. Perhaps one of the more difficult tasks that autistic children face is learning how to shift perspective as a strategy for understanding and responding to the intentions of others, which has been identified as a key factor in developing social skills (Dawson and Fernald 1987). For neurotypical people, these shifts happen automatically. People with autism tend to have a difficult time switching perspective between self and other. With practice, though, new drivers eventually learn to shift gears more fluently, with smoother transitions and more comfortable acclimation to navigating the roads they travel.

Neuroplasticity, which allows the brain to rewire itself and develop new neural pathways in order to adapt to an ever-changing world, suggests that autistic children can gain competence in shifting the gears of perspective. Researchers at UNC Chapel Hill found that toddlers with autism are more likely to have an enlarged amygdala, the region of the brain that helps to control emotions, regulate attention and read social cues from eye contact. The largest amygdalae were found in the highest functioning children leading scientists to believe that the area overgrows to compensate for deficits in other areas of the brain that also coordinate these functions (Cody-Hazlett *et al.* 2009). Reports that find that the rapid expanse by age two of the normal-sized brains of autistic children (Akshoomoff, Carper and Courchesne 2003), and local areas of an autistic child's brain becoming over connected, possibly in response to other poorly connected regions (Herbert 2005), suggest that the brains of autistic children are not set in stone and have the capacity to neurologically coordinate and construct avenues for improved functioning.

Classic models of development identify the ability to shift perspective as a key operation that empowers cognitive and social emotional functioning. Piaget's reversibility moves individuals back and forth between perceptual contexts, prompting them to link previously polarized aspects of information in order to generate new knowledge (1951), while Erikson identifies an alternating focus between polarized states of awareness that individuals move between in order to link previously disparate contexts of experience and resolve intrapersonal conflict (1968). The lack of interconnectivity between left and right hemispheres of the brains of autistic people (Just 2004) indicates the degree to which autistic children struggle to engage these critical operations that switch perspective in order to connect, synchronize and coordinate sources of seemingly disconnected information.

Developing skills of emotional intelligence, the ability to identify and express emotion in a manner that alleviates emotional distress while enhancing cognitive processing (Chasen 2009), has been shown to support neural interconnectivity and perspective taking. Articulating and verbalizing emotion creates pathways between cognitive and affective domains, providing a common language by which individuals may express their own emotional states and understand the emotional experiences of others. The processing of emotion has also been identified as a key factor in prompting shifts in perspective that generate cognitive development, as well as the more obvious social emotional development. By tracking patterns of biochemical brain activity, researchers have found that cognitive functions do not and cannot operate properly without engaging a methodical approach to processing emotion (Damasio 1999).

Autistic children rely on concrete tools for emotional expression to navigate shifts in perspective and help organize thoughts, feelings and behaviors. A boy refused to enter the group room unless he was able to hold a sign used in a previous activity printed with the word *sad* during the time that his father was receiving treatment for cancer. Other children have requested to hold these signs printed with words describing emotion as a way of coping with distress that they were otherwise unable to articulate. Another well-spoken boy regularly used our power words blackboard wall containing phrases such as *I am... I feel... I know... I can...* when he became overwhelmed with anxiety and emotion. Rather than tantrum or run out of the room, he asked to use the board and would write, *I am scared other kids won't let me have a turn...*, *I know Dr. Lee will stop them...* and *I can wait for a turn...* to help shift perspective and cope with the anxiety brought about by social interaction. Providing tools for autistic children to develop skills of emotional intelligence is a key component of promoting neural interconnectivity.

The autism spectrum, while presenting a certain set of symptoms and conditions, manifests many different types and subsets of behavior, affect and personality. Classification within the spectrum is not an exact science, and children may present with various aspects found in the different categories during the course of their development. One prevalent feature we often see among the children who attend our groups is the attraction to mechanical objects and concepts, especially among boys, who outnumber girls on the spectrum by a ratio of 4:1 (Medscape 1997). Beginning with Thomas the Tank Engine and later moving toward science and engineering-themed characters, programs and toys, such as Star Wars, Legos and Bionicles, many autistic children are attracted to machine-like figures that have personalities, expressing a strong affinity for encounters with objects that embody an intersect between humanity and technology. Perhaps this fascination is a function of their search for tangible mirrors, reflections that allow them to perceive, juxtapose and shift perspective between operation of the brain as computer and calculator, and as a facilitator of personal feeling and social connection.

While each autistic child presents a unique personality, traits are often influenced, as they are in all of us, by developmental and neurological conditions. Some of us are more right-brain oriented, while others' strengths emanate from abilities more associated with the left side. These various strengths and weaknesses are more pronounced and influential in autistic children, who lack the more comprehensive connection, integration and balance among brain functions seen in neurotypical brains, causing a more restricted range and stereotypical modes of expression. An autistic child may be either excessively silly or overly serious. They may offer no eye gaze or maintain unending eye gaze. They may constantly seek out physical contact or completely avoid it. Different individuals may portray a consistently flat, calm, overly emotional, seemingly emotionless, loving, happy, confused, anxious, detached or agitated affect. With some exceptions, there is usually adherence to one of these traits without the typical range of expression between the various affects; the range is more expansive with higher functioning children.

There are patterns of traits that appear consistently among certain autistic children. They may be extremely uncomfortable with and resistant to sharing whether or not they have brothers or sisters, the names of their teachers, where they went on vacation or other personal information if the interaction is, in their perception, out of context, occurring in a setting different than the one in which it is being discussed. This discomfort is based in cognition rather than affect, as the child might vehemently exclaim, with regard to the concepts, "They don't go together!"

Many autistic children have difficulty stating opinions and exploring grey areas, and are more comfortable sharing information grounded in black-and-white concepts. Most have some degree of difficulty transitioning between settings as well as activities, as their heightened and sensitized sensory systems react and attempt to adjust to the shift. These traits can make it extremely challenging for parents and teachers to facilitate learning and socialization for autistic children—but we need to first embrace and align with who they are, rather than merely rejecting and extinguishing behavior, if we are to guide them toward more effective perspective shifting, emotional adaptation and enhanced functioning.

Early opportunities to learn concepts and practice operations that prompt perspective shifting and emotional intelligence can take advantage of parallel opportunities for neurological remediation afforded by the neuroplasticity of the brain. Otherwise, symptoms of PDD, many of which resemble neurotypical traits of early childhood, may become more challenging to adjust as the brain matures and the basic structure of neural pathways becomes relatively set toward adulthood. A diagnosis of PDD, especially in higher functioning children, can be difficult to establish in young children, though, because of the age-appropriateness of many of the symptoms. Perseveration, fantastical ideation, singsong or mechanical speaking tones, stereotypical behaviors and limited perspective are common and expected in toddlers. As higher functioning Asperger's children who have not been diagnosed become elementary-school aged, the gap in developmental appropriateness begins to widen, and behaviors can seem regressed and oppositional, causing frustrated teachers and school officials to react, all too often, in damage-control mode, further exasperating the child's situation and grinding those gears necessary for optimum manual transmission.

Positive intervention

Despite criticism leveled in previous sections regarding behavioral applications, it is imperative that parents and teachers provide autistic children with comprehensive management systems that establish concise guidelines for independent self-care, expressive language, adaptive behavior and social interaction using specific measurements that determine rewards and natural consequences to reinforce successful outcomes and promote neural connectivity. These systems need to be set up, though, in the context of a purely positive and empathetic partnership with the child and not as a result of reactionary frustration and power struggle.

Too often, parents and teachers take an oppositional stance with autistic children, prompting the child, in turn, to become withdrawn, distracted or equally oppositional. Accusatory anger from someone in a position of authority directed at an autistic child who is reacting from a developmental deficit rather than malicious intent will likely provoke further undesirable behavior in that child, and possibly plant the seeds for future displays of otherwise nonexistent malicious intent. Some of our nicest, most well-behaved children who have been in our groups for years without incident have been suspended from their schools for hitting teachers who have most likely unwittingly provoked them. It is not a good idea to angrily penalize a child who expresses joy by harmlessly flapping his arms while laughing. An approach toward modifying the flapping through alternative strategies for expression is fair enough, but punitive measures authoritatively enforced will accomplish nothing and likely backfire.

Conversely, some of our angriest, most oppositional children come from households where there are no constructive boundaries, allowing the impulses, compulsions and perseverative demands of the children to apparently rule the home as well as the burgeoning neural structure, leaving no opportunity or need to shift perspective and create new connections. These particular children who happen to be quite mild-mannered by nature, are thrown into perceptual and sensory disarray, antagonized by unclear expectations and ambiguous, unpredictable emotional reactions from authority figures. A third, fourth and fifth warning to a child that he may not receive a toy if he continues to purposely spit because he is not getting his way is not at all helpful to him. Letting a child play four hours of video games because he likes them (and will tantrum if parents attempt to turn them off) does little to lay the foundation for neuroplastic adaptation that can prompt coping skills and enhance personal and social growth. Parenting and supervising an autistic child with few limits or confusing boundaries is an equally contentious recipe for developmental disaster.

Along these same lines, parents need to be wary of working too hard when helping their child adjust to challenging situations, as they could unknowingly rob them of opportunities for building self-soothing skills and independently generated, solution-oriented thought. Rescuing children from situations they need to learn to handle on their own will make them overly dependent and may be even more damaging than reactionary anger. It is difficult but necessary to strike a balance where autistic children are held accountable for their behavior while being guided in partnership with a positive stance of potential and accomplishment. Standards and support need to be high and reciprocal, with an eye toward developing independence, self-management and problem-solving skills in the child.

Parents and teachers need to use calm, business-like tones whenever possible, especially when attempting to address negative behavior. They need to elicit response from the child rather than lecture him, so that the child's expressive language can function as a tool for understanding and adaptation and provide opportunities to reflect on and reconfigure behavior and choices. A specific, concrete and consistent system of support and measurement using charts, tokens, contracts, game boards, poster lists and interesting challenges will help position the parent and teacher outside of the power struggle, while keeping the child responsible for progressing toward his or her goals. A visible, accessible system that everybody has agreed upon takes the burden of enforcement off the backs of parents and teachers, allowing the people in charge to play a more positive role. Once the system is established by mutual agreement, it becomes bigger than its participants, allowing facilitators to, in a sense, empathetically shrug their shoulders during enforcement as they defer to the co-created "laws of the land."

When identifying realistic and meaningful goals for the child, the behavioral "yes" needs to be established and documented, rather than the "no". Instead of "no hitting," the goal would be "using power words to say how mad and frustrated I am." This keeps the approach moving in a positive direction, allowing parents and teachers to act as coach, mentor and cheerleader, rather than adversary and warden. Along with sparse inclusion of small trinkets and prizes for notable accomplishments, rewards should focus on the more intrinsic benefits of cooperative behavior and be comprised of the child's basic recreational choices, such as access to television and electronics, especially when dealing with issues of control and oppositional behavior. Logical consequences with which parents and teachers can follow through, rather than threats and punishments, should be administered when necessary, as per the agreed-upon system, with an empathetic eye toward opportunity to be more successful next time.

Parents and teachers need to align and empathize with the child throughout the behavior management process. All interventions must be undertaken with the purposeful tone and spirit of empowering the child. Yelling, arguing and berating, as well as pleading, begging and bribing, undercut this important agenda. Parents and teachers need to take the time to revisit and replay situations with the child in a non-judgmental, conflict-free exchange, so that the child can reflect on behavior with a supportive authority figure serving as an ally. Adverse reactions to food, seasonal allergies and a myriad of other sensory factors, while not used as an excuse, should be taken in account when strategizing for an improved and empowered behavioral response.

Teachers and parents need to prepare, from their adult mindsets, for a marathon rather than a sprint. Autistic children respond well (as do all children!) to pragmatically sequenced, honest information presented in a matter-of-fact, businesslike, supportive fashion whenever possible. Dealing with difficult issues by avoiding, placating or explaining something away will likely cause anxiety or confusion for all involved in the short term, and deepen dysfunction with management and coping skills in the longer term. There are no "quick fixes" in the big picture, especially when it comes to developmental and neurological issues. Organization, consistency and proactive, empathetic vision are key when it comes to modifying behavior and implementing change.

During one of our video-modeling activities, a boy was thrilled with his onscreen success, saying over and over, "I did it! I did it! I left the door alone!" after watching himself perform. When group was over, he burst into the waiting room, waving his certificate, happily exclaiming, "Look, mom! I left the door!" I followed him out to support his enthusiasm, only to find his mother scowling at the boy, telling him, "No you didn't." She turned to me and described how frustrated the family is because of his compulsive need to open and close the front door of his house whenever someone enters or exits and the tantrums that ensue when he is unable to. I was aware of this because she wrote it down on the sheet we handed out the previous week asking for challenging situations the children could work on. Even though the video activity was also described on the sheet, I explained the process again to her, in which he envisions himself being successful, enacts the vision to engage the experience and creates a positive, tangible image of that success he can replay in his mind as a step toward modifying the behavior. Without even allowing for the opportunity to take the in-vitro skill home for a test run reenactment, she discredited his accomplishment by saying that it was just a video and not real. Parents and teachers need to be positive and patient when it comes to the long-term development needs of autistic children.

Back through the looking glass

One of the more promising developments toward understanding and remediating challenges that autistic children face, as well as providing new insight into how we all learn, interact and develop, emerged with the recent discovery of the mirror-neuron system. The mirror-neuron system is a neural network that automatically activates, or fires, when an individual perceives an action performed by another, just as it would if the individual were performing the action him- or herself. Because these neurons fire in similar fashion whether we are taking action or merely perceiving others performing those same actions, we are able to personally experience and gain understanding with regard to the actions and intentions of others (Iacoboni 2008).

If I passively sit and watch someone bake a cake, build a house or perform any activity, my mirror neurons will fire, just as if I were actively involved in those same activities, providing me with a visceral sense of what it is like to perform those actions. This embodied simulation of others' experiences that causes us, when very stimulated, to cringe if we see someone getting hurt or hide our eyes during scary movies, comprises the neurological foundation for developing a sense of self, other, social connection and empathy, enrolling us in the same moment as participant and observer. Thus we get an ongoing biochemical rehearsal of sorts for adapting and empowering our own calls to action.

This new awareness of how the brain perceives and interacts with others supplants the concept of "theory theory" which states that individuals come to understand the social world by analyzing the actions of other people, constructing theories about those actions and then testing those theories through trial and error (Iacoboni 2008). Instead, neuroscientists have found that the simultaneous experience of perception and action that occurs in the mirror-neuron system is unified and integrated, not separate and linear. Rather than gaining understanding about self and others through a distanced analytical process of conceptual reasoning, our brains are built to actively gain understanding by neurologically mirroring and imitating all that we perceive.

Along with merely imitating the motor actions of others, mirror neurons are also able to distinguish and fire with regard to the goals and intentions of those actions (Iacoboni 2008). Perceiving a person who is waving their arms while dancing will fire that particular set of neurons in the observing individual. Different neurons would fire in the observer if the observed person were waving arms to get someone's attention, or to shoo away mosquitoes—even if, in each example, the arms were waving with the same speed, frequency and direction. As we perceive the goals of the actions we neurologically imitate, our brains encode the intentions of others, giving us a profound understanding of their mental states. As our mirror neurons fire in sync with the perceived actions of another and we internalize those intentions, the other becomes, in a sense, another self, allowing our brains to reenact the mental state of the other, creating intimacy between the two. This internalized relationship between self and other may provide the mechanism through which we become able us to see ourselves as others see us, establishing the foundation for self-awareness and introspection (Oberman and Ramachandran 2006).

Mirror neurons develop throughout early infancy as others, especially primary caretakers, imitate the actions of newborns, creating a self/other perceptual merge in infants that becomes differentiated as the baby develops (Iacoboni 2008). The intimacy between self and other bestowed by neurological imitation is a key building block for the development of language during infancy, as mirror neurons that fire when observing gesture and sound ultimately transform bodily actions from an internal reflex to a social experience that can be shared with other people. In a similar process, the infant's firing of automatic motor mirror neurons in response to others' facial expressions triggers the limbic system that processes emotional feeling, connecting the feeling with the facial expression and allowing the identification and expression of emotion. The reflexive neural mimicry of gesture and facial expression eventually becomes associated with meaningful expression and social interaction.

Within this model, the mirror-neuron system provides a technical blueprint for the greater development of social ties and empathy. Our brains react to the pain of others, physical as well as affective, as if it were a shared experience (Iacoboni 2008). We come to understand and experience the emotions of other people because the sight of a smiling or frowning face automatically activates the same mirror neurons that fire in ourselves when we are performing those actions, as if we were smiling or frowning. It is through mirroring, the simulation in our brains of the felt experience of other minds, that we come to understand what others are feeling. We become able to deeply understand others through mirroring because it is the reciprocal and ongoing process through which we come to understand ourselves.

As the mirror-neuron system matures, the cortical midline structure of the brain, an area where mirror neurons overlap with social cognition neurons in order to evaluate information, allows the individual to distinguish between neural firings resulting from actions taken by the self and firings related to others' actions (Uddin *et al.* 2007). A gradual process that begins at birth cues mirror neurons of the perceived self to resonate more strongly and find a better "fit" in relation to the perceived other within the existing neural map, allowing the individual to identify self and differentiate from others' actions. As might be expected, researchers have found deficiencies in some of these processes and structures related to the mirror-neuron system in the brains of autistic children.

Typically, when not responding to social stimuli, the brain falls into what is referred to as a "default" state of self-referential thought and internal awareness regarding the self/other connection prompted by this resonance of mirror neurons (Dapretto and Iacoboni 2006; Iacoboni 2006). When performing a task or responding socially, the self-aware absorption of the default state deactivates and shuts down, in effect allowing individuals to "move out of their own head" and respond accurately to social stimuli. This recalls the description of the constantly running surveillance camera in the back of my head that perceives and monitors actions of the self in relation to others, as discussed in the introduction. As described in the neurological model, when I perform a task and interact and respond to others, the more inward, ongoing default state of self-surveillance deactivates as I tend to the external task at hand. Lab tests have shown that the brains of autistic children fail to deactivate the default state, causing them to remain in a more self-referential and less socially responsive state (Iacoboni 2006).

As the autistic brain fails to suppress self-stimulating mirror-neuron activity firing in relation to others' responses, the system receives a contradictory stream of sensory stimuli and information, hampering the individual's ability to construct a pragmatic, meaningful and balanced response that simultaneously represents self and connects to other. We have seen members from our groups tip toward either side of this imbalance. Some autistic children, rather than sharing their own interests as a way to connect with others, ask obsessive and socially invasive questions about others' personal lives in order to stimulate themselves, without much, if any, consideration of the other. Other children in the group associate and communicate with others in a state of purely self-referential information that has little, if any, meaning for the other.

So the camera is on and the programs are running, but it's hard for autistic brains to strategically channel surf, switching from the network that stars episodes of self/other, to the station of other/self, as needed. It is the switching between these neurological states, the purposeful deactivation and reactivation that monitors and coordinates self-awareness with perceptions of others, that allows for meaningful and pragmatic understanding of an interactive self as it relates to other, and understanding of others as they relate to self. The imbalance is neurologically rather than emotionally driven, creating a dynamic that is ego-less rather than narcissistically ego-centered. The difficulty with interactive processing and lack of "automatic transmission," the ability to easily shift between concepts of self and other, actually promotes very little ego, allowing, for better or worse, an almost complete lack of a judgmental and/or critical social stance in autistic children.

Other related dysfunctions and irregularities regarding the mirror-neuron system have been found in the brains of autistic children. Along with similar electroencephalogram (EEG) results that demonstrate lower response when relating to others (Oberman and Ramachandran 2006), a diminished "self response" and ability to represent one's own intentions has also been found in autistic children (Chiu *et al.* 2008). An abnormal thinning of grey matter affecting the mirror-neuron system has been identified in the cortical areas of autistic brains that manage emotion recognition and social cognition (Gallese 2006); the degree of thinning in this area correlates with symptom severity in autistic children (Hadjikhani *et al.* 2006).

The breakdown of the mirror-neuron system could very well explain deficits in social skills that autistic people experience (Iacoboni 2008; Oberman and Ramachandran 2006). Research suggests though that the mirror-neuron system is not entirely static or inflexible once patterns are learned and, since they develop through sensory-motor associational learning, may in fact be able to "dynamically adjust" in accordance with changing inputs (Pineda 2008). And, by virtue of neuroplasticity, these deficits could be understood more as delays rather than absolute and irreversible conditions (Oberman and Ramachandran 2006). Activities that increase individuals' representations of the role of the self in goal-directed social interactions have been suggested as potentially valuable tools that could help autistic children better negotiate the self/other relationship brokered by the mirror-neuron system (Chiu *et al.* 2008)

While there are detractors from the notion that dysfunction in the mirror-neuron system is a major cause of autism, and while scientists question whether mirror-neuron dysfunction causes autism and if autism in fact causes mirror-neuron dysfunction (Altschuler *et al.* 2005), there appears to be potential for active intervention to further developing this neural network. It is as clear now as it was years ago in our musty basement, when we reluctantly pulled kids away from that giant floor-to-ceiling mirror by which they were so transfixed. Our brains have these built-in mirrors that automatically reflect and neurologically reenact everything we perceive in order to empower a sense of self and connection with other, generating a more automatic transmission that smoothly switches the gears of perception between the two. Autistic children need opportunities to practice manual shifting so they can override a faulty and unreliable automatic transmission, keeping them on the road toward clearly representing self while successfully constructing a pragmatic response to the world.

So what happens when we hold a mirror up to the mirror?

Chapter 3

Drama: Mirroring the Neurological Soul

Reflection for the ages

Sitting in the Performing Arts Center of my daughters' high school, watching the drama club's production of *Footloose*, I am flooded with thoughts and feelings that go beyond pride for my children's accomplishments. Although I have known most of the kids performing in the show, my daughters' friends, for years, and I have seen this production three times, I feel genuinely concerned for the characters they are playing. I choke up hearing Ren tell Ariel about his father's leaving him during the scene by the railroad bridge. I start to think about my relationship with my father. I am excited and hopeful as the kids challenge the reactionary, close-minded preacher and make their case for allowing dancing in the town. I feel the pain of the preacher's loss and come to understand how he got to that place. As my own 17-year-old daughter makes her entrance, I feel compassion for the single parent middle-aged woman she portrays.

Even though I know most of the kids on stage and their "real life" stories pretty well, and I am consciously aware that the situations and roles they play are not real, my emotions and thoughts are moved, sometimes powerfully, by the fictional characters and simulated circumstances they are creating. I drive home from the experience invigorated and calmed by the emotional and intellectual workout, feeling more empowered and in sync with my particular understanding of the world within and around me. Mirror neurons, meet the magic of drama and theatre.

Shakespeare's Hamlet articulates the purpose of theatre as holding "the mirror up to nature" (Act III Scene II) to reflect the human condition. When you hold a mirror up to another mirror, you gain access to sides of yourself you are not usually able to see. Whether it's the three-paneled mirror on the medicine cabinet in your bathroom that opens up to let you check how bald you are getting, or the full-length multi-sided wardrobe mirror in the dressing room of the department store that allows you to see how the dress fits in places otherwise unavailable for viewing, mirrors held up to mirrors provide us with a greater range of perception. The power of the mirror-neuron system— with its inherently dramatic functions of imitation and reenactment for understanding self and other—is increased exponentially when the mirror of drama and theatre, which purposefully imitates and reenacts social and emotional events in order to establish a greater, deeper sense of self and social understanding, is held up to those mirror neurons.

Mirror neurons fire for all perceived actions, emotions and intentions. Theatre and drama portray a given set of circumstances that purposefully reflect a particular sequence of actions, emotions and intentions, providing an advanced starting point of perception that prompts our mirror neurons to explore, through imitation and reenactment of the perceived dramatic circumstances, the next, deeper level of self-perception and social understanding regarding those circumstances. In 1983, a movie titled *The Day After* debuted on network television. It depicted, in a realistic style that was graphic but not overly sensationalized, the effects of a nuclear war on the residents of Lawrence, Kansas and Kansas City, Missouri. As a young man, I remember feeling as if the mood and perception of the entire country shifted with regard to the possibility and consequences of nuclear war after the popular movie aired. On the night of its showing, thousands held a candlelight vigil in Kansas City, and people filled the streets of Lawrence, gazing in horror at buildings that had just been fictionally annihilated on their television sets (Helliker 1983; Trowbridge and Hoenk 1983).

The function of the mirror-neuron system tells us that this was more than just an intellectual or even an emotional shift. The fictional, dramatic presentation prompted viewers of the movie to embody and simulate what the actors were portraying; the experience of living through a nuclear war suddenly became real. Soon after, the political winds started blowing in a more conciliatory and less threatening direction in America's dealings with the Soviet Union. Before the movie, we all had an intellectual and emotional understanding of the concept of nuclear war, but the internal simulation of the experience engaged by the dramatization caused us to collectively respond as if the tragedy had occurred, because, neurologically, for the 100 million Americans who watched the movie, it had.

Drama, whether viewed on Broadway, the high school stage or cable television, presents images and situations that allow us to experience expanded dimensions of who we are and what we can be, individually and collectively. Theatre, movies and television shows that imitate and reenact dramatized accounts of personal conflict and social challenge mirror the neurological processes of the mirror-neuron system, providing a unique integration of thought and feeling that simultaneously suspends and enhances reality by firing neurons relative to the dramatized conflicts and challenges. The deeper understanding initiated by the embodied simulation creates a polarized dynamic between existing understanding of self and other, and the perceived dramatic circumstances in relation to self and other, prompting us to move between the two and construct and consider potential actions we might take that can empower our lives. We perceive and reenact the dramatic information, assimilate new, unexplored aspects relative to self and other presented in the drama, and then we accommodate our circumstances accordingly.

Theatre visionaries and practitioners, long before the advent of neuroscience, intuited and celebrated theatre's unique ability to purposefully mirror. Aristotle (1920) described drama as the imitation of an action that brings about a catharsis or purification of difficult emotions. Shakespeare's mirror reflects the truth of our nature, the full range of human virtue and scorn. Brecht, concerned that merely purging difficult emotion through reflection would lull audiences into complacency with social injustice, rejected the notion of Aristotelian catharsis and sought to alienate the audience into taking action, stating, "If art reflects life it does so with special mirrors" (1964, pp.203–204). Mindful of cultural manipulation that sells superficial happy endings, sex, violence and other stimuli to placate and coerce audiences into compliance, Brecht called for a more active mirror:

a hammer to shape a society plagued by commercial contrivance. Similarly, Boal (2005) sought to ascribe the mirror with interactive properties to allow participants to penetrate and transform the image as well as corresponding socio-political oppression.

Amongst the many genres available for playing and presenting theatre and drama, a common theme resonates in the concept of theatre as a purposeful mirror that engages and integrates cognitive and emotional processes. The question of what and how the mirror should reflect for theatre-going audiences is, for the purposes of this text, secondary. George Bernard Shaw provides what may be considered a unifying view in *Back to Methuselah*, when the She-Ancient exclaims, "You use a glass mirror to see your face: you use works of art to see your soul" (1921, p.254). Whatever style or media are reflected, theatre and drama, by purposefully imitating and reenacting human encounters, mirror the function of the mirror-neuron system, creating, when these two mirrors are held up to each other, a powerful tool for expanding perception and deepening understanding of self and relation to other.

Drama is therapy

In her introduction to Robert Landy's book *The Couch and the Stage*, Zerka Moreno states that all forms of psychotherapy "should respond to one universal criterion: to touch the autonomous healing center of the client(s) involved" (2008, p.ix). For thousands of years, this has been the function of drama. From ancient rituals that shaped identity, understanding and emotional security through the use of masks, movement, role and dramatic enactment, to recent research in neuroscience identifying imitation and reenactment as the foundation for understanding self and other, drama provides an operational scaffold that facilitates therapeutic processing. The dynamic of drama naturally reflects and engages key developmental functions, integrating perceptions of self, other, cognition and emotion, generating potential for deep understanding and self-empowering activity.

Throughout history, drama has imitated and reenacted conflicted aspects of the human psyche as a means for promoting self-awareness, social understanding and general well-being. It reaches back before history, when the earliest cultures gathered for strength and comfort, telling stories and enacting dramatic rituals that integrated their hopes and anxieties about life's challenges, supporting participants toward strategizing pragmatic approaches for survival. Evidence of dramatic representation and ritual has been found in artifacts that date as far back as three million years (Courtney 1989).

Along with the obvious place of drama in modern culture as a powerful art form that can move and inspire personal and social action as discussed in the previous section, drama has had a profound impact on modern approaches to psychotherapy (Landy 2008). Approximately 2500 years after the first production of *Oedipus Rex* in Athens, Freud, the father of psychoanalysis, used the title character and content of the play to build upon his influential theory of personality and psycho-sexual development (Freud 1965). The concept of *catharsis*, also originating with early Greek tragedy, was introduced as a central component of psychoanalysis as well (Breur and Freud 2000). Early psychoanalyst Otto Rank, a contemporary of Freud, formally introduced Narcissus, a character from Greek mythology who could not pull his gaze away from the mirror image of himself, to the early world of psychoanalysis in 1911 (Millon 2004). A few years later, Freud firmly established the role that Narcissus continues to play in psychodynamic theory (1914).

Discussing the influences of art, drama and spiritual existence on the first psychoanalysts, Landy cites pioneers in the young field who attempted to maintain an action-oriented approach to psychotherapeutic treatment in the wake of the growing tide toward scientific rationale. Landy compares concerns of early practitioner Rank to traditional shamanic healers who "seek to repair a rupture in the whole fabric," rather than "thinkers who seek to reduce the whole to its parts" (2008, p.29). Noting that shamanism, the ancient source of healing expressed through dramatic enactment, had been rejected by the scientific rational modern world, Landy speculates that dramatic action as a healing agent persists because of its holistic nature, a component now supported by neuroscience research.

Identified by neuroscientists as whole and holistic (Iacoboni 2008), the mirror-neuron system has transformed our basic understanding of how development and connection to self and other occurs, bringing the fragmented approach of Western scientific thought full circle, back to what the ancients knew. On the heels of this new and old understanding, drama, with its inherent ability to engage, embody and integrate whole systems of development and processing, reaffirms its role as a form that not only touches but also fully embraces the autonomous healing mechanism of the individual, intensifying its operation and enhancing its effectiveness. The mirror-neuron system provides drama, alongside its mystical and creative credentials, with a biological testament to its healing and therapeutic powers.

Drama therapy, a field that emerged in its own right in the 1970s, uses techniques from drama and theatre, including role-playing, directing, individualized scripting, improvisation, costume, set construction, puppets, masks, and other forms of creative expression and enactment to reflect, engage and empower therapeutic and developmental processes. According to the National Association for Drama Therapy (undated), established in 1979, therapeutic goals may include personal growth, catharsis, emotional and physical integration, behavioral change and enhancement of interpersonal relationship skills. The active process encompasses movement, imagination, expressive language and playful encounter.

The most significant developments in the new field of drama therapy occurred in the United Kingdom and the United States, with practitioners coming from related backgrounds including theatre, drama-in-education, psychology, psychoanalysis and psychodrama (Landy 2008). Jacob Levy Moreno, the creator of psychodrama, was the first psychotherapist in the early twentieth century to employ drama as a primary approach to healing, providing an important foundation for the development of drama therapy. In his theory of child development depicting the unfolding of awareness and differentiation between self and other, Moreno, after identifying the first stage in which mother and infant are one, describes the second stage, the mirror, where there is a recognition of self separate from mother, achieved by seeing the self in the reflection of the other (Moreno 1994). Moreno's theory, clearly reflected 50 years later by the mirror-neuron system, affirms his capability for envisioning larger-than-life, far-reaching concepts. Perhaps one day, a healthy and vibrant society artistically co-created by spontaneous and empowered individuals will credit Moreno for the accuracy of other positive visions that he unrelentingly prophesized (1978).

Landy lists a number of drama-therapy approaches and practitioners, focusing upon two, David Read Johnson's developmental transformations, and his own role theory/role method that have generated, along with psychodrama, the most research and descriptive literature in the field (2008). Landy's earlier distancing theory identifies movement along a polarized continuum that seeks a balance between thought and feeling, allowing for catharsis to occur (1986). The distancing dynamic that would later inform and expand Landy's approach to role-theory inspired research that looks at related systems in which polarized states of awareness and being interact to generate enhanced functioning and explores their connection to dramatic operation (Chasen 2003, 2005, 2009).

What became apparent is that dramatic enactment provides an ideal template through which similarly occurring strands of polarized information can be purposefully guided toward increased interaction within developmental systems, enhancing processes to empower optimum functioning. New scientific understanding that now sees systems previously thought of as separate, most notably cognitive and emotion-affective, as components of a larger integrated system (Damasio 1994), is also indicative of the healing and remedial power of drama. Drama's propensity for integrating polarized information within various systems includes coordinating and realigning fragmented states of information between cognition and emotion, systematically severed by a misguided approach to "rational" thought that gained prominence as cultures became industrialized. Participation in dramatic enactment naturally restores integration among processes and a measure of wholeness to the experience and treatment of the individual, an approach that is increasingly advocated by mounting scientific evidence.

The mirror-neuron system, by neurologically imitating and reenacting all that is perceived to generate understanding of self and other as a means for preparing individuals to act in the world, affirms drama's therapeutic key function as a form and approach that reflects and enacts critical developmental processes and operations. Drama's ability to integrate information within and between developmental systems by imitating and reenacting conflicting circumstances provides a remedial roadmap for treatment of a variety of conditions. A drama-therapy approach to social skills and emotional growth in autistic children enacts processes that mirror critical functions within developmental systems, prompting psychodynamic awareness and insight, and, perhaps more significantly for this particular population, integrates processes that support competence with the manual shifting of gears between perception of and pragmatic response to self and other.

Process Reflective Enactment

As stated throughout this chapter, theatre and drama reflect, engage and enact processes and operations that occur within related systems of cognitive, emotional and social development, purposefully integrating polarized states of information and being. They coordinate the functioning of a whole system, enhancing and empowering the individual's ability to successfully respond to and participate in self and other encounters in a manner that represents a more fully integrated and aware being. A *Process Reflective Enactment* approach to drama therapy immerses autistic children in activity critical to developmental integrity and well-being.

The essence of drama provides the source of these critical operations. Landy describes the dramatic "paradox," in which the individual actor or group chorus function simultaneously in two separate and seemingly opposing realities: past and present, fiction and nonfiction, internal and external, real and imagined, me and not-me, as the "heart of the dramatic experience" (1993, p.11). The realities exist in polarized relationship, opposites seeking connection, ideally merging in a place of balanced coexistence via "an interaction or intrapsychic process characterized by a range of closeness and separation" (1994, p.111). Landy cites the important role polarities play in theories of personality and approaches to psychotherapy (2008).

Richard Courtney defines tension as the "essential characteristic of drama" that "pulls between two poles: between imagining and action: and also between inner and outer" (1980, p. 23). Rather than functioning in conflicted opposition to each other, the "inner dynamics both pull together and pull apart" along the poles, constituting the wholeness of drama (p.23). Play, the medium of dramatic enactment that allows us to act as if we were someone or something else, is the "thing between" that moves us in, around and between the poles (1989, p.32). When we are acting "as if," "we think and act in [a] fiction, while, simultaneously, we are engaged in the living process" (1995, p.4). Courtney identifies oscillation, the movement that occurs within these polarized states of information and perception during dramatic enactment, as "characteristic of all the dynamics of thought" (1995, p.88).

Gavin Bolton describes the dramatic process of movement along the polarities as "thought-in-action; its purpose is the creation of meaning; its medium is the interaction between two concrete contexts" (1979, p.21). Perceptions move between "two aspects of the same experience": the actual and the make-believe, the personal and the objective, each becoming a "pivot" for the other during dramatic enactment, bringing together otherwise disparate sources of information from previously separate contexts into a new and meaningful relationship of understanding (p.21).

This primary operation of drama, navigating movement between polarized states of information, concepts, experiences and perceptions of self and other, subject and object, past and present, concrete and symbolic, and real and imagined, represented within a unifying framework and context, initiates a process of interaction and integration that creates new meaningful contexts of understanding. The individual consciously and pre-consciously moves, guided by the dramatic enactment, between opposing perceptions and perspectives, finding commonalities and creating links among the polarized states of information. The resulting dramatic paradox and tension established by the polarized contexts of fiction and reality, and the perceptual movement that occurs between the two, provide a template for navigating similar movement identified by theorists in fields of cognitive and social-emotional development.

Citing imitation and play as the foundation for cognitive development, Jean Piaget describes a sequence of events and conditions that move individuals between polarized contexts of information to generate and integrate intellectual processing. Perceived information and events are organized, retained and represented within the schema by classifying and then merging together similarities, allowing them to be reviewed as a "speeded-up film" (1951, p.238). Unknown materials and concepts encountered in new events are integrated into the schema through the process of assimilation, where qualities from past familiar experiences, recalled from the "film," are compared and related to any similar qualities presenting in the new experience, for purposes of recognition and understanding. When recognition and classification occurs, new materials and concepts are integrated into the existing schema by the process of accommodation (Piaget 1951).

Conceptual intelligence with regard to new encounters and experiences is able to develop, according to Piaget, when a state of equilibrium exists between the processes of assimilation and accommodation, which integrates the previously polarized contexts of information. He asks, "What, in fact, constitutes an operation such as uniting or separating, placing or displacing, arranging or disarranging...?" and answers by describing "reversibility" as the operation that links one object, experience or concept with another "in such a way that movement in either direction is possible" (p.240). Piaget goes on to say that it is a "mobile reversible equilibrium that ensures the conservation of concepts and judgments...and governs... the interior conceptual system of the individual" (p.240), establishing reversible movement between concepts and perspectives as a key component of cognitive development.

Building on Piaget's model, constructivist theorists identify "multiple perspectives" facilitating a "simultaneous changing of our internal representations in response to those perspectives as well as through cumulative experience" (Duffy and Jonassen 1992, p.21). Deep conceptual understanding develops in response to a "dynamic 'dance' of...adaptation and organization" in which "we assert ourselves and our logical constructs on new experiences and information" on one pole, while "our reflective, integrative, accommodative nature is the other pole." The "dynamic interplay" that occurs along the poles generates an "intrinsic, self-organizing nature [that] serves to keep the system in an open, flexible, growth-producing state" (p.14).

During dramatic enactment, then, the participant applies existing knowledge to unknown objects and concepts encountered in the drama, foam tubes or sheets for example, to create new understandings within the dramatic context. Reversible movement between perceptions of self and role, subject and object, past and present, concrete and symbolic and real and imagined that occurs during enactment prompts the participant to move between the two polarized contexts—properties of the unknown objects and the known content of the drama—to explore the potential for meaningful connection. Size, shape, color and other classifications of the tubes and sheets are reviewed for similarities between the two contexts and possibilities for purposeful application and function within the dramatic encounter. Motivated by the quest for dramatic wholeness and the intrinsic force to create "as if," the unknown objects are assimilated into the drama and accommodated as furniture, food, roofs for houses or other functions that fulfill the dramatic context and criteria. The movement between polarized contexts of information that occurs in drama engages an active operational partnership with these similarly structured cognitive processes, providing purposeful navigation for mobile reversibility and meaningful choreography in the dynamic dance of adaptation.

Citing dramatic play as "the most natural self-healing measure childhood affords" (1950, p.222), Erik Erikson's theory of social and emotional development describes polarized contexts of being that individuals navigate to facilitate a sense of identity. As the child moves through a sequence of developmental stages, each one interpreted within the context of one overriding conflict, he or she is confronted with a new function of identity, instigating a "crucial period of increased vulnerability and heightened potential...a potential crisis because of radical change in perspective" (p.96). Conflicts within the stages are represented by two opposing concepts, or polarized extremes of one concept, such as trust vs. mistrust and initiative vs. guilt (1950).

The child plays, according to Erikson, as a means for moving between the two extremes, developing balance, understanding and acceptance of both potentials, ideally prompting successful mastery of the stage and averting a potential crisis of personality development (1950). Erikson notes that "the interpersonal perspective...changes rapidly and often radically, as is testified by the proximity in time of such opposites" (1968, p.96). Social and emotional growth occurs as movement between the polarized contexts alleviates "conflicts, inner and outer, which the vital personality weathers, re-emerging from each crisis with an increased sense of inner unity" (p.92).

In his theory of emotional catharsis, sociologist T.J. Scheff describes "an arrangement of stimuli which contains a balance of distressful and reassuring stimuli...a balance between involvement in past distress and present safety" (1979, p.66). If the individual is able, based on perceptions of the stimuli, to navigate the distance between the present safety of reality and re-experienced past emotion, a "rapid alternation" occurs as the individual becomes involved in a "cycle of participation and observation" (p.62). At the point of "aesthetic distance" along the continuum of opposing states, there is a "balance of thought and feeling" (p.64), followed by cathartic emotional expression, resulting in "a decrease in tension, increases in mental clarity and feelings of well-being" (p.66).

During dramatic enactment, then, the participant is able to experience past emotional distress in the safety of the dramatic moment through the use of puppets, for example, to manage emotional vulnerability and explore related identity conflicts. Movement between perceptions of self and role, subject and object, past and present, concrete and symbolic and real and imagined that occurs during enactment allows the participant to project emotion onto the puppet and rapidly alternate perspectives between opposing states of personal re-experience of the real emotion, and the more distanced, imagined expression through the role of the puppet. The participant uses the role of the puppet to move as close to or as far away from the emotion as is necessary, negotiating the balance between thought and feeling. The movement between polarized contexts that occurs in drama engages an active operational partnership with similarly structured social and emotional processes, allowing purposeful navigation between polarized states of potential conflict necessary for identity formation and the rapid alternation between perspectives needed for achieving aesthetic distance and catharsis.

While advances in neuroscience technology have rendered some aspects of cognitive, social-emotional and other classic models of development obsolete, newly discovered information shines more light on the relevance of drama as a model for therapeutic functioning and neurobiological development. By comparing cognitive and emotional behavior in patients and then tracking patterns of biochemical brain activity, neuroscientist Antonio Damasio (1999) challenges the historically popular scientific notion that functions of emotion and reason are separate and largely unrelated processes. Determining that cognitive functions do not and cannot operate properly without processing an emotional component, he explains how organisms construct knowledge about their environment through awareness of biological regulatory systems contingent on emotional response.

Rejecting the belief that emotion is too subjective, elusive and vague to be considered in cognitive functioning, Damasio asserts, "emotion is integral to the processes of reasoning and decision-making" (p.41). While distinct cognitive and emotional "states" are present within this process, an organism, Damasio concludes, cannot relate to an object, event or concept in the environment and construct knowledge about it without first registering a response from its emotional state, thereby integrating the process of emotional regulation with cognitive development.

Pioneers and leaders in the field of drama therapy, Peter Slade (1954), Brian Way (1967), Richard Courtney (1980, 1989, 1995), Sue Jennings (1978, 1994), David Read Johnson (1982), Robert Landy (1986) and Renee Emunah (1994), to name a few, have consistently defined drama as a modality that engages, facilitates and integrates emotional and cognitive functioning. "Imagination," writes Courtney, "by relating emotion and knowledge, brings about an affective-cognitive synthesis" and "provides a unique kind of knowing that is felt" (1995, pp.118–119). Drama is, perhaps, unique in its ability to integrate within a unified structure equally important elements of thought and emotion in order to create a whole experience.

Damasio identifies a "convergence zone" in the brain, a "reciprocally interconnected...third-party neuron ensemble" that coordinates emotional and cognitive input, sorts the subsequent meanings that are created by such facilitation and estimates potential action that may need to be taken by the organism (1994, p.242). This appears to be an area of the brain in which the operations of drama are especially resonant, pulling in, converging and integrating otherwise polarized aspects of emotional and cognitive functioning, empowering the individual's awareness and ability to successfully respond to and participate in the encounters and challenges of life.

Damasio describes the convergence zone as not exclusively supportive of images of the object or of the self, but a place of perceptual mediation between the two (1994). In 2007, cortical midline structures of the brain overlapping the mirror-neuron system were identified as processors of information regarding self and others in more abstract evaluative terms, with researchers citing the "domain of imagination" as the "representational domain in which both neural systems might cooperate" (Uddin *et al.* 2007, p.156). These neurological processes reflect the key function of drama, purposefully moving participants between and mediating perceptions of self and other, prompting neuroscientists to identify imagination, a fundamental component of drama, as a distinct neurological domain where such mediation and integration can occur.

The discovery of the mirror-neuron system has further eroded the notion that self-awareness, social development and conceptual thought are acquired solely through a sequential formulation of hypothesis and analysis. Neuroscientists now postulate that individuals build awareness and understanding within whole and holistic neurobiological acts of imitation and reenactment that "unify" perception and action and spontaneously incorporate many aspects of development (Iacoboni 2008). Drama is no stranger to whole and holistic acts of imitation and reenactment that unify perception and action and spontaneously incorporate many aspects of development.

Brian Way's (1967) developmental drama focuses on "the whole person" with exercises and activities that seek to enhance concentration and sensory, imaginative, physical, speech, emotional and intellectual capabilities, so that the individual may "practice living" (p.6). Way describes the function of drama as leading the participant "to moments of direct experience, transcending mere knowledge, enriching the imagination, possibly touching the heart and soul as well as the mind" (p.1). Courtney discusses the "holistic effect" and transformative quality of drama, declaring it to be "the developmental unifier" enhancing the "personal, social, intellectual, emotional, aesthetic and psychomotor growths of the total organism" (1995, p.117). Like Moreno, practitioners who have used drama for purposes of healing and development have resisted the rational tide, remaining historically tuned-in to the holistic and integrative power of drama—essential qualities now backed up by neurobiological research.

The operation of drama mirrors operations described by pioneers and leaders in fields related to cognitive, social and emotional development for decades. After nearly four centuries of the Ages of Rationalism, Reason and Enlightenment, during which emotional functioning has been systematically extracted from scientific procedure and related social institutions, findings in neuroscience have swung the pendulum back in the direction of integrating emotion into our understanding with regard to development and functioning. The synchronization of cognition and emotion to bring about new understanding within a unifying structure is at the very core of dramatic enactment.

The discovery of the mirror-neuron system, in which "imitation and synchrony is the glue that binds us together" (Iacoboni 2008, p.130), is reminiscent of the basic dramatic function of imitation and reenactment identified by Aristotle 2500 years ago. It is reasonable to assume that participating in drama and engaging its operations and processes provides individuals with, at the very least, valuable practice for shifting perceptions between polarized perspectives existing within cognitive and affective systems. More ideally, participation in drama provides a template for guided processing that integrates culturally fragmented and neurobiologically challenged development occurring within related systems, moving individuals toward optimum functioning. The following concepts explore a Process Reflective Enactment approach to drama therapy that prompts individuals to enact and embody a range of developmental and therapeutic operations. For the purposes of this text, the discussion will highlight group participation and the response of autistic children.

Spectacle

Aristotle identified "spectacle" as all the visual elements on stage that serve to maintain the drama as a whole (1996). Spectacle in a process reflective approach to drama therapy refers to applied elements of lighting, sound, set pieces, props, costumes, puppets, masks and other objects that attract and hold the attention of participants, most notably children who are inattentive and neurologically impaired, in order to facilitate participation in the drama (Chasen 2005). Contrary to David Read Johnson's "poor drama therapy" approach to developmental transformations that use virtually no supportive materials (Dintino *et al.* 1996), simple colored track lighting, voice amplifying microphones, tents and other eye-catching materials invite participants to connect with the dramatic process and engage operations that enact developmental and therapeutic processing.

Otherwise disconnected and non-responsive children, upon seeing colors change and hearing voices echo on stage, become intrigued with the unusual display and show enthusiastic interest in related activities that connect them with other group members. A study showing how specifically applied sensory stimuli, such as flashing lights and sound, positively influence the imitation performance of autistic children speaks to the impact that spectacle has with regard to engaging therapeutic process through drama. The sensory effects positively influenced all the children in the study, although typical children tended to be influenced more by the social properties of the environment, while autistic children were more impacted by the sensory effects (Ingersoll, Schreibman and Tran 2003). Studies also show that providing opportunities for autistic children to develop joint attention, the ability to coordinate attention between an object and a person in a social context, leads to improvement in a variety of social and communication skills (Ingersoll, Screibman and Whalen 2006). The sensory elements of spectacle send a message to the thalamus, amygdala and frontal lobes of our brains indicating that something attractive, unusual or interesting is occurring, initiating a focused impulse to connect to and explore the environment, as well as the people and processes that are part of it.

Spontaneity

Moreno again foresaw what neuroscientists discovered a century later, stating, "spontaneity, as a cerebral function, shows a more rudimentary development than any other important, fundamental function of the central nervous system" (1994, p.47). Spontaneity prompts drama therapy participants, without overly defining preconceived notions, to interact freely with materials, techniques and concepts that move individuals between polarized states of being and information. Landy defines spontaneity as "the creative moment…when the unconscious is accessible and ready to be symbolized through dramatic action…the midpoint between compulsive, inhibited styles…and impulsive, over-involved styles" (1994, p.118). The concept of spontaneity is especially relevant for autistic children who are so often trapped between extreme fluctuations of these styles, demonstrated in part by tendencies toward echolalia, or "television talk": sudden unexplainable actions, and repetitive, idiosyncratic patterns of behavior. An environment that encourages spontaneity prompts autistic children to freely explore, interact and engage movement between extreme styles in order to find the developmental midpoint where new understandings and connections can be created.

Spontaneity in general is perhaps a little unnerving for people and a culture comforted by predictable and seemingly manageable circumstances, especially when it comes to the behavior of children. Not many homes or classrooms, unfortunately, operate from a principle of spontaneity. The unusual and eccentric manner in which autistic children express themselves exacerbates this sentiment, causing parents and teachers, with misguided intentions, to censor the emergence of an already difficult-to-cultivate sense of spontaneity, due to perceived inappropriateness. A Process Reflective Enactment approach to drama therapy provides an environment of lights, colors, objects, tolerance and clear boundaries that invite spontaneous interaction and expression in order to engage developmental and therapeutic operations.

Ritual

Once an initial connection to the drama-therapy group is established through spectacle and spontaneous interaction, extended connections among group members, established and expressed through ritual, start to appear. Rituals initiated by the group leader support safe encounters and transitions. Maintaining certain protocols and materials from session to session provides a sense of consistency and safety, especially for autistic children who deal with stimuli often perceived as unpredictable and unsafe. Ritual helps contain perceived chaos and create order within the encounter (Emunah 1994). Landy notes that ritual "is a conservative activity...repeated in a prescribed way to perpetuate the status quo...and to defend an individual or group against danger" (1994, p.69). Rituals and ritualistic behavior performed by autistic children—for example arranging a pile of magic markers, inhabiting a particular spot in the room or needing a certain cushion or toy—reflect attempts to manage the social environment and remain present within all the unsettling sensory, perceptual and emotional stimulation that comes with it.

Landy also sees ritual as a way to "affirm a common bond among members of a community" (1994, p.69). While group leaders create rituals that define the rhythm of the group as a whole, group members enact parallel solitary rituals and ultimately merge within the unifying group rituals set forth by the group leader, spontaneously generating new collective and connective rituals among group members. Arranging the pile of markers becomes a shared game that brings laughter to an otherwise isolated and silent boy. Unintelligible song-like vocalizations and hand movements exhibited by one boy in his own world become a weekly duet with another group member, performed regularly with happy laughter and sustained eye contact between the two. A lone wanderer who moves clockwise around the perimeter of the room in the same manner session after session eventually is joined by three or four, all moving together in synchronized and comforting formation. The previously lone wanderer now looks for his companions each week and smiles at them as they undertake their journey. For these children, ritualistic behavior represents a more primal, sensory-motor response to an unpredictable and uncomfortably stimulating world. By providing dramatic rituals for defining space, time and other boundaries that guide appropriate enactment, these self-soothing rituals of autistic children are able to spontaneously transform from isolated events into something new, a shared experience representing authentic connection with other people.

Ensemble

As connections with other people begin to emerge, the drama-therapy group ideally takes on qualities of an ensemble, in which "a sense of wholeness and cohesion...facilitates empowered development of the individual in a reaffirming social context" (Chasen 2005, p.170). The creation of ensemble mirrors polarized operations of development as disparate pieces of information, in this case, individual group members, are integrated within a unifying context to create something new and uniquely meaningful. A distinctly supportive and empowered shared identity emerges from the collection of individuals in the group, exuding feelings of safety, acceptance and meaningful encounter. Ensemble empowers individuals by guiding them to experience operations that reflect developmental and therapeutic processes. Empowered individuals go on to inform and strengthen the identity of the ensemble in an ongoing reciprocal relationship. The purposeful and supportive energy generated by the ensemble allows participants, in a number of circumstances and in groups for autistic as well as typical children, to find success after other settings have failed them, expelled them or labeled them as having uncontrollable behavior problems (Chasen 2005).

Neuroscientific underpinnings of ensemble can be found in the concept of intentional attunement, in which mirror neurons imitate actions and intentions of others while perceiving aspects of ourselves in others, generating a "peculiar quality of familiarity" with other individuals, produced by the "collapse" of others' intentions into our own. A "shared manifold" develops from activation of what is perceived as a shared neural system, merging perceptions of what others do and feel with what we do and feel, resulting in an experiential understanding of others coinciding with connection to self occurring in a shared meaningful interpersonal space. Social identity, defined as the "'self-ness' we readily attribute to others, the inner feeling of 'being like you,'" is the result of interacting within the shared "we-centric" space. (Gallese 2006, p.16). The ensemble of drama therapy embraces all participants, inviting autistic children to experience and affirm shared aspects of identity in a safe and supportive environment that reflects and enacts developmental and therapeutic processing.

Empowerment

As the individual connects to the group, opportunity for empowerment through drama therapy is generated on a number of levels. Neurologically, operations of drama engage a range of developmental and therapeutic processing, synchronizing and integrating an otherwise fragmented system, inadvertently wired by developmental challenges and systematically dismantled by cultural decree. Autistic children in particular are empowered by pragmatic experience with the manual shifting of cognitive and social-emotional gears that determine perception of and response to self and other, providing a technical blueprint for more successful functioning and interaction.

Personally and socially, drama therapy empowers participants to envision, enact and embody personalized images of a healthy and productive life, placing them in the role of producer, playwright, director, lead actor and audience in the quest to realize that vision. It provides opportunities to explore, express and create on one's own terms, potentially expanding roles and increasing the ability to be seen and heard by self and others in a different or enhanced light. Problems can be solved and powerful words can be documented. Participants are liberated to be whomever they see fit within the parameters of the ensemble.

Globally, a Process Reflective Enactment approach to drama therapy empowers a worldview that seeks to re-integrate whole and holistic measures of functioning discussed in previous sections, recognizing the mirror of dysfunction and disease that exists between individuals, aspects of culture and the Earth. In too many respects, global and cultural institutions operate in depersonalized and self-destructive manners, isolating feeling from thought and thought from feeling, resulting in the manipulation and distortion of both (Chasen 2009).

This fragmentation prompts people, for example, to protest the evils of government-run health care by demanding that government keep its hands off Medicare, a popular government-run healthcare program; it enables oil companies, soon after a devastating spill, to rally public support for drilling deep in the ocean with no established backup plan or technology for managing catastrophic spills; it allows publicly influential anti-gay crusaders to privately justify indulgences with same-sex prostitutes; and it makes it OK for soccer moms and dads to chat with each other and complain about the price of gas from the open windows of their parked SUVs, while their engines idle for another ten minutes until practice ends, on a perfectly fine evening that needs no air conditioning or heat, on an otherwise increasingly warming globe—another layer of fragmented irony that does not, I suspect, find its way into their conversations. These events, just a few of which are occurring at the time of this writing, exemplify how we, as a society, dissociate thought from feeling and feeling from thought in a manner that threatens our well-being.

Issues such as these refer more to conditions of broad psychosocial dysfunction than political persuasion. As Moreno states, "A truly therapeutic procedure cannot have less an objective than the whole of mankind" (1978, p.3). We all participate in a world-wide system where "so many of the basic things we need to do to nurture and take care of ourselves, like eating, breathing, managing waste, and pursuing health, operate in a manner that actually leads us more quickly to our own demise" (Chasen 2009, p.221). The emotional/cognitive disconnect is profoundly dysfunctional and alarmingly epidemic.

Following the logic that led the Supreme Court to rule that corporations can be considered as individuals,[1] our society, if it was an individual, clearly meets the *DSM-IV* criteria for Antisocial Personality Disorder. But that only (partially) covers Axis II. Axis I could include a host of Dissociative and Substance-Related Disorders, while Axis III would need to describe various injuries and poisonings, many of them self-inflicted (making a case for the inclusion of Borderline Personality Disorder on Axis II). Axis IV would indicate each of the psychosocial and environmental problems listed in the *DSM-IV*, and Mr./Ms. Society's GAF might hover somewhere in the mid- to lower-50s.

Many who seek and obtain power do so through these fragmented strands of self-deprecation and depersonalization, riding waves of violence, corruption and destruction that provide a false sense of empowerment to positions of influence, confusing the collective narrative and perpetuating the dysfunctional system. Participation in drama therapy allows us to explore, manage and become aware of our darker impulses within safe and nurturing contexts. A Process Reflective Enactment approach empowers systemic change, reintegrating thought and feeling, effecting realignment within related systems and channeling energy in a positive, visionary direction.

Action

"Dramatic action" according to Landy, is "an essential means of healing" (2008, p.197). Understanding self and other begins and progresses with the unified process of perceiving and imitating action (Iacoboni 2008). Since autistic children perceive and experience action in a manner that can overload sensory systems, immersion in ensemble activity and structured dramatic action defined by the quest

---

1   *Citizens United v Federal Election Commission* [2010] US Supreme Court.

for empowered well-being can be particularly beneficial in connecting them to developmental and therapeutic processes. Action occurring in the drama-therapy group differs from enactment, discussed below, in that it refers to active experiences surrounding the participant that can be perceived for purposes of engaging neurologically embodied simulation as preparation for enactment, rather than to the roles or actions he or she imitates and reenacts within a dramatic activity. Access to an environment that facilitates and reflects ensemble activity and dramatic action provides participants with the opportunity to perceive and simulate a range of action and experiences structured for empowered functioning.

Imitation

From Aristotle's musings to the mirror-neuron system, imitation of action has been identified as the foundation for development of deep understanding and emotional processing. The multi-mirrored experience of imitation in drama reflects and heightens the neurological function of imitation and embodied simulation. Neuroscience research demonstrates that imitation, for which we are "hard-wired" (Oberman and Ramachandran 2007, p.25), can make someone slow, fast, smart, stupid, rude, polite, aggressive, cooperative, neat or sloppy; merely thinking about college professors and neurologically imitating them can make a person smarter, while thinking about soccer "hooligans" can make a person "dumber" (Iacoboni 2008, p.201). In the anterior insula section of the brain, visual information concerning the emotions of others is directly mapped, as a result of imitation, onto the same motor neural structures that determine the experience of that emotion in the observer (Gallese, Keysers and Rizzolatti 2004). Imitation of an action empowers a basic understanding of self, connection to others and management of the subsequent interactive cognitive, emotional and social relationships. Imitation through Process Reflective Enactment reenacts key components of a range of developmental and therapeutic processes.

Symbolic representation

Symbolic representation in drama therapy, the ability to compare qualities of objects and concepts to imagine them as another thing, operates the vehicle that moves between polarized developmental and therapeutic contexts. It provides the key that engages critical components of functioning, allowing for the reversible and alternating focus between sources of information and affect identified by classic theoretical models (Chasen 2009). Neuroscientists note that symbolic representation is the primary function within the "domain of imagination" where neural systems bringing different sources of information are able to interact and cooperate (Uddin *et al.* 2007, p.156).

Opportunities to practice and gain experience with symbolic representation are critical for autistic children, as they encapsulate the challenge presented by the switching of gears through manual vs. automatic transmission. The literal, black-and-white thinking demonstrated by autistic children is indicative of the difficulty they face with moving between polarized concepts. They are most comfortable at either end of the poles and can be at a loss to understand all the relative areas in between. By exercising the operation of symbolic representation through imaginative and dramatic play and improvisation, autistic children are able to increase their ability to move between contexts of information. The operation is often delayed or dormant in autistic children, who need guided experiences with projective techniques that can counteract repetitive and restrictive modes of processing (Landy 1994). By projecting qualities of emotion and story onto otherwise inanimate play objects, autistic children are able to break perseverative patterns and increase their ability to interact. One mother expressed astonishment that her ten-year-old son, after exposure to parallel group activities and processes, was initiating imaginary play, when he had never shown any previous interest in that type of activity. Symbolic representation in Process Reflective Enactment engages functions that provide a pragmatic approach to initiating and exercising shifts in perspective, the operational movement between contexts critical to developmental processing.

Envisioning

Similar to the notion of imagining discussed in context of symbolic representation, envisioning looks more specifically at the individual's ability to visualize self. Neurotypical people may have difficulty visualizing a balanced sense of self due to personal or affectively driven issues. Autistic people, although they rely heavily on visualization to compensate for other underdeveloped parts of their brain (Medical News Today 2006), also experience technical difficulty with interpreting and constructing visual images of self (Chiu *et al.* 2008).

In an unpublished study undertaken at Kid Esteem, autistic teenagers, when asked to describe images of self in relation to certain situations, had a difficult time articulating physical characteristics of their bodies, such as what their face or stance might look like, or where they might be situated in relation to others, when visualizing hypothetical as well as actual circumstances. They easily described and related to objects such as clocks, food, tables, chairs and other details in the visualizations, and they were able to articulate different personal feelings about the situations through description of these objects, but they could not, at the outset of the study, describe how their physical self might appear. The neurotypical teenage respondent in the study was able to describe images of self in detail, stating, "It's like a movie of what is happening, playing in my mind with me as the lead role." The autistic teenagers were not able to describe images of self from the visualizations, responding with phrases such as, "I don't know," "I can't tell," "a million different pieces of things floating in my head" and "little bits of pictures moving by too quickly to see."

Self-modeling, video and visualization techniques of drama therapy supported the autistic teenagers' enhancing of their ability to visualize and describe a sense of self within a range of social situations. Once they became more competent with constructing a representation of self, they became able to ascribe positive characteristics to the images of self that could potentially impact the situational context of the visualization. This brings us back to Jason, the little boy discussed in Chapter 1 who was "beside himself" when he did not receive his certificate. After seeing others receive the certificate, Jason was apparently able to visualize and/or perceive himself receiving the certificate as well. When this positive image was not actualized, Jason was able to be "beside himself," moving between the image of receiving the certificate and the reality of not receiving it, prompting expression of his frustration. Although this was a difficult encounter for Jason, it was a relatively healthy one, in that he was able to construct an image of self interacting socially, rather than remaining isolated within an object-image orientation that disconnected him from others. A Process Reflective Enactment approach to drama therapy provides tools and techniques through which participants may envision, construct and manage technical as well as affectively driven images of self, including visions that support the yet-unseen potential of the individual participant.

Enactment

Enactment comprises the climactic activity in which all processes become integrated through some form of presentation of self within a dramatic activity. In the mirror-neuron system, this occurs simultaneously with perception and imitation as an integrated process, when the neural system recreates the experience by simulating what is being perceived (Iacoboni 2008). Enactment in drama therapy, along with imitating, reenacting and integrating key components of developmental and therapeutic processing, provides structured opportunities for building ensemble, generating spontaneity, engaging symbolic representation, exploring personal and social relationships, acquiring models for appropriate response to behavioral and social encounters and challenges, and developing emotional expression and pragmatic language skills toward constructing and actualizing a vision of self that is, in the moment, transformative and whole.

Autistic children, like most children, process challenging concepts and affect through play and enactment. Unlike most neurotypical children, autistic children tend to enact in isolation, playing out all the different roles and parts of a story by themselves. They often perseverate on a particular aspect of the enactment, repeating the same language or actions over and over again. A Process Reflective Enactment approach to enactment places participants in relation to each other as parts of a structured and meaningful whole, causing autistic children to break out of isolating, limiting patterns of engagement and initiating processes that generate and facilitate interaction.

Plot

Aristotle (1996) referred to plot as the organization of events that imitate an action of magnitude. The concept of plot in drama therapy, the content of the story enacted, provides participants with an empowering, pragmatic context for reflecting, organizing, constructing, enacting, understanding and responding to significant life episodes. For autistic children who have difficulty internally structuring and verbalizing sequences of events in a manner that is cohesive and easily shared, activities and techniques of drama therapy facilitate a variety of formats through which they can clearly and systematically construct, share and explore personally meaningful incidents.

Aristotle lists a number of components within and related to plot that support the pragmatic needs of autistic children. The notion of "unity" maintains that a cohesive theme and/or set of ideas be presented throughout the enactment, reflecting a "completeness...a whole which has a beginning, a middle and an end" (1996, p.12). "Character" in this context alludes more to a degree of consistency and connection with other elements of the enactment, while also reflecting "the kind of thing which discloses the nature of a choice," a basic perspective of "goodness...[and] appropriateness" (p.24). "Recognition" indicates a "change from ignorance to knowledge" resulting from memory, inference and/or emotional impact (p.13). "Reasoning" speaks to "the ability to say what is implicit in a situation and appropriate to it...the means by which people argue that something is or is not the case, or put forward some universal proposition" (pp.12–13). "Diction" refers to the manner in which the words and phrases are articulated and enunciated (p.12), and "universality" reflects the plot's relevance to and expressed understanding by the larger ensemble (p.16). These components, organized more readily or automatically by neurotypical participants, represent fictional and non-fiction events that support participants in building social skills and responding more effectively to life's challenges. Elements of plot, expressed through the activities, tools and techniques of a Process Reflective Enactment approach to drama therapy, are a significant source of pragmatic support for autistic children, prompting them to structure meaningful life experiences for purposes of reflection and empowered response.

Emotional intelligence

Emotional intelligence "indicates an ability to be aware of and express emotional states of being, using self-identified language, in a manner that assists with the task of fulfilling individual needs and solving problems, be they personal, social, or intellectual" (Chasen 2009, p.12). Autistic children, managing heightened anxiety from having to coordinate an over-stimulated input of sensory information, developmentally fragmented perceptions of affect and difficulties with verbal communication and articulation, have an especially hard time identifying and expressing emotion in a pragmatic and task-supportive manner. Specific tools and techniques of drama therapy, such as sociometry signs discussed previously and formatted language models that prompt empowered emotional response provide participants with concrete experiences that build emotional intelligence skills.

By imitating facial expressions, mirror neurons "lead us to experience a particular affective state" directly understood by embodied simulation (Gallese 2006, p.19). This process establishes the neurological foundation for generating emotional intelligence. By providing safely structured contexts within which autistic children can experience and explore feelings and construct accurate, self-supporting expressions of emotion, drama therapy reflects, guides, enacts and informs neurological functions, processes and pragmatic experiences that enhance and empower emotional intelligence and subsequent social interaction.

Catharsis

Emotional intelligence acquired through participation in drama therapy creates opportunity for catharsis, discussed earlier, in which there is a balance between previously distressful and presently reassuring stimuli, and between thought and feeling (Scheff 1979). Drama therapy integrates these elements within one unified structure, generating operational movement, synchronizing functions, and facilitating emotional release, understanding and feelings of well-being.

When considering Landy's model of distancing (1994), an autistic child may at times appear to be over-distanced, with an analytical, object-focused, disconnected affect, and other times under-distanced, demonstrating emotional overreaction and loss of boundaries between self and other. These fluctuations between extremes are more a result of cognitively driven developmental and neurological conditions rather than affectively driven emotional imbalances. Reenactment and exploration of meaningful events through drama therapy serves to counteract fragmented perceptions and stereotypical, idiosyncratic affects exhibited by autistic children, bringing cognitive and emotional functioning more into balance with regard to the situation being explored. When autistic children achieve aesthetic distance, catharsis is usually demonstrated in more subtle fashion, through clear verbal and reflective articulation that accurately identifies the emotion occurring in the situation, rather than the more intensified reactions of crying, laughing or raging, as atypical affects are brought into balance and pragmatically voiced with reasoned and insightful expression. Participation in drama therapy empowers autistic children to construct personally meaningful aspects of plot that bring emotional expression and intellectual understanding more into balance, prompting opportunities for emotional self-awareness and catharsis.

Rehearsal

Participants in drama therapy become involved in an ongoing process that, on one level, integrates perceptions of self, other, cognition and emotion, naturally reflecting and engaging a range of related therapeutic and developmental processing, and, on another level, reenacts meaningful life events, generating potential for deep understanding and self-empowerment. Drama therapy provides guided rehearsal for enhancing functions within both these levels. Rehearsal, critical to development in neuroscientific terms, is described as "constant automatic simulation and reenactment" with the purpose of "making us ready when action is really needed" (Iacoboni 2008, pp.128–129). The mirror-neuron system provides a built-in rehearsal process that is mirrored by the activities, tools and techniques of drama therapy, supporting competence with the manual shifting of gears between the perception of and pragmatic response to self and other, integrating fragmented domains of functioning, and prompting psychodynamic awareness and insight. Rehearsal in a Process Reflective Enactment approach to drama therapy coordinates, over a period of time, a whole system of functioning with the goal of representing a more fully integrated and aware being.

Transformation

Moments and opportunities for transformation through the rehearsal process in drama therapy facilitate the emergence of a more fully integrated and aware being. In his discussion of drama as an agent of transformation, Courtney defines transformation as "change from one thing to another," a person into a character through acting, or one idea into another through learning (1989, p.15). Transformation is also described as the result of a spontaneous encounter in which "the therapist deconstructs the story to break up constraining narratives... The emphasis in this model involves the removal of obstacles rather than a gathering of insight" (Galway, Hurd and Johnson 2003, p.137). Engaging participants in playful encounters to empower transformation is especially relevant for autistic children, as their ability to interact verbally as a tool for gaining insight can be underdeveloped, and, as is the case with all children, potentially counterproductive. Transformations that occur within the dramatic enactment have a direct impact on the demeanor and outlook of the participant.

During a group session with four-year-old autistic children, a particularly combative boy monopolized a toy toaster, repeatedly popping up pieces of toy toast a bit too close to the other children's faces. The look of steely, guarded determination on his face as the group leader called his name told us that he was going to continue this activity and was prepared to fight the inevitably punitive interventions he likely, and understandably, received in other settings. The group leader approached him and situated her hands so that they were in between the toaster and the face of the next child into which he was preparing to pop toast, exclaiming, in an animated fashion, "Yes! I need toast! Please! I'm so hungry! Is it hot? Oh, no! Is it too hot?" The boy's sullen face with furrowed brow loosened into a mischievous smile as he popped the toast into her hands. The group leader bobbled the toast and danced around a bit, exclaiming "Ah! Hot! Hot!" As the toast "cooled," so did the boy's demeanor. His smile was no longer mischievous; it became joyful, reflecting the delight of the play. He sought to repeat the encounter, loading the toast again and warning the group leader, "It's hot!" The boy was able to share the toaster with other children, and the game lasted a few more rounds until it was time to clean up.

Even if the boy's transformative experience only lasted for the duration of the playful encounter, it added that much more positive, cooperative, joyful interaction to his schema than there had been before, and for the moment, it thwarted yet another negative punitive social encounter that would have been piled on top of his four short years of life experience. In later sessions, while the boy continued to have his moments, he participated with a more open and playful demeanor, occasionally seeking out the group leader as well as other children to play the hot-toast game in a manner that was more cooperative than aggressive.

The group leader instinctually appealed to the boy's desire to act aggressively by suggesting that the hot toast would have an adverse effect on her as a strategy for eliciting and transforming his negative interaction. Approaching oppositional and potentially aggressive behavior in this way is tricky and requires sharp instincts and skills that can ensure the safety of all group members, especially when working with young atypical children. But, whenever possible, interventions regarding undesirable behavior and general empowerment are best accomplished through playful encounters that elicit transformation and expand response, rather than imposing yet more constraining narratives that limit response. The tools and techniques of drama therapy are defined by their ability to facilitate transformation.

Role

In a model of drama therapy that reflects and enacts developmental and therapeutic processes to cultivate social skills in autistic children, establishment and evolution of new and existing roles that promote social interaction, such as friend and playmate, is the desired outcome. Spectacle, ritual, ensemble, action, imitation, symbolic representation, envisioning, enactment, plot, emotional intelligence and catharsis integrate to generate a rehearsal process that transforms and expands the otherwise isolated role repertoire of the autistic individual, reflecting a healthy sense of self successfully interacting with others in a manner that empowers social connectedness and a general sense of well-being.

Landy defines "role" as "one of many parts of the personality that is animated as one acts in the mind and in the world" (2008, p.104). Alluding to "both the actor on stage and the actor in everyday life," the theatrical and sociological meanings of role compliment each other, representing types of behavior that are "more prototype than stereotype" (p.104). Landy states, "once the separation between 'me' and 'not me' is made, role taking as such begins" (1993, p.34). He describes the ability to play roles as coming from "one's need to assert oneself in the world…to get in and out of oneself and to master both that which is situated inside, the role taken, and outside, the objective world" (pp.39–40). Herein lies the challenge of working with autistic children toward developing new social roles. Neurological conditions hamper the ability to clearly separate the "me" from the "not me" and the inside from the outside, diminishing, to some extent, the conscious need to assert oneself in the world and subsequently promoting styles of behavior that are more self-related stereotype than other-related prototype.

While everyday roles, organized by Landy within somatic, cognitive, affective, social/cultural, spiritual and aesthetic categories (1994), are all impacted by the neurological makeup of the autistic child, opportunity for transformation can be found within spiritual and aesthetic engagement, where "spiritual roles of the epic dimension often intersect with aesthetic roles, those pertaining to the creative process" (1994, p.161). In comparison to existing medical and behavioral approaches that pathologize autism with procedures seeking to control rather than transform somatic, cognitive, affective and social/cultural conditions, the spiritual approach, reflecting the joyful and playful spirit of the child, and aesthetic, reflecting the natural creative instinct of the child, are perhaps the more "pristine" categories of engagement, the last frontiers that have not as yet been completely dominated and "dumbed down" by institutionalized practices.

Developing social roles through the aesthetic spirit of drama therapy provides a model of treatment that recognizes, without judgment, a duality and diverse range of roles that can coexist and thrive, rather than assessing and categorizing individuals within the more linear and limiting criteria of normal or abnormal, diseased or well, good or bad. This approach reflects and supports the notion of neurodiversity, in which atypical neural development, instead of needing to be "fixed," is accepted, respected and empowered to full potential, as with any other regular variation of human traits and abilities.

In neuroscientific terms, "role" refers to a commonly shared function existing and occurring within the social world that is able to be represented by convergent neural states realized in two different bodies, allowing the "objectual other" to become "another self" (Gallese 2006). An individual observes another individual functioning in the role of student, for example, and coordinates that perception of the other with awareness of his or her own actions and intentions when functioning as a student. This prompts the individual to understand the experience of the other, as it activates similar responses when actions are taken by the self, neurologically merging the two separate experiences within the one objective but intimately shared and understood role of student. This ability of the mirror-neuron system to imitate and take on the role of other as it relates to self is the foundational strategy for building understanding of the roles of self, other and the interactive relationship between the two. As Landy asserts, "The more competently one plays out one's roles, the more one will develop an ease in navigating the sometimes difficult boundaries between internal and external experience" (2008, p.40).

Process Reflective Enactment in drama therapy social-skills groups for autistic children empowers individuals, through a spirited aesthetic experience, to perceive and construct pragmatic understandings, approaches and responses to established and emerging roles such as friend, playmate, classmate, son, daughter, sibling and other roles that initiate and engage spontaneous and creative social interaction. By engaging in enjoyable encounters and experiences with others that empower the joyful and playful child's spirit, the individual becomes naturally inclined to focus on enhancing somatic, cognitive, affective and social/cultural components of the role in order to gain fuller access to the desired experience. A child who is having fun with others on the playground will likely speak and behave in a manner that will attempt to enhance that fun. While the child may or may not be so successful from a pragmatic standpoint, the infusion of spirited creative energy provides an invaluable resource for pursuing remediation.

The enactment of pragmatic skills and operations within relevant dramatic contexts prompts expansion of the enhanced roles, as well as exploration of new roles, connecting self to other and immersing participants in what it means and how it feels to function in these roles. The choice to play a particular role, reflecting a desired or declined aspect of self, provides, through enactment, deeper understanding, management and opportunity for taking purposeful action. The following Process Reflective Enactment tools and techniques empower individuals to rehearse and embody developmental and therapeutic processes that establish, expand and enhance desired roles.

Guided play—facilitated at the outset of each group, open access to costumes, puppets, props, toy family houses and people, action figures and other play objects prompt projection, presentation of self to other, and interaction, providing participants with self-guided opportunities to transition to the group session, establish ritual and manage stimuli at their own pace.

Drama games—interactive games of movement and enactment for learning names, establishing ensemble, exchanging information and developing connections.

Locograms / Sociometry—originated by Moreno (1994), various criteria move participants around the space to facilitate and measure emotional expression, connection to ensemble, and individual and group perspective.

Puppetry—for facilitating greetings and related social skills, projective play, empowered emotional expression and catharsis, plot construction, symbolic representation and pragmatic language skills.

Masks—for identifying emotional expression, reading facial cues and prompting related pragmatic language.

Set construction—uses tables, chairs, sheets, tents and objects to create ritual, ensemble and symbolic representation; establishes concrete foundation for construction and enactment of plot.

Improvisation—alternative use of objects for generating symbolic representation, perspective-building, transformation, connection between self and other, pragmatic interactive skills, reading face and body cues.

Narration—verbal reflection and description of plot, ensemble activity, dramatic action occurring in the environment and story, to prompt imitation, sequencing skills and sustain pragmatic, reality-based connection to others.

Role-play—envisioning and enacting self as another, or portraying self in another time frame or setting, through language and movement, individually or in groups, within a prescribed boundary of shared meanings and contexts, with or without the use of costumes and props, for rehearsing pragmatic language, social interaction and problem-solving skills.

Storytelling—reflecting fictional and non-fiction events supporting plot construction, symbolic representation, projection, envisioning, imitation, enactment and pragmatic language skills.

Movie-making—small groups use elements of spectacle to construct plots, take on roles and create videos that facilitate envisioning, dramatic enactment, imitation, pragmatic interaction, emotional intelligence and self-assessment associated with process-oriented social skills.

Power Lines scripting—documented verbal expressions constructed through enactment that prompt, reflect and empower pragmatic language of emotional intelligence, problem-solving and self-empowerment skills.

Simulation—reenactment of particular social events and encounters to empower imitation and rehearsal of pragmatic interaction and response.

Director's Chair—derived from Playback Theatre (Fox 1999); participants rely on previous group experiences with ensemble, envisioning, plot, and rehearsal to direct reenactments of reality-based scenes from personal, real-life experiences, casting group members in significant roles to empower plot construction, pragmatic language response, emotional intelligence, catharsis, empathy, transformation and role enhancement. Reflects notion that "sensory motor system appears to support reconstruction of what it would feel like to be in a particular emotion, by means of simulation of the related body state" (Gallese 2006, p.19).

Video-modeling—videotaped role-play approaches for enacting, envisioning, rehearsing, perceiving and self-assessing social and emotional intelligence skills, including reenactments of specific events depicting personal challenges from participants' real-life experiences to empower pragmatic response, transformation and role enhancement.

Theatre, drama and PDD children

Brian, a 13-year-old boy with low self-esteem and mild, undiagnosed signs of PDD, enters the individual session and starts talking about his school play. Usually we enact scenes, improvisations and role-plays around the bullying he regularly receives while walking the halls and attending classes in his junior high school. He struggles with self-image, stuck on the question of why kids act that way and why they choose him as their target. It's apparent that he despises the way he is treated, but he also seems to cling to the role of victim as a way of organizing and maintaining his avoidant and sullen outlook. Today, though, as he announces he got a part in the school play, his affect suddenly brightens and he is eager to perform some of his lines during our sessions. His part is secondary but substantial: a somewhat one-dimensional, not-especially-likeable teacher in a version of *High School Musical*. When I ask him how he feels about the character he is playing, he leans toward me and pronounces, with a presence of mind and spirit full of exuberance, "I LOVE him!"

Theatre and drama is an ideal activity for children with autism. Participating in his school play allows Brian to create a surrogate role through which he can express love for himself. He is able to channel aspects of his eccentric affect into the role and receive positive attention from his peer group, rather than the usual disdain for these aspects of his personality. Many higher functioning autistic children, because of their uniquely idiosyncratic verbal and physical behaviors, can reproduce specific vocal intonations and qualities and have a natural affinity for theatrics. They are able to effectively apply their "quirks" toward building an interesting and responsive character through the discipline of the rehearsal process. Even if they aren't cast for performance, participating in drama as a school activity, building sets, painting scenery and working on stage crew are mechanical and artistic activities that utilize particular skill sets in which high-functioning autistic children often excel. Moreover, junior high and high school drama clubs are populated by students generally more tolerant and understanding of people considered to be outside the social norm, creating an accepting and interactive environment that naturally promotes socialization.

The flair for the dramatic can also be found in the play of younger autistic children, who tend to demonstrate stronger, more sustained connections, bordering on obsessions, with popular roles and characters from entertainment media than most typical children. This may be a result of reliance on visual stimuli to create understanding and connection to self and other, or perhaps it is due to the mirror created by idiosyncratic machine/person hybrids discussed earlier and seen in shows and toys like Thomas the Tank Engine and Pokémon, or maybe it's a combination of these and other factors. Whatever the reason, autistic children seem to connect to characters in a way that helps them build a sense of self and response to other, providing the brain with a meaningful subject/object to synchronize operations around.

The brain's thalamus likely takes notice of the unusually stimulating visual and auditory sensory information that makes up the character and sends it to the emotion-processing amygdala, which, as stated earlier, is oversized in autistic children, causing a heightened response. The rational processing of the frontal lobes coordinates the reality around what is being perceived, that the character is also a conscious, responsive and interactive being, and communicates this information back to the excited amygdala, creating a balance between emotional stimulation and rational thought that keeps the child highly interested in and engaged with the character.

Autistic children often repeat dialogue and relate plot lines from their favorite characters' episodes, possibly as a strategy for generating meaningful communication and connection. A context for processing this tendency for echolalia, or "television talk" related to favorite characters, may be found in *The New Science of Learning: Brain Fitness for Kids* (National Public Television 2009) airing periodically on Public Television stations around the nation since June of 2009. Neurobiologists present a model organized around the acronym MAPS (Memory, Attention, Processing, Sequencing) that explains how different parts of the brain coordinate aspects of information and create the neurological foundation for learning.

Memory, the ability to retrieve and apply information, works with and is guided by the notion of attention, which needs, according to the model, some unpredictability to remain undistracted. "Processing rate" refers to the degree that learners can understand, coordinate and act on verbal and nonverbal cues, while sequencing—organizing and tying all the information together—is seen as the fundamental building block of learning. When remembering and sharing events from a particular show or story that has caught their attention, all children process and sequence relevant information. Autistic children, by perseverating on and repeating dialogue and episodic information over an extended period of time, are perhaps attempting to engage aspects of the MAPS paradigm in an effort to bridge the disconnect between self and other, and manually shift between gears in which they otherwise find themselves stuck.

Along with enacting operations that reflect developmental and therapeutic processes, the structure of drama provides a template for engaging components of MAPS as well as other models of learning based on neuroscientific research. A *New York Times* article titled "The Make-Believe Solution: Can imaginary play teach children to control their impulses—and be better students?" (Tough 2009, pp. 31–35) alludes to the recent influx of neurologically based research identifying play and pretend as a primary organizing activity for enhancing cognitive functions and learning styles.

Drama engages meaningful, spontaneous activity that mirrors and integrates cognitive and emotional functioning within a paradigm that empowers development of the whole person. Ideally, the dramatic action is child-centered, child-initiated and child-directed. Drama is fun, dynamic and larger than life, igniting interest and illuminating neurological pathways not previously accessible and providing emotionally intelligent scripts for taking on real-life challenges. Anecdotes from parents describing the first time their child noticed and said hello to another child at a playground, or how their child was dancing with his cousins at the family party, or how their child asks, "Can we go every day to play school?" or commenting that our group is "the only place we go where I don't have to fight him to get there" adds to a body of circumstantial evidence that speaks to the power of drama as a modality for engaging autistic children, combining the liberating spirit of joyful play with clinical methodology for developing self and other awareness and connection, interactive skills and behavioral transformation.

But it is not always a smooth and easy process. Adjustment and adaptation is hard work for autistic children, as they tend to be much more interested in staying safely in their own heads and being entertained by their own ideas. The act of making a choice and managing concepts that do not offer rigidly fixed black-and-white contexts can be difficult for them. While they perseverate on existing dramatic stories and characters, transitioning toward the creation of new stories can be challenging. Autistic children often enter the drama-therapy group, or any group, for that matter, with developmental resistance to the natural give and take of group interaction, emotional resistance due in part to anxiety caused by developmental resistance as well as a host of other personal emotional factors, and behavioral resistance caused by the combination of developmental and emotional resistance and years of mismanagement.

Ian, a ten-year-old boy who has been with our program since he was six, had been fixated for a number of years, ironically, on the different genres of drama, interpreting every interaction that occurred in group (and at home and in school, according to his mother) in terms of its relevance to action, comedy, horror, fantasy, drama or romance. Prior to developing this language, Ian rarely communicated with others, echoing in isolation, for the most part, dialogue from television shows. As we reached in to meet him at his place of reference, this new interactive and conceptual language began to emerge, providing tremendous opportunities to create reciprocal and meaningful dialogue, first with leaders and then with others in the group, empowering him to be much more present. Perhaps being subjected to years of drama therapy prompted development of the dramatic language!

Ian always loved the Director's Chair activity but consistently resisted its purpose, which is to present and work with situations occurring in the director's real life. Year after year, Ian insisted on directing "fiction," and although flexibility is an important aspect of drama therapy and leadership, we stick to the parameters of non-fiction situations to facilitate the clinical goals of this particular activity. Ian would initially refuse to comply, one time storming out of the room and another time becoming physically aggressive to another child, but most times just shutting down and refusing to participate. Eventually, though, he would come around, often by doing a scene about his difficulty with the activity that was occurring in the moment. Now that he is older, Ian begrudgingly responds with a mildly annoyed "I know... I know..." when we remind him that he needs to direct a show about a real-life event as he takes his place on the director's chair.

Neuroplastic adaptation and developmental transformation doesn't happen overnight. It takes time, a lifetime, and the changes that do occur are often more subtle than sensational. While the universal language of joy and fun expressed through drama inspires spontaneous connection, years of developmental, emotional and behavioral inconsistency experienced by autistic children will certainly have an impact on their play and the group with which they play. Some children enter group predisposed to being oppositional, angry and aggressive. They will act out and test limits in a way that has worked for (or rather, against) them for years. Faced with a willful rigidity that is not necessarily open or cognitively responsive to reasonable compromises and/or conceptual negotiations, the drama-therapy group must balance a free-spirited approach with strong group parameters, a dynamic that will be discussed in the next chapter.

The majority of high-functioning autistic children who attend our groups, though, are relatively compliant with basic group protocol and respond with enthusiastic excitement at the spectacle of the drama-therapy group room and the activities that hold a mirror up to their most capable selves. The operations of a Process Reflective Enactment approach to drama therapy serve as a template for imitating and reenacting mirror-neuron activity and engineering manual transmission shifts between perspectives of self and others. It reintegrates functions that have been developmentally and culturally fragmented, providing opportunities for generating empowered self-awareness, interaction and connections with others through meaningful, pragmatic language and enhanced levels of processing. Drama celebrates the autonomous healing center of the individual by throwing a party and inviting all the related therapeutic models, developmental paradigms and processing systems to attend.

Part II—Center Stage: Theory in Action

Constructing a Drama-Therapy Approach to Social Skills

Space and materials

Five-year-old Jimmy stands tentatively at the entrance of the room, cringing and grimacing, holding his shaking arms in front of his body while repeatedly bending at the waist, lurching forward and moving back again. A smile peaks through his facial contortions as he shifts between the hallway and the doorway of the room. We approach him gently as his mother becomes increasingly annoyed with him, rolling her eyes and nervously commenting that "he always does this." She explains, in frustrated and depleted tones, that teachers and practitioners at his school are attempting to modify his behavior. From the way she describes it, Jimmy seems to receive consequences for dancing his dance of approach and avoidance. Our approach, as we gently escort him into the room over the next few weeks, is to support him toward representing his experience through language. We ask, as he ducks in and out of the hall, slowly making his way into the room, "What do you see, Jimmy?" With hands balled into fists held out in front of him, and every muscle of his body seemingly clenched as tight as they can be, he half responds, half asks, in a voice that strains through smiling cringes and grimaces, "It's the party room?"

Jimmy's reaction embodies an overwhelming mix of excitement and anxiety, an extreme physical response to the visual stimuli that invite him to enter the space and participate. As the months progress, he enters the room more smoothly, with less physical contortion, simultaneously asking and stating, "It's the party room...!?" as his transitional activity. We reiterate that it is the party room, and Jimmy eventually moves comfortably in and around the space, naming all the items and materials that are so stimulating to him. Sometimes he holds back at the entrance, moving into the space only after leaders, and eventually some group members, encourage him to "Come on in to the party room, Jimmy!"

A space used to engage a Process Reflective Enactment approach to drama therapy should be a party room. Accessible sights and sounds should stimulate and inspire children to engage and connect with objects that can potentially reflect an empowered sense of self and facilitate interaction with other group members. The main group room that is presently used for social skills at Kid Esteem is approximately 20 feet by 18 feet (6 meters by 5 meters). The floors are covered with industrial carpet with a mix of deep-blue and earth-toned colors, and the walls are a soothing sandy color. There are seven large vinyl banners hanging on the walls, depicting images of stars, moons, suns, dolphins, koala bears, dragonflies and other animals, purchased online. Brightly colored posters hang as well, listing emotions with corresponding child-friendly illustrations, purchased at a local teacher supply store. A mural of a child's shadow quietly plays in a small alcove. The Power Lines poster created by Marianne and the local office-supply store hangs above the stage, boldly cueing expressive language beginning with phrases *I am...*, *I feel...*, *I know...*, *I need...*, *I don't...*, *I want...*, *I think...*, *I can...* and *I will...* to prompt empowered responses. Small magnets glued to the wall and cork strips help to quickly and easily secure and display sociometry signs and other materials used to support activities.

The stage, skillfully built by Dan Montefusco, the husband of my assistant and co-leader Doreen, is simple but elegant, crafted with different levels, aesthetic contours and room for storage underneath. I finished the stage with the help of a friend: black carpet remnants and black duct tape for the edges. The "stage lights" hanging above, simple track lighting purchased at a discount department store, were installed by my brother-in-law and master electrician, Steven Napolitano, with colored bulbs found at a local electrician's store completing the effect. Cheap stick lights with adjustable lamps plugged in on either side of the stage suffice as spotlights.

Lined up against parts of two walls rounding out a corner across from and facing the stage are 12 red chairs, having foldable frames with no legs and covered in foam and fabric, used to gather the group when transitioning between activities, discussing a topic or sitting as an audience. Usually sold as college dorm accessories, I found them on clearance in September. Next to the red chairs are four body pillows also used for seating, although sometimes they need to be removed if group members become overly possessive, stimulated or distracted by them. Usable cushions collected from broken chairs are piled on the stage, and a large (clean) garbage container holding a bunch of foam tubes, connectors and sheets for building and improvising stands next to an old coffee table that acts as a supplies center and work desk. Here are markers, scissors, rosters and other administrative necessities. A large roll of white paper is stored under the table, and a stack of folding play tents are hidden underneath the stage.

A shoe rack hooked onto a closet door doubles as a conveniently inviting display and storage area for puppets. A brightly colored puppet stage leans against a nearby wall. Old Halloween costumes and random clothing articles hanging on a wardrobe rack, also purchased at a discount department store, round out another corner of the room. An overflowing hamper of colored scarves and fabrics sits next to it. Bins and baskets underneath and alongside the costume rack are filled with various props and objects used during play and enactment. There are felt figures and felt boards to arrange them on, finger puppets, old phones and cameras, purses, different styles of glasses, doctor kits, jewelry, gladiator shields, hats, masks (a favorite is the elaborate talking Darth Vader helmet donated by Doreen's son Nick) and other odds and ends used regularly by the children.

Other materials used for the autistic children's social-skills groups that are periodically put out for use and then stored away in the closet include a collection of Rescue Hero action figures, ships, planes and accessories, a doll house with family figures and furniture, a toy karaoke machine and microphone, sociometry signs, large appliance boxes for set construction, and other objects not always used on a weekly basis. The waiting room is child friendly, with a large jungle-themed mural that was purchased online and glued in sections, like wallpaper, to one wall. Murals of children's shadows playing and moving around the space, along with a "tree of life" painted by Doreen's daughter Rosa, decorate the Center. A Power Lines themed hopscotch designed and painted on the cement walkway by Doreen and previous intern Jennie Smith greet group members with a power word phrase in each of the boxes as they walk, and hop, toward the building.

An inviting, brightly colored and comfortably homey approach to decorating and providing materials for the space need not cost a lot of money. Many of the toys and play items listed above were purchased at garage sales and thrift shops or donated by my children and family members as they outgrew them. We still use the animal potholders we purchased from the supermarket for $3.00 each 15 years ago, when we could not afford $20.00 puppets. As drama therapists, we need to be resourceful, able to improvise and willing to call upon members of our community, our own extended ensemble, to create an inspiring space that reflects joyful and empowered functioning.

Roles of leadership

One of the most important and clinically effective qualities that a social-skills group leader should have when engaging a Process Reflective Enactment approach to drama therapy, in light of information generated by the discovery of the mirror-neuron system, is the ability to interact with co-leaders and group members in a manner that reflects excitement, happiness, fun, a degree of silliness, a desire to be present and a genuine interest in connecting with others. Hearing vocalizations of "amusement and triumph, laughter and excited shouts" activates identical motor neurons and intentions in others perceiving the activity—staff as well as participants—laying a foundation "essential for establishing cohesive bonds within social groups" (Iacoboni 2008, p.105). The simple act of smiling fires the same neural mechanisms in those who perceive the smile. Autistic children, like all children, sense, on a number of levels, the degree of enjoyment and connection experienced and expressed by group leaders. Authentically promoting this type of atmosphere not only generates feelings of comfort and acceptance while serving as a behavioral model, but also provides a workout for neural responses that will ideally support similar activity among group members.

The positive reflection and response exhibited by group leaders needs to come from a place that is genuine and authentic; even monkeys are able to differentiate between actions and intentions (Iacoboni 2008). Moreover, leaders need to view group members as fully functioning equals with regard to certain key areas of being. This does not mean leaders should pretend that group members do not have physical and developmental limitations that need to be addressed in a methodical and pragmatic manner; however, there needs to be a general understanding that on a higher, metaphysical or soul level of functioning, everyone in the room is on the same playing field and worthy of the deepest levels of respect afforded to any other individual. Too many stories abound about lower functioning children who appear to be profoundly retarded and are treated poorly, with unpleasant and hurtful comments made by unwitting caretakers, only to find that the children had been cognitively perceptive of what was occurring around them all along, as new communication technologies gave them the means to finally express themselves. Even if the child's neurological functions actually are so low that they are unaware of emotional mistreatment, all people on all levels of functioning deserve to be treated not with disdain or pity but with a dignity and respect that recognizes the universal power and equality of their being— especially in the case of the more vulnerable members of our community.

In this light, the group leader, in addition to reflecting and projecting happiness and social connectedness as a neurological model for group imitation and reenactment, also reflects the basic goodness of the group and individuals within the group, providing a mirror through which individuals may see and experience the best of who they are. Along with the more obvious roles of activities facilitator, safety manager and understanding caretaker necessitated by the position of social-skills group leader for autistic children, the intersect of drama therapy and the mirror-neuron system also inspires leadership roles of animated playmate, silly performer and cosmic compatriot.

The assistants or co-leaders in the group, while taking on all the above roles, also capture and record specific language and phrases expressed by members during enactment, to create supportive documents that celebrate and reinforce triumphant and empowered communication. Assistants and co-leaders help set up materials for set construction and other activities, and guide interaction, in and out of dramatic roles, among individuals during small group and whole group enactment. When facilitating activities that may be chaotic with a group of children who are somewhat unpredictable, it is important that one primary leader not take on any involved dramatic roles during enactment that will distract his or her attention from overseeing and responding to the group as a whole. The group leader in a process reflective approach to drama therapy functions, as well as producer and director, as the stage manager, a mechanic of sorts, keeping the engine of the drama running smoothly, tinkering with manual transmission shifts and amplifying moments of critical operation that occur within the dramatic action.

Group protocols and interventions

The social-skills groups for high-functioning autistic children run in three successive ten-week cycles, from September through June, meeting once a week on Saturdays for 45 minutes for a total of 30 sessions, with a six-week "summer fun" program in July and August. Participants between the ages of 3 and 17 are placed according to age among six different groups, limited to 12 children each. The staff-to-child ratio varies depending on the number of interns and volunteers participating, but there are always at least two professional leaders from the creative arts therapies, special education or related fields. There are usually one to four adult interns in the room from local graduate programs as well, along with volunteers from area high schools. Typical peer models from junior high and elementary schools occasionally participate. More staff allow for expanded one-on-one coaching and guided interaction opportunities within the context of the group activities.

There is no formal evaluation process for prospective group members. Interested parties and parents are informed that the groups work best for children diagnosed on the higher functioning end of the autism spectrum who have at least some interactive, receptive-expressive language skills, or are compliant with basic group protocol, such as transitioning between activities, sitting with the group and respecting the rights of others. If a child has difficulty complying but can be approached through language, or if he or she has little response to language but moves easily and independently with the flow of the group, then the child is likely to be a good fit for the group. We explain to parents that while the group is structured for a methodical approach to clinical engagement and remediation, our presentation to the children connotes a playful, rather than pedantic, experience. Parents are welcome to bring their child by for a more informal evaluation, a visit to see the space and a quick chat, or, if they choose, a full individual session, before signing up.

Parents fill out an intake form that lists all contact information, their child's diagnoses, any medical or allergy information, a personality outline of the child including likes, dislikes, interests, social strengths and challenges, ways of handling social conflicts, and any other social, emotional and behavioral information parents feel is relevant to their child's successful participation in the group. While members sign up at the beginning of each ten-week cycle, they are encouraged at the outset to stay with the program from September through June, since best results come from participation in the full 30-week program. New participants may begin the program at the start of the second ten-week cycle in January, but we discourage parents from starting their child in the third ten-week cycle beginning in March, as too many foundations and skills have already been established in the group without their child's participation, and we don't want to set anyone up for failure.

Each group leader and assistant in our social-skills program works with a small number of individuals during an initial ten-minute period of guided open play through an "individualized socialization plan," in which skill levels are established regarding language, physical activity, play, social interaction and general behavior, and goals are set to map a course for increasing functioning levels and improving skills. Through playful encounters with their assigned group leader, individuals are coached and guided to interact in a manner that generates self-awareness and management of pragmatic issues with regard to the aforementioned skills, including language articulation; volume modulation and expressive content; physical boundary awareness; self-stimulation; personal space management; interactive, imaginative and expressive play; social connection with others; attendance to environmental cues; problem-solving; behavioral compliance; and cooperation and participation, along with the highlighted group skill from the previous week's session. A formatted rubric allows group leaders to record and organize observations and progress over each ten-week cycle. During Sessions 9 and 19, leaders hold five-minute conferences with each parent and provide them with a report summarizing their child's progress. A final progress report is handed out to parents on Session 30.

New skills are presented to the group and integrated within the activities of the program over the course of the sessions. Parents are provided with weekly follow-up skills sheets listing procedures they can implement at home to reinforce progress. Each skill builds upon the previous week's skill, following a pragmatic parallel to what occurs during a social encounter. At the end of every session, ten points are added to each child's name on a chart hanging on the wall, which the children decorate with colored markers at the outset of the program, if the child participates in the activities and can recall some relevant aspect of their participation. Small prizes are awarded at five-week intervals, if the child earns 50 points over the period. We rarely, if ever, deny a child the opportunity to pick a prize. We will withhold a member's ten points for the day if they remain noncompliant, after exhausting all efforts at getting them to participate or behave at the level at which they are capable, but we offer the opportunity to earn it back the next week. There was one time, I believe, when we did not allow a child to pick a prize one particular week, but he was on his best behavior and worked hard upon his return in order to pick his prize the following week.

Our approach to managing disruptive, negative or aggressive behavior, as indicated in the "Positive intervention" section (see p.53), strives to maintain a positive tone. Behavioral intervention strategies begin by establishing a preemptive and proactive foundation that builds excitement among group members and appeals to a child's desire for fun. This positive child-centered atmosphere, combined with the prospect of participating to earn points for prizes, serves as a healthy deterrent to behavioral problems. When problems and issues do emerge, we attempt to support the children by appealing to their strengths and abilities with regard to the task at hand. We coach them with cognitive strategies to engage positive self-talk for implementing "good ideas...true ideas...real ideas" that can guide them toward better choices. We point out the posters and signs listing emotions and feelings around the room to help ground and connect them to their actions through expressive language. We refer them to the Power Lines poster to prompt language that can address the situation in a more empowered manner. We use key words and phrases provided by parents that support appropriate behavior at home. Group leaders in a Process Reflective Enactment approach to drama therapy attempt to "double" (Landy 1994, p.141), rather than condemn, members' disruptive actions.

If the problem persists, we may then have a staff member spend a few minutes with the child outside of the room, away from the source, to review the situation and have a conversation about possible alternative approaches. Problems, for the most part, emerge from more typical incidents such as grabbing and sharing toys, personal space invasion and general compliance. More difficult issues arise from chronic patterns of anxious and oppositional behavior that intersect with the rigidity of the PDD mindset. We may then go to the Reflections space down the hall described earlier, where squares on the wall made from blackboard paint headed by Power Lines phrases *I am...*, *I feel...*, *I need...*, *I think...*, *I know...*, *I can...* and *I will...* prompt the children to ground themselves cognitively by using chalk to complete the sentences in a manner that will support them toward more successful management of the situation. The act of writing is not meant to be punitive; children can draw pictures about the situation in the squares or ask the accompanying group leader to write their words. Finally, if none of these approaches solve the problem or calm the situation, we ask the parents to speak with their child and possibly spend some time shadowing him or her in the group. All the while, as much as humanely possible, group leaders attempting to intervene and address the situation present themselves to the child as a positive ally, rather than an oppositional adversary.

Compliance with the program needs to be measured and implemented on an individual basis. While most children are expected to make transitions, clean up, sit with the group and participate in activities, there may be some exceptions. A particularly angry and oppositional boy (with extremely ineffective parents) resisted any type of procedure or protocol implemented by the group. He would not initially participate in structured activities, nor would he sit with the group when it was time to come together. For months, he would moan and cry and roll around the floor when he did not get his way.

When it was time to clean up the toys and meet at the red chairs, he would defiantly hide under cushions on the opposite side of the room. Although sitting away from the group is not usually tolerated, the leaders chose to ignore his stance as long as it did not distract the rest of the group, with the understanding that just being present in the room was as much as his fragile nature was able to accomplish at that time.

Other group members did ask about his behavior, to which a leader explained that he just wasn't able to have fun and be with us yet. If other children had begun to follow his example and move away from the group, we would not have been able to accommodate the boy's need to sit separately. At one point, he emerged from his cushions and moved toward the toys while the rest of the group was involved in a discussion. This move was immediately shot down, with the very clear and firm rationale that he was being afforded much leniency by being allowed to remain separate, but he certainly would not be allowed to play with toys that the rest of the group had just put away. He sulked back to his cushion. If he continued and began taking out and playing with the toys, we would have brought his parent in to assist in enforcing this boundary, which likely would have been unsuccessful and resulted in his removal from the group, at least for the day. An ongoing juggling act can be required on a session-to-session basis when attempting to balance the needs of different individuals in the group with the needs of the group as a whole. As the months progressed, the boy slowly moved toward the red chairs and eventually began to participate in structured activities.

The majority of children attending the program are not as challenging as this boy. Most children are captivated by the tools and techniques of a Process Reflective Enactment approach to drama therapy and respond accordingly to the degree of empowerment and mantle of respect they are unconditionally afforded by the group ensemble. At the outset of the program, parents are strongly encouraged to adopt some form of management system at home, using charts, tokens, checks, stickers, contracts or other means of documentation and organization that measures, rewards and reinforces progress with our weekly skill as well as other social, emotional, behavioral, expressive language and daily life skills identified by the parent that enhance growth and development. As indicated previously, doling out prizes and special events as reinforcement and rewards should be done sparingly, and reserved for modifying non-aggressive behaviors such as developing calmer reactions to anxiety provoking situations, tolerating sensory challenges and trying out new social skills. When dealing with oppositional and defiant behavior, basic privileges such as television and computer time should be used as the reward. A small, special prize may also be offered if the child performs above and beyond expectations over an extended period of time.

Whether the management system is set up to develop and reinforce new skills or to transform negative behavior, a positive approach that emphasizes fun and partnership is the most efficient and effective way to generate a sense of individual responsibility and accountability. All group protocols and interventions are structured to reflect and enact processes leading to self-awareness, self-empowerment and successful social interaction.

Process-oriented social skills: Three layers of engagement

A process-oriented approach to social skills considers the broader social experience in an integrated and holistic light. While behavioral approaches to social skills emphasize structured lessons in a classroom setting, and developmental approaches follow the lead of the child with little behavioral direction, social-skills practitioners note that there "needs to be time both for a skill lesson and to play or talk in less structured, naturalistic settings as a way of practicing the skills" (Baker 2003, p.6). A Process Reflective Enactment approach to social skills uses the power of the group, the ensemble, to engage processes that support the pragmatic development of social skills while creating a reciprocal dynamic in which the instruction of mechanical skills generates and enhances developmental processing.

The structure of drama allows behavioral, developmental and other components of social learning to occur simultaneously, naturally facilitating operations associated with understanding self and other while recreating naturalistic settings in which specific skills, presented through plot, can be meaningfully enacted, rehearsed and scripted. Dramatic play and enactment, highly valued and purposefully initiated by children, integrates a multi-layered and interactive approach to social skills in which remedial processes are activated while specific skills are taught, empowering a deeper level of social learning. While Yalom (2005), discussing the therapeutic power of groups, reminds us that "therapeutic factors are arbitrary constructs" and "no explanatory process system can encompass all of therapy" (p.2), three layers of social-skills learning come to mind, each layer reflecting, supporting and containing elements of the others.

Social encounter

The social encounter satisfies a basic biological need and primal desire for social connection. Moreno understands this as a "psycho-organic...unity of mankind," a closer physical relationship that early people depended on for survival before the development of language and other "social organs" that ultimately perpetuated more "psycho-social" interaction (1978, pp.3–4). Neuroscience illustrates how we are organically hard-wired for basic connection with others, citing the manner in which newborns automatically imitate caretakers by sticking their tongues out (Oberman and Ramachandran 2006). Goleman describes how we are "wired to connect...our brain's very design makes it sociable" (2006, p.4). Our very existence, survival and ability to thrive appear to depend on basic encounters with others.

Moreno, in discussing the transition from psycho-organic to psycho-social interaction, describes a process of individualization and differentiation among groups that parallels the advancement of society, "a gradual evolution from simpler to more complex patterns" causing the social unity to pull "at one time apart" and then "at another time together" (1978, pp.3–4) in order to maintain a sense of balanced connection. As early society began to differentiate and physically "pull apart" in one respect, it came together in another respect: for example, the development of language. As our society becomes increasingly complex and technologically advanced, opportunities for face-to-face encounters seem to be pulled farther apart while, perhaps, opportunities for deeper, more meaningful communication and self-expression pull us closer together through the use of social media and technology. By pulling together social learning groups that focus on meaningful communication and self-expression through face-to-face encounters, a degree of balance can be restored to the social unity pulled apart by technological advances.

Yalom (2005), in describing the group as a social microcosm, identifies 11 primary therapeutic factors that impact an individual's ability to change through participation in group. Three of these factors inform an understanding of the social encounter layer. Yalom begins with the "installation of hope," in which participants are able to conceptualize and maintain a "faith in treatment mode" (p.4). The initial encounter with the space and the leaders can "make or break" this factor, especially when working with children. It establishes for Jimmy, as he moves in and out of the room, whether his excitement or his anxiety about the group will be confirmed, whether he will be embraced or rejected by the experience, whether he will be punished for his behavior or provided with strategies to address his over-stimulated sensory system.

Yalom states that the task of installing hope begins before the group actually starts, and that group therapists should do "whatever we can to increase clients' belief and confidence in the efficacy of the group mode" (2005, p.5). Parents often call before their child's group starts and ask, "What should I tell him about where he is going?" I tell them to tell their child that he is "going to a fun playgroup that will help you become more powerful." In typical groups that focus on anger management, I add that parents should also say to their children "…and they told me they teach the parents how to behave better!" That is sometimes met with a moment of silence or a chuckle on the other end of the line, but their resistant and angry children, upon hearing this objective relayed by their parents, more often than not arrive at group ready to work, or at least intrigued.

Yalom's concept of "universality" speaks to the degree that participation in group counters the disquieting notion that clients are "unique in their wretchedness" providing "a powerful source of relief" when it is discovered that others have similar feelings, concerns, impulses and secrets (2005, p.6). While this sort of disclosure may not be as relevant for a social-skills group of autistic children, there is definitely a sense of relief and universal freedom that comes with participating in a group where members operate on a similar frequency. Within this dynamic, autistic children can let their guards down a bit and allow for a fuller range of joyous interaction.

"Existential factors" according to Yalom, "relate to existence...a confrontation that informs us of the harsh existential facts of life...our freedom and responsibility for constructing our own life design...and our search for life meaning" (2005, p.98). As organisms hard-wired for social encounters, this is where coming together as an ensemble to create a "we-centric" space in which we can experience the "self-ness" of others within a shared manifold informed by the embodied simulation of the mirror-neuron system serves such an essential purpose. The simple act of encountering others within a group helps us to make biological as well as metaphysical sense of our own existence.

The social-encounter layer of the social-skills experience provides participants with a foundation through which all social learning can take place. By separating from parents and entering the group space, autistic children automatically make themselves available to a host of organic and conceptual processes, initiating and empowering operations accessed by merely being present, that contribute to the synergetic development of the individual as well as the group, piquing interests and sparking desire for further connection.

Social engagement

Social engagement, by virtue of the social encounter, initiates processes of imitation and reenactment generated by the mirror-neuron system that empowers development and understanding of self, others and the interactive relationship between the two. Engagement within the ensemble, perceiving smiles, happy, playful interactions and sounds of laughter and joy, as discussed in previous sections, activate neural mechanisms essential for establishing cohesive bonds in a social group. As group members perceive aspects of themselves in other members' actions, they become able to gain a clearer sense of self as well as an understanding of others' intentions. The process of intentional attunement, a direct form of experiential understanding of others through embodied simulation activated by the mirror-neuron system, empowers individuals to become more aware of and responsive to the social environment. The perception of others in a positive group environment begins a natural organic process of neurologically based social engagement.

Engagement needs to unfold as spontaneously and naturally as possible, so that the range of organic processes may connect and interact in a manner that best suits the individual's neurological makeup. Moreno, advocating for the empowerment of individuals through spontaneity and creativity, calls for the establishment of groups that do "not center primarily in the idea of sublimation but which leave man in the state in which he is spontaneously inclined to be and to join the groups he is spontaneously inclined to join" (1978, p.5). By sublimation, Moreno is talking about the imposition of a philosophy or set of ideas in group treatment or experience that would override natural inclinations and deplete the healing spontaneous energy of the individual.

Moreno instead calls for an experience "which does not appeal to man either through suggestion or through confessional analysis" and "does not forcibly transgress the development of individuals and groups beyond their spontaneous strivings," seeking to keep individuals "as near as possible to the level of natural growth and as free as possible from indoctrination" (1978, p.5). A group formation that provides opportunities for naturally occurring, spontaneous and playful interaction establishes a more individualized and authentic engagement of neurological processes that facilitate intentional attunement to the social environment.

Seven of Yalom's 11 therapeutic factors inform an understanding of the social engagement layer. In the "corrective recapitulation of the primary family group," clients engage relationships with other group members that resemble dysfunctional relationships experienced in their primary families, creating the opportunity to resolve issues through guided and structured encounters within the group (2005, p.15). For the purposes of the social-skills group with autistic children, this dynamic can be understood as a corrective recapitulation of the primary play and social group. Children often enter the social-skills group, like Jimmy or the boy who popped the play toast, hopeful but defensive, prepared to struggle either with other children or the grownups in charge, based on past negative experiences. Guided and structured encounters can help children learn to tolerate and enjoy playing with and being with each other, "correcting," perhaps, a previously established negative perception of what it means to play with other children.

Yalom's "imitative behavior" refers to how members identify with therapists and other group members (2005, p.18), a concept that is underscored by the neuroscientific relevance of imitation discussed throughout this text. *Interpersonal learning*, a "broad and complex therapeutic factor" empowers "group members, through feedback from others, self-reflection, and self-observation, [to] become aware of significant aspects of their interpersonal behavior: their strengths, their limitations, their inter-personal distortions, and…maladaptive behavior" (p.48). Yalom provides a detailed and comprehensive definition of the psychodynamics of interpersonal learning, which, similar to the concept of imitative behavior, has been interpreted within a neuroscientific paradigm throughout this text.

The concept of "group cohesiveness," the relationships among group members, group leaders and to the group as a whole (Yalom 2005, p.53), has been presented in terms of developing the ensemble, while *catharsis* the "open expression of affect vital to the group process" (p.91) has been discussed as well. The concept of altruism, in which "members gain through giving, not only in receiving help as part of the reciprocal giving-receiving sequence, but also in profiting from something intrinsic to the act of giving" (p.13), is a therapeutic factor unique to social engagement.

Yalom's "development of socializing techniques" concept includes social learning that is not a direct result of social-skills instruction but pertains instead to socialization that naturally occurs when groups of people interact (2005, p.16). This incorporates all previously discussed neurological processes of social interaction, including self- and other awareness, establishing and shifting perspective and integration of cognitive and emotional functions, as well as the more pragmatic byproducts of engaging with others in a group, such as sharing and taking turns. The layer of social engagement provides opportunities for establishing healing connections to group processes, adapting and adjusting to the demands of basic group protocol, navigating the social nuances of interacting, playing and working together, and managing the tasks of collective undertakings.

Social learning

Social learning ideally occurs when specific skills of social interaction, the cognitive- and behavior-oriented "lessons" presented and facilitated during the sessions, are neurologically imitated, reenacted and integrated cognitively and affectively in accordance with the beneficial processing facilitated by the social encounter and social engagement. As discussed previously, merely thinking about certain individuals and imitating their actions through embodied simulation can have a profound impact on a person's sense of self, intellectual and emotional outlook and behavioral response to self and others (Iacoboni 2008). By presenting social skills in a positive and dynamic group context, group members encounter, engage and enact pragmatic information regarding how to interact more successfully in social situations, creating opportunity for deeper levels of social learning.

While warning against groups' indoctrinating members through a set of fixed ideas that would stifle spontaneity, Moreno recognizes the inherent strength of the individual and concludes that "sublimation in a modified form could...be called back to function again as an agent" of therapeutic change (1978, p.5). He refers to this approach as "*active* sublimation, productive as well as curative, productive of individuality...which does not arise through analysis backward towards the past trauma but through the training of the individual's spontaneity based on the analysis of present performance" (pp.5–6). It is within this context, along with Yalom's therapeutic factor of "imparting information" that incorporates "didactic instruction... advice, suggestions, or direct guidance from either the therapist or other group members" (pp.8–9), that the specific skills component of social learning is facilitated.

The progression of skills presented over the course of the 30-week program follows a pragmatic sequence of what a successful social interaction might look like. Weekly themes such as greetings and responses, using group members' names, self-identification, and expression of emotion, opinions and ideas begin the season. The skill set then moves toward noticing others, sharing likes and interests, finding commonalities with others, playing together and working cooperatively. After that, the group looks at conversation skills and interpreting and constructing social language, including facial and nonverbal body cues, in response to commonly occurring social situations. Individual group members then explore and enact personal challenges and empowered responses to specific social situations with the participation and support of the group. In its final phase, the group uses comedy as a tool for broadening perspective and simulates various social experiences to practice and reinforce skills.

Each skill facilitated during a session naturally extends and builds upon the skill from the previous week. Throughout the process, members are coached to acknowledge and think about social interaction taking place in the group and encouraged to construct social realities that successfully respond to the collective well-being of self and others. Additional social behaviors that emerge spontaneously during the course of the action and enactments of the ensemble are guided and structured for positive outcomes. In this respect, assessment occurs throughout the program, with an emphasis on self-assessment as an ongoing clinical tool. Group members use child-friendly checklists to determine their own pragmatic functioning with regard to eye contact, volume modulation, use of gesture, language and other skills of social communication, when watching videos of their enactments. At end of each session, the group comes together by the chart so individuals can review and reflect upon their actions during the session and their relation to the skill of the week. At the end of each ten-week cycle, parents participate in a conference with the group leader and receive a skills rubric assessment of their child.

In determining success with regard to the three layers of social encounter, engagement and learning of social skills, a Venn diagram comes to mind, with transformation and development of new roles related to social functioning and relationship inhabiting the center, where the three layers intersect and overlap. Participation in the group over a number of years results in a process, rather than a product, of neuroplasticity, in which "repeated experiences sculpt the shape, size, and number of neurons and their synaptic connections" and "relationships…gradually mold certain neural circuitry" (Goleman 2006, p.11).

By incorporating operational concepts from social encounters and social engagements within a social learning environment, a process-oriented rather than one-dimensional approach to social-skills instruction is established, creating a dynamic in which members are, in addition to talking and walking through the mechanics of the skills, experiencing the neurological and inspirational relevance of connecting and interacting with others.

Revisiting Aristotle

Upon reviewing old notes, papers and ideas in preparation for writing this book, I realized that Aristotle's depiction of drama presents a useful vehicle for organizing the program, the 30 sessions for the five-to-eleven-year-olds put forward in the remainder of this text, within thematic chapters. While some of these terms are also used to inform Process Reflective Enactment concepts listed earlier, Aristotle's pragmatic analysis of dramatic components conveniently parallels pragmatic skills facilitated in the program, providing sources for chapter headings and a rationale for constructing a drama-therapy approach to social skills.

Beginning with "recognition," a basic element of plot describing a simple relationship change "from ignorance to knowledge" (Aristotle 1996, p.18), group members meet and become familiar with other members of the ensemble during the initial encounters of the first few sessions. Recognition can also "come about...with respect to inanimate and chance objects; and it is also possible to recognize whether someone has or has not performed some action" (p.19). Group activity during the early phase of recognition acclimates and connects members to the people, materials, routines and protocols of the program and the roles that individuals in the group play to maintain them.

The more "artistic" forms of recognition occur "by means of memory, when someone grasps the significance of something that he sees" and when similar events prompt one to recognize through "inference" (p.26), rather than specific, concrete information. The "best recognition of all," according to Aristotle, is "that which arises out of the actual course of events" (pp.26–27). Recognition, prompting connection to members and activities early in the program, continues throughout the sessions, generating insight and awareness with regard to social functioning that emerges from the action and enactments of the ensemble.

"Unity," a "basic concept" of plot referring to the conceptual cohesion of ideas and actions occurring within the drama (p.15), guides members during the early part of the program toward expression and enactment that is purposefully connected to the skill set of the week. The ensemble forms and concepts regarding social learning become more tangible as a result of integrating a sense of unity within the group. The cluster of sessions organized by "character" illuminates the individuals within the group and focuses them, through the structure of the unified action, on accessing and sharing an authentic sense of self that reflects "goodness...appropriateness...[and] consistency" (p.24). Sessions focusing on "plot," the primary component of drama (p.13), organize the unity of character and action to support enactment of a sequence of meaningful events that posses "a certain magnitude" (p.13) with regard to social skills and functioning encountered in earlier sessions toward the end of the first ten-week cycle.

The next group of sessions explores pragmatic expression through "diction" and "reasoning" (1996, pp.12–13), focusing group members on the power of language as a tool for managing challenging social situations. "Diction...the forms of utterance" (p.31) performed within the drama, supports empowered "verbal expression" (p.13) relevant to plot, articulation and enunciation of words and phrases, while "reasoning" prompts "the ability to say what is implicit in a situation and appropriate to it" (p.12). A session on interpreting, expressing and responding to facial cues and body language provides guidance and practice since "one should also, as far as possible, work plots out using gestures" (p.27). Sessions grouped in the chapter defined by the "complication and resolution" of which every drama consists (p.29) continue the focus on interactive language, guiding the ensemble to build conversation skills, address social complications and enact relevant problem-solving strategies.

Sessions focusing on comedy as a tool for understanding and shifting perspective, and plot once again, organize and reflect skills and events of the second ten-week cycle. Moving into the third ten-week cycle, the initial group of sessions enact "not an imitation of persons, but of actions and of life" (p.11), simulating playful events and social practices that members may encounter outside of group. "Reversal," a component of plot indicating "a change to the opposite in the actions being performed" (p.18), facilitates a series of sessions described in Chapter 13 in which group members create videos of themselves successfully enacting social and emotional management tasks they have otherwise been unable to accomplish in their lives. Finally, during the last sessions described in the episodic outline chapter, stories are "set out in universal terms [to make] use of them oneself," empowering individuals to reflect on their experiences in group, "then turn the story into episodes and elaborate it" (p.28), creating and narrating a yearbook as a personal tool for reflection, closure and maintaining connection.

The social-skills program for five-to-eleven-year-old high-functioning autistic children presented in the remaining chapters, organized by Aristotle's analysis of the components of drama, is a work in progress that will continue to be tweaked, altered and adapted to better serve the needs of the children. The following chapters may be viewed as a reflection of process, rather than a proclamation of product, so that the reader/practitioner may tweak, alter and adapt as well, and apply the program in a manner that most aptly suits the needs of the children served.

Chapter 5

Recognition: Establishing Roles

Orientation

We begin the program with a half-hour orientation for children and parents the week before the start of Session 1, on the same day and time the program will be meeting throughout the year. While the children participate in introductory activities in the group room, parents receive an overview of how the group will operate, along with an information sheet outlining program dates, skill themes and approaches, behavioral protocols for group, and parenting strategies for implementing and organizing a supplemental social and emotional skills management system at home.

Along with providing an opportunity for the children and parents to view the space, familiarize themselves with the materials and meet the other participants, we also use the orientation session to assess and evaluate children who might either be too high- or too low-functioning for the group. It is a tricky encounter, with anxious and sensitive parents wanting to make sure their children won't be in an environment where they will "learn bad habits." Parents often begin the program visibly distraught over their child's diagnosis and all the subsequent fallout they have had to deal with in the relatively short period of their child's life, and they can be understandably hyper-vigilant about any type of placement for their child.

We explain to all the parents that while there may be some children who need to be placed in a different group with either higher or lower functioning children, the structure of the program tends to elicit and facilitate more positive behavior while "containing" less desirable reactions. We reassure the parents that all decisions will be made in the best interest of their children. In the ten years that our social-skills groups for high-functioning autistic children have been running, there have been maybe four instances in which children were moved to different groups after participating in the orientation session.

The children, in many ways, are much easier to manage than the parents. The space, discussed in the previous chapter, invites them to come in and play on their own terms and in their own time during the first ten minutes of the session. They enter the room, sometimes tentatively, like Jimmy, and begin exploring on their own. Co-leaders and interns engage the children as they interact with toys and objects, sometimes keeping their distance if they sense a child is not ready to "let them in" just yet. Some of the children sort through the materials with an intently serious affect, while others openly delight at the array of puppets, costumes, props and toys. Some stay securely in one spot, while others move freely around the room. Any minor conflicts over sharing and taking turns are quickly diffused and redirected during this first encounter before the group sits together.

We call the children to the red chairs, looking to see who comes quickly and easily and who will need a number of prompts or perhaps an escort to transition from open play to more structured activity. Jack needs an escort. Seven-year-old Jack entered the room ten minutes earlier, smiling and singing out loud to himself with little if any acknowledgement of the newness of the people or things surrounding him. He walks around the room during the open-play period, continuing to sing and smile, sometimes uttering an unintelligible word or two to describe what he sees on the walls or in the baskets. As different group leaders attempt to join him in singing, he smiles uneasily and moves away. We ask the group to help clean up and "meet us at the red chairs." As we try to explain to Jack that it is time to sit down together, we can see, as he resists, that his receptive and expressive language is very limited. Jack's difficulty with following simple directions combined with his language delay might preclude him from staying with the group.

As the rest of the group moves to the red chairs, some children absent-mindedly sit on the legs or arms of other children. Some, stimulated from the play and newness of the situation, excitedly grab at the bodies of their new playmates as they sit. Responses to both of these encounters from other prospective group members range from passive oblivion to angry words and pushes. We usher the group through this initial phase of physically settling in with each other by narrating and doubling (repeating) what is occurring. We look at William and say, "Ow! That hurts!" or "Ooh! I don't like that!" and then toward Ian and say, "But you didn't mean to hurt William—you were just playing," or, "But you were just trying to find a place to sit" (if, in fact, that's what seemed to occur), then back at William to suggestively ask, "You're OK?"

When we finally get Jack to sit with the group, we ask the children "How come we all came here today?" Depending on the age of the group, the leader might join the question with an exaggerated shrug of shoulders and arms along with a quizzical or confused facial expression. While animated body, facial and verbal expression serves to engage the children, the leader must be sure to also access and project authenticity and genuine interest. Some of the children respond with answers like "To play!" and "Have fun!" Others laugh or make noises associated with excitement, while others appear to be disinterested and mildly disaffected, seeming to pay no regard to the question. Jack continues to sing and recite idiosyncratic fragments of dialogue toward the leader sitting next to him, who gently tries to quiet him and redirect his attention toward the discussion.

The group leader affirms and reiterates all the pragmatically relevant responses from the children and extends the discussion, saying "Yes! We are here to play and have fun and be friends with each other! And we can learn how to be stronger and more powerful friends by using the puppets and costumes and toys you were all looking at and playing with before! We're also going to make movies and get prizes and do a lot of cool stuff when we come here to play with each other on Saturday mornings!" The group leader transitions into the activity by continuing with, "A great way to be powerful is to say your name to your friends and tell them what you like to do!"

We explain that the children, when it is their turn, will get up on stage, choose the color lights they wish to shine upon themselves, and use the microphone to tell the group their name and something they like to play, an activity we call "Your Name in Lights." A leader turns on the side stick lights and the colored stage lights, and turns off the main overhead fluorescents, explaining, "These are our show lights we put on when we act and pretend stuff." The leader demonstrates the activity, modeling through self-directing soliloquy, choosing colors and using the microphone, emphasizing pragmatic response using the full sentences "My name is…" and "I like to play…" rather than responding with one word.

The spectacle of the colored lights and voice amplification through the microphone captures the attention and interest of all the children at this very early and critical phase of group development, including Jack, who immediately gets up and says, "Jack red!" We sit him back down and use his investment in the activity to build a little tolerance for delaying gratification, calling on him to take a turn after three or four children have gone. Up on stage, Jack takes the microphone, smiles at the group, says his name and points at the colors. He is not able to say what he likes to play, or perhaps he is and we are just unable to understand him. We praise him and he sits back down.

Most children need some prompting to successfully verbalize the complete phrases representing their names and interests. The "audience" is encouraged to raise their hands to share any commonalities or ask any questions of the person on stage. Some express typical impatience while eagerly awaiting their turn. Children may, if it feels right for the particular group, choose the next person to go. This approach, usually initiated at the request of a group member, may be too much for some groups.

The group leader also explains that the children do not have to use the microphone if they do not want to. About a third of the group chooses not to use the microphone. Responses with regard to what the children like to play are, for the most part, typical, listing activities like video games and playground visits. Some responses, like Jack's, do not fit the criteria and prompting does not help much, but the excitement and enjoyment demonstrated by the children when they get on stage, choose a color and verbalize with the microphone fulfills the most important goal of this first structured activity of the program: to inspire participation that establishes a positive connection between group members and the activities, materials and intentions of the program.

Hannah, a quiet girl also in the seven-and-eight-year-old group, sits with her arms wrapped around her knees pulled into her chest, and shakes her head when all the other children have gone and it is her turn. Her shy and withdrawn demeanor, displayed since she came in, hints that coming up onto the stage might be too much for her at this point. We gently encourage her, but she declines our offer to go up with a group leader or a friend. Finally, we ask if she can tell us her name and what she likes to do from where she is sitting, and she does. Decisions regarding whether or not or how much to push a child to participate in an activity are made on an individual basis, taking into account a number of considerations, including newness of the encounter, developmental capability, sensory tolerance, past performance, general behavior and any other challenges that the child may be facing at that time. Since it is the first day of our meeting as a group, we reluctantly and good-naturedly let members off the hook if they seem too intimidated or unsure of the activity.

While individuals take their turns on stage, an assistant records the responses of the group (if there is time) in preparation for the next activity, which we call "Name Tag." We ask the children to stand up and spread around the room. We explain that we are going to ask them to "find the boy or girl who told us that they like to…" filling in the blank with one of the things listed in the previous activity. The group then has to find that person and point to his or her shoulder. We demonstrate, using a leader as an example, how to leave at least a foot or two of space between the tip of the person's finger and the other person's shoulder when they remember who said they liked the particular activity. We encourage them to "watch the group if you're not sure, and see who other kids are pointing to." For Jack, we say, "Find the boy who likes red!" We time their reactions to see how quickly the whole group can find the right person, and if we can "beat our record" when the next activity preference is called out and we try and find the boy or girl who said it. After sitting, attending and waiting for a period of time during Your Name in Lights, we want to facilitate interaction by moving the children around a bit.

Name Tag and Your Name in Lights, along with other activities facilitated in the social-skills group, can be provocative on a number of levels. The movement of up to ten other children coming your way can feel threatening and intimidating. Group leaders need to be on top of children with spatial and physical boundary issues who may jam their fingers right into the shoulders of the children they are happily identifying. More competitive children may get annoyed with those who do not respond or pay attention, when a group effort is needed to beat the clock and improve their time. Sensory overload from the different lights, colors and sounds can stir up over-stimulation and behavioral fallout. Problems occurring from these types of activities are managed in the spirit of providing opportunities that guide the children toward more empowered responses. The excitement, participation and connection facilitated by the activities ideally counteract any potential negativity provoked by the level of stimulation. In these situations, it is helpful to have a number of interns and volunteers.

We gather back at the red chairs and go over the fun things we have done in the past half hour. We reiterate that we will be playing together on a regular basis, doing fun things like puppet shows, making movies and earning prizes. We ask if anybody has any questions or wants to say anything, which usually results in exclamations like "This was fun!" and "We can come back?" We say goodbye for now and walk them down to their anxiously awaiting parents in the lobby.

Most parents, especially ones new to the program, want to "check in" and make sure the program is right for their children. While I understand and respond professionally to their concerns, in my head I think, *What could be wrong? A bunch of kids are playing and having fun together...* Jack's parents wait until everyone else has cleared out. They approach me with eyebrows raised and taut, worried smiles on their faces. They tentatively ask, "So...?" knowing that their son is on the lower end of the children's functioning range. I look to Jack and say, "Jack! Did you have fun? What did we do today?" He responds with a smile and some unintelligible phrasing. I tell them that it was a little rough getting Jack to follow group protocol, but he participated and had fun and it should be fine. They release their tension as they breathlessly say, "Thank you!" and walk down the hall with their smiling, singing son.

Session 1: Naming Names

Session 1 uses spectacle, puppetry, drama games and improvisation to promote symbolic representation, development of the ensemble and remembering the names of other group members. Within the spectrum of high-functioning autistic children, some remember the names of every person in the group after the first five minutes, and some will still have to ask after 30 weeks. As we pull out the toys and set up the room, we hear little voices drifting down the hall asking, "Are they ready yet? Is it time?" Along with the always-accessible puppets, costumes and props, we pull out a limited number of materials, the Rescue Hero action figures, the dollhouse and accessories, to create two centers of interaction where children can congregate. We also put our large paper points chart grid on the floor with a bunch of colored markers so the children can write their names on one of the rows. We assign an intern to sit by the chart and supervise their signing in.

Group leaders and interns get a feel for individuals in the group during the open-play period and decide who they want to follow and coach for the individualized socialization plans discussed in the "Group protocols and interventions" section of Chapter 4. Depending on the amount of staff and children, each leader will follow approximately three individuals, using the table format of the plan to document goals, observations and progress with regard to language and physical, social, behavioral and play skills over the ten-session period. Leaders play interactively with or parallel to their individuals, gradually engaging them in a manner that facilitates the goals. For children who are already engaging interactively with others, leaders hang back and positively intervene as needed.

Our parent information sheet available in the lobby describes the session's activities and reiterates the importance of following up our system with a system at home that reinforces skills and builds neurological development throughout the week. Parents are asked to create a routine during snack time, bedtime or other convenient time during which children tell about "something real" that happened in school or on the bus that day, using the names of the children and/or teachers involved. Depending on the functioning level of the child, the retelling of the event may be very detailed or two sentences long, and parents should be prepared to offer prompts such as "What were some things that happened at lunch?" It is important that the child becomes connected and comfortable recalling and describing meaningful events using people's names. Parents are also instructed to ask their children, "Whose name do you remember from your new friends in the playgroup?"

As we walk down the hall to get the children, we see their faces eagerly pressed against the glass window of the door separating the lobby from the play and treatment rooms. We greet them, along with new children who did not make it to the orientation, with enthusiastic welcoming smiles, words and eye contact. They enter the room and move with purpose toward objects they encountered and familiarized themselves with the week before. Seven-year-old AJ comes in with a huge basket of trains and tracks that he dumps on the floor five steps into the room. This may present a problem if he is territorial with his toys and other children want to use them. The trains do attract a group of children, and AJ seems to be accepting of them, for now, as they begin to put the tracks together.

Six-year-old Stevey, along with a bunch of other children, heads for the puppets. He sees another boy with a dragon puppet similar to the one he has and exclaims, "Your puppet is a dragon too!?" The older children in the nine-to-eleven-year-old age group seem to love the dog puppet with a microphone from a recently popular ad campaign. They walk around interviewing other group members and leaders, when they're not dressed in Star Wars masks and capes engaging in light-saber duels. Children who have participated in the program in previous years interact with each other more readily, setting a good tone for the room.

Ritchie, a six-year-old boy who has been with us for a number of years, demands to be provided with paper so he can draw his sea animals. We prompt a more appropriate way for him to ask for what he needs. He complies, and we give him the paper. Ritchie has had a number of meltdowns in group since he began with us, and we try to balance our response to his often-demanding and inappropriate behavior. Five-year-old Jason, discussed in Chapter 1, tentatively moves toward the bucket of markers that Ritchie is now hoarding. He reaches in to take some for his marker line up ritual, and Ritchie jerks the bucket away from him with an aggressive and defiant grunt. Jason, who is barely verbal, jumps back and starts nervously vocalizing and fluttering his fingers. After being in the groups with us for two years, all we need to say is "Ritchie," and he puts the bucket back within reach, saying, with attitude, "Fine. But don't take all the blues." We say, "That's fair. Good job, Ritchie," and encourage Jason to take his markers.

We give the two-minute warning and then call for clean up. There is some mild moaning and complaining from a couple of children, but everyone pitches in, some with a little extra prompting, and we gather at the red chairs. We explain the points chart now hanging on the wall with all their names colorfully represented, and tell them that whoever participates in today's activities will receive ten points and a prize, and that prizes will be given every five weeks. Our prize box is filled with toys from fast-food restaurants, donations of small toys from people looking to clear out closets, and valuable-looking knickknacks accumulated by the resourcefully gifted and connected Doreen.

Our structured whole-group activities begin with a game we call "Name Hopping." Starting with the younger groups, we ask the children to recall last week's games before turning on the pretend, or show, lights and placing two round cushions in the center of the room. As we cover the cushions with blue scarves, we tell the group, "This is the pond where our frog lives. He likes to visit his friends, but he needs lily pads to hop on to—so come on over, pick a color for your lily pad and find a spot for it at the edge of the pond!" After the children pick their scarves, group leaders guide them to find a spot around the edge of the cushions and sit with their bunched-up scarf placed in front of them on the "pond." The leader finds a spot as well and introduces the beanbag frog that wants to visit everybody in the group. The leader explains that the person with the frog will help the frog hop to another lily pad, saying the name of the group member as he or she tosses the frog to their lily pad. That person will then toss the frog to the lily pad of someone who hasn't gone yet, saying the name of that person. The children are encouraged to ask for each other's names if necessary.

From this activity we move the children back to the red chairs, keeping the show lights on and asking, "I wonder how the puppets would tell everyone their names?" We set up the puppet stage on the main stage across from the chairs and ask the children to look at the puppets hanging next to the stage on the closet door. We tell them, "When it is your turn, you're going to come up, pick a puppet, go into the puppet stage and help your puppet say its name to everyone! And maybe someone will ask your puppet a question that you can answer." The leader chooses the children who are more likely to understand the concept to go first and serve as models for the rest of the group. We keep the activity moving quickly, prompting and assisting children who get a little stuck when choosing their puppets. The group is engaged and engrossed by the parade of puppets introducing themselves and offering tidbits like "I'm Tiger, and I eat zebras!" Questions from the audience, which we limit to one or two per puppet, are enthusiastic and typically repetitive, like, "Where do you live?" Sometimes a silly theme of questioning will emerge, such as "Do you like beef jerky?" that makes the group laugh, even after the tenth time it's asked. Silly and fun encounters like these generated by group interaction begin to shape the nature of the ensemble.

Jason doesn't volunteer to go up to the puppet stage, but he has been watching the other children's enactments, sometimes with a smile on his face. We prompt him to go to the puppet display and find a puppet. A leader escorts him, and he picks a frog, possibly connecting with the previous activity. With the leader's help, he holds the frog up in the puppet stage. We say, "Hi! Who are you?" He responds, surprisingly, with, "I'm a frog." We are impressed with the full, accurately constructed sentence. We ask, "Do you live in a pond?" and he, as the frog, answers, "Yes." We want to keep the pragmatic momentum going and ask, "What color are you?" At this point, Jason pulls his frog down, looks out from the stage and says, with a mixture of confusion and conviction, "I'm Jason." We answer, "Yes, you are Jason!" happily affirming his proclamation of reality as he moves through this new territory of imaginative and symbolic representation of self through role.

Our final activity with the younger group is a version of Name Tag, where we ask, "Where's [name of one of the group members]?" Upon hearing their names, group members respond with, "Here I am!" The rest of the group points at the group member and says, "There's [name of the group member]!" We playfully time the responses to see how long it takes for all the children to look at, point to and say the name of the member whose name was called, seeing if we can beat our record. We may not get to this activity, since we want to leave time, at least ten minutes at the end of the group, if we are picking prizes, or five minutes if we are just recording points, to go over the activities of the day and make connections. Today, we ask each child back at the red chairs to tell us how many playgroup friends' names they can remember. If they can't remember any, we prompt them to ask one of the other children what their name is and then repeat it back to us.

The older groups begin with a more involved discussion around how we remember names and why it helps us to be friends with each other. After eliciting and affirming responses that are even remotely feasible, we lead the discussion toward the concept of connecting with each other, using names and interests as a way of making and remembering connections. We ask, "What does it mean when things connect?" usually receiving answers having to do with Legos or other building pieces that fit together. We relate that concept to the notion of connecting as friends and as a group, using names and common interests as a way of fitting together. Group leaders need to determine the maturity and functional level of the seven-and-eight-year-old groups, as they may be more successful with the Name Hopping and puppetry activities.

We introduce the "Connect the Names" activity, where children construct objects with connecting foam tubes and scarves that represent a personal interest, something they like to do or play. The foam tubes, similar to pool noodles, come in a set that includes small plastic connectors. It can take a few different versions of explanation for the group to understand that they are going to choose something they like to do or play, and then show us what it is by creating and representing their ideas using the materials. A concrete example offered by the group leader can help: "So, if I like to read, I may use these to make a book, like this!" The leader holds the materials as if they were a book, pretending to turn the pages. The children spread out, collect their materials and start building. After a few minutes, we tell the group that we are going to take turns showing everybody what we made and trying to guess what other people like to do. They show their creations while the rest of the group calls out their guesses. After a few guesses are called out, we prompt the person who's taking a turn to use full sentences to state, "I'm [name] and I like to [what the creation is showing about the person's interests]." The leader asks the group, "Who can connect? Who also likes to do that?" and individuals are prompted, if it's the case, to respond with, "I'm [name] and I like to [activity], too!"

The leader then challenges the group with a more daunting task, asking, "Lets see if we can connect all these cool creations you've made into one thing," prompting the group to find a way to make one interconnected creation. Leaders gently coach members to communicate with each other and share ideas, work through resistance and intolerance, alleviate the desire to control others and manage territorial impulses and physical boundaries as creations are combined and connected. This may be too much for some group members, as the anxiety of having their creations deconstructed or morphed into something else in a manner that is not entirely under their control may be too challenging. Encouraging individuals to push a little beyond their self-imposed limitations is balanced with respect for the individual's developmental and emotional capabilities.

We clean up the tubes and play Name Tag, asking the group to remember and "Find the friend who liked to [activity represented by creation]," attempting to beat the record of how long it takes all group members to respond. Finally, if there's time, we divide the group into two or three teams, place them in different parts of the room and ask each team to see how many names of group members they can remember. We leave time for points and prizes at the red chairs, asking each individual to tell us how many friends' names he or she can remember from the group. We write *Using our friends' names* on top of a sheet of chart paper that will be displayed throughout the season, coach them to say goodbye using their friends' names and dismiss them with prizes in hand.

Session 2: Greeting Others/Saying Hello

Session 2 uses video to enact and rehearse different ways of greeting each other while creating opportunities for self-modeling and self-assessment. The videos also empower perception and construction of a more cohesive perspective of self, reflecting mirror images critical to neurological processing. The parent information sheet directs parents to practice making eye contact and use appropriate gestures, spatial distance, language and names with their children when greeting people. Using a variety of settings and circumstances that are both planned and spontaneous, parents are encouraged to use other members of the family and available friends to create opportunities to practice effective greetings, rewarding success with special treats such as a trip to the playground or a little extra time at night with dad.

This week, AJ enters the room with a plastic dinosaur that must be at least two and a half feet (almost a meter) tall. Tommy seems to be highly stimulated by the toy and starts grabbing angrily at it. He is not able to tell us why. We explain to AJ, with the help of his mother, that he won't be able to bring toys into the room anymore and that he'll have to leave them with his mother. After a bit of resistance, we agree that he can leave the dinosaur just outside the door in the hallway. It waits there, on the other side of the door, looking like it's going to attack whoever walks by.

Jack walks in singing and smiling. He stops by one of the leaders, looks right at her and says, "Hi, Krista! I remember you!" in mechanical, idiosyncratic tones but with pragmatically accurate syntax. He walks by another child and says, "Hello! What's your name?" but doesn't wait for an answer. He proceeds to where the colored lights are hanging from the ceiling and starts pointing and talking about them. Kenny is also preoccupied with and speaking about the lights, as well as the television in the corner that will be used later. Like Jack, Kenny pays little attention to the leader that tries to engage him. They seem to prefer intra-acting in their own worlds rather than interacting in the shared space, and appear to be inconvenienced and/or uncomfortable when others attempt to enter those worlds. Hannah arrives and heads straight for the dollhouse, where she'll remain until it's time to sit at the red chairs. Ten-year-old Walter walks in on his tippy-toes during his group and watches Ian practice lightsaber dueling with Mike.

Ritchie is developing an especially rude habit of pointing and wiggling his rear end at people while sticking out his tongue and making a nasty face when he is unhappy with something. An alumnus, he is quietly but sternly reminded that we don't tolerate that type of behavior, especially in front of impressionable new members, and to use his power words if he has a problem. He backs down. Ian, after asking Mike for a turn with the Darth Vader mask, decides to pull the mask off Mike's head when he gets no response. Mike submits to the somewhat rough retrieval, but he is a bit rattled. We double the probable intentions and responses of both parties, looking at Mike and saying, "Aah! That hurts! That wasn't fair!" and then look at Ian, saying, "But he never answered!" Then to both boys: "What could we have done to make this work out better?" Ian says, "He could have given it to me." We respond: "But what else could *you* have done when

Mike didn't give it to you or answer you?" He says, "Ask for help." Mike says, "I could've said, 'In a little bit.'" We praise their responses and give the group the two-minute warning for clean up.

We gather together at the red chairs and excitedly tell the group that we have to start practicing for when we make our movies. We explain that we are going to start with a screen test to see what we like and how we'll look in the movies. We say, "Let's start by practicing what people do when they meet each other" and ask, "What do we do when we first see each other?" We process their answers and continue with, "What do we use to say hello to each other?" We elicit and guide their responses, prompting them with, "I'm using one of the things right now," as we lean toward them and widen our eyes to exaggerate eye contact. When the children guess, "Your eyes!" we reply, "Yes! We use our eyes to say hello!" Comfort with eye contact and eye gaze can be difficult due to an overactive limbic system identified in autistic children. This apparently harkens back to our primal natures, when direct stares agitated the amygdala and were perceived as a threat, as they are in the animal kingdom, making it difficult to mirror and simulate facial expressions which are key to developing empathy. Reassuring exposure and practice through enactment and rehearsal helps alleviate some of the anxiety of making eye contact.

We continue: "Here's another thing we use when we meet each other!" We wave at them and model other gestures people use for greetings, such as high fives and shaking hands to illustrate use of the body. After we clarify the use of body language and gestures, we use names and different words to model a variety of ways to greet each other through language.

We explain that, as practice for our movies, we are going to videotape how we use our eyes, bodies, words and names to find different ways to greet each other, and then we'll watch ourselves to see what we liked about what we did. The child who goes first chooses another group member to greet. Each child is placed at either end of the stage and instructed to walk toward each other, when the leader calls, "Action!" The two greet each other using the assortment of tools we discussed, while a leader videotapes the encounter. During the enactment, the leader can quietly pose questions picked up by the camera's audio, like, "Is Mike too loud? Is Ian too close?" to prompt discussion and aid assessment when the videos are viewed by the group. The group member chosen by the child who went first will then be the "greeter" and choose the next child to approach. After all the children have a turn approaching someone and greeting them with eye contact, gestures and language, we watch the videos together and respond with a self-assessment checklist.

The checklist criterion asks, *Did I look at my friend's eyes?*, *Did I use my body to say hello to my friend?*, *Was my body too close to my friend?*, *Was my body too far away from my friend?*, *Did my words say hello to my friend?*, *Was I too loud?*, *Was I too quiet?* and *Do I know the name of the friend I said hello to?* The children check boxes organized by columns indicating *Yes*, *No* and *Almost* to answer. Under that, the question *How did I do when I said hello to my friend?* is answered by checking boxes labeled *Great*, *Good*, *OK* or *I need to try harder.* Underneath that, group members write answers to *Which part was I good at?* and *What do I need to get better at?* Group leaders help the children fill out the sheets as needed.

The children are excited to make and watch the videos. We might do a warm-up activity with the older group before we videotape them, in which we divide them into two teams that come up with as many phrases and gestures for saying hello as they can think of, and then present their ideas in round-robin format. The leaders playfully award scores for appropriateness, effectiveness, eye contact, space management, language, volume and use of names. After we film the individual encounters, we sit at the red chairs and roll in the television cart where everyone can see it. Even Jack, Billy and Kenny, group members who are least responsive to receptive-expressive language and interaction (Jason is absent today), are tuned-in and eager to see themselves. We hand out the checklists and pencils and maneuver leaders to sit next to individuals who will probably need help focusing and writing. We hook the camera to the television, and the children watch intently.

Kenny eagerly watches himself hop toward his friend in the video, look at his eyes and say, "Hi!" Kenny in the video then looks up and says, "I'm standing next to the red lights and the blue lights!" This is pretty successful for Kenny, and he does even better responding to the next boy, Stevey, by looking directly at him, waving and saying, "Hi, Stevey," in response to Stevey's greeting. Ritchie does well, as does AJ, maintaining eye contact and appropriate distance. Jack, also distracted by the lights, looks toward his friend and smiles but does not initiate any type of greeting. He is engrossed, though, when watching himself on the television, excitedly pointing out and exclaiming, "There's Jack!" Hannah is still not ready to get up on stage, but we film her saying hello to the group leader sitting next to her at the red chairs. She also seems thrilled to see herself.

The children do surprisingly well with the checklists. After each individual segment, we ask the children how they thought they did. We are stunned to hear Billy accurately say, after watching his enactment, "I was too close to my friend," as he checks the corresponding box. The children are engaged and responsive as they finish up their checklists. We add the skill of the week, *Saying hello to our friends*, to our chart paper and walk the children into the lobby, where many of them excitedly wave their checklists at their parents, eager to share their experiences.

As we establish and recognize the role of friend within the ensemble, this activity empowers group members to envision, enact, perceive and imitate images of an interactive self. For children like Jack, participating in a structured activity and then watching himself participate through the video prompts a degree of attunement to and construction of a more cohesive perspective of self-functioning in a social environment. Billy surprised us with his more sophisticated level of cognitive self-awareness. For Hannah the benefits are also effective, providing her with a positive image of self responding relatively successfully to an uncomfortable task. By enacting approaches to greeting others and viewing themselves on video, group members reflect and integrate mirror-neuron processes, gain pragmatic experience and assess their own performance. Before they leave, we ask them who they said hello to and record their points on the chart.

Session 3: Listening and Responding to Greetings

Session 3 uses video-modeling to enact and rehearse different ways of attending and responding to greetings. The activity of consciously shifting perspective from self to other to respond to a greeting provides a concrete macrocosm that mirrors the operational neurological microcosm of alternation and sorting between perceptions of self and other. This week's skill sheet asks parents to engage in activities with their children similar to the previous week's, although this time the children will respond to greetings from others. Through rehearsed and spontaneous encounters within a variety of settings, such as churches and playgrounds, family members and friends can use different approaches and language to help the child practice appropriate responses to greetings in different circumstances, switch perspective from self to other and attend to environmental cues, rather than getting stuck in self-absorbed play and thoughts. Parents are provided with an outline of steps prompting them to plan and reflect with their child around enactment and evaluation of skills.

We hang a big sign with illustrations in the group room reminding the children to "Look at your friend's eyes! Say hello with your body. Say hello with your words. Use your friend's name, or ask if you don't remember." As the children enter the space, AJ aggressively tosses an armload of toys into the room with a big smile on his face. When we remind him that he has to keep his things outside the door, his smile fades to frustration. He kicks off his shoes and starts throwing the hard, sharp toys around. We try to take a walk to calm him down, but he hits a group leader, so we get assistance from his mother. Upon seeing his mother approach, he rolls around the floor of the hallway and spits, as the corners of his mouth lift into a slight smile. His mother tells him that if he stops spitting, she will buy him a toy after group. As he continues to spit and writhe on the floor, she increases the offer, adding on a special lunch and a trip to the playground if he stops. It continues to escalate. The leader attempts to tactfully override her misguided intervention, saying to AJ with empathetic concern, "Oh, no! Maybe mom won't get you anything if you don't stop!" Thankfully she takes the cue and says, "That's right, AJ! We'll go right home and there will be no movie tonight." Eventually he calms down and pulls it together. At the end of group, the leader speaks with AJ's mother about how her initial intervention rewarded his negative behavior and set up a self-defeating strategy. She explains her adherence to using what she called "positive reinforcement" as a tactic, but she is receptive to this broader perspective.

Walter enters the room asking when we are going to make our movies. We remind him, as we told the group last week, that we will be practicing for about five more weeks and then we will film our movies. He is not happy about this and begins to whine, loudly, that he doesn't want to be here and wants to leave. A leader intervenes, repeating Walter's frustration about having to wait to make the movies, and telling him, "I'm glad to hear your words!" They walk down to the Reflections room where Walter writes, "I am mad. I feel mad that we're not making movies. I need to make movies. I think I can make movies. I know I will make movies. I can wait to make movies. I will make movies on another day" on the blackboard squares on the wall. He integrates the self-generated information, calms down and returns to group. Meanwhile, another leader speaks with Walter's mother, who feels helpless and has no system for managing Walter's sometimes "out-of-control" behavior.

These behavioral displays often come with the territory of establishing deeper, more comfortable connections. While the majority of the children find relatively positive ways to channel their investment in the group and build an ensemble, some members have a more difficult time moving through the process. All are affected in some way by the stimulation of closer connection. A group of boys with puppets begin playing together in a manner that prompts a leader to say, "Boys, try and help those puppets calm down a little— we don't want any of them to get hurt!" The boys settle in with each other. If they continued to play too aggressively, we would attempt to empower their roles as arbitrators of the activity, telling them something to the effect of, "Uh oh, you may have to put [puppet] in a time out if [puppet] can't stop..." Aligning with, rather than opposing, the child in this manner usually serves to manage the activity, as well as reinforcing the child's ability to comfortably align with authority and practice self-control.

Children who have been playing alone for the past three weeks start to engage with others, greet them, ask their names, and eventually find ways to play and interact. Jonathon giggles as he takes a scarf, uses it like a fishing pole and "reels in" a playfully cooperative Billy. They repeat the activity a number of times. Seven-year-old Eddie plays next to Hannah at the dollhouse. Art imitates life as the little people they use in their play slowly warm up to each other's presence. Five-year-old Gary enthusiastically enters the room with big smiles and happy greetings for everyone. His openness toward positive interaction and connection quickly dissolves into frustrated tears as he initiates numerous power struggles with various children over the use of different toys. The choice of toys and children has little to do with Gary's difficulties; the stimulation from the potential for positive social encounter ultimately "short-circuited" his initial open stance, causing him to implode and react in a manner opposite what his original intentions seemed to be. Episodes such as these are the short-term fallout resulting from the long-term process of establishing deeper, more comfortable connections. We give the two-minute warning and call for clean up.

We meet at the red chairs, talk a bit about what we did last week and segue into this week's theme by asking, "What do we use when we answer someone's 'Hello'?" We move through the discussion, again incorporating the use of eyes, body, words and names, as we did the previous week. We explain to the children that for this week's activity, we are going to put the toys back out. They respond with muted happy cheers. The older group, which does not have toys during open play, will be supplied with some age-appropriate objects and games to be used along with the costumes, puppets and props. During the play, the children will be called one at a time to sit with the group leader for a minute and narrate what they see occurring in the play space. The leader will ask them questions like, "What do you see? Who's playing alone? Who looks like they're having fun?" The child will then choose someone involved in the play to approach and greet.

The respondent, the child who is being approached, must interrupt their playing and use their eyes, words and body to appropriately acknowledge the child who greets them, while the leader videotapes the encounter. If the respondent does not acknowledge the greeter, the approach is repeated. The child who responds then takes a turn sitting with the leader, narrating what is occurring in the play space and then choosing someone else to approach and greet. Depending how much time is left after everyone has a turn, general play can be videoed for reflection and self-assessment, if there is enough time left in the session to watch the videos.

Leaders can warm up the activity by role-playing and modeling inappropriate responses to greetings on stage, such as making no eye contact, ignoring and using inappropriate words while prompting the children in the audience to correct the leaders. While the children enjoy watching the leaders act inappropriately and are able to accurately correct their actions, this can, depending on individuals in the groups, stimulate unwanted imitation of the inappropriate behaviors being presented.

We begin the activity. Ritchie gives a detailed description of the interaction going on in the room. He approaches Gary who is playing with cars. Gary does not look up or respond when Ritchie greets him. He turns his body as he steers the car away from Ritchie. Ritchie positions himself back in front of Gary and tries again, looking at him, waving and saying, "Hi, Gary, What are you playing?" Gary looks up and says, "Cars." Gary goes next. Kenny looks right at him, waves and says, "Hi!" when Gary greets him.

Stevey initially has a tough time narrating what he sees in the play space, perseverating instead on the dragon he was playing with. Jason does not respond to the greeting directed at him. Jason also has a tough time narrating and needs a lot of prompting. He approaches a leader and again, with much prompting, mechanically greets the leader. Billy, focused on the object he is playing with, does not respond to Tommy's greeting until we call his name and say, "Billy! Tommy is saying 'Hi' to you!" He happily waves back and says, "Hi, Tommy!" Hannah is more comfortable this week, moving freely across the room to greet Eddie, who enthusiastically responds. Jack does not spontaneously respond to the child who is greeting him, nor does he do so when prompted, and he is not able to narrate what he sees in the play space. He is more successful with the mechanical act of greeting someone else.

When everybody has had a turn, we sit together and watch the videos, assessing and commenting on what we see. We don't use a checklist this week but apply much of the same criteria used last week. Jack and Jason, who seemed so disconnected during the activity, watch themselves intently along with the rest of the group. We excitedly call attention to any positive interaction they displayed during the enactment. They smile as we cheer them on. While Jack and Jason were barely able to demonstrate a shift in perspective portraying response to another, they remained engaged and focused on recognizing images of self presented in the video. We ask the group to recall who greeted them during the activity as we tally up their points, add the skill *Answering our friends' greetings* to our chart list and say goodbye for the week.

Chapter 6

Unity: Building Ensemble

Session 4: Finding Myself

Session 4 uses locogram sociometry and puppetry to empower self-awareness, identification and expression of personal opinion, and the pragmatic use of emotionally intelligent language, unifying affective components of plot for enactment by the ensemble. This week's skill sheet asks parents to encourage their children to identify and express emotions and feelings on various topics while watching television shows, telling pretend stories, and recalling real events that have occurred. It explains how we often negate and deny important and useful states of being concerning our children's emotions with statements like "Don't be mad" or "You have nothing to be sad about." The strong and clear expression of emotion is an important and necessary pragmatic skill that keeps children grounded in and communicating from a realistic and more integrated sense of who they are.

We ask parents to start a daily routine in which their children identify emotions that occurred during the day, using magazine pictures or by creating paper plate drawings depicting mad, sad, scared, frustrated and happy faces that can prompt appropriate language as needed. We suggest that the whole family practice using the Power Lines, strong statements beginning with phrases such as "I am" and "I feel" that can accurately describe their emotions. We provide examples of how to intervene if their children start to whine or act out by modeling expressive language like "I am *so mad* about that! That feels *so unfair!*" then asking their child, "Did I get it right?" and prompting the child to repeat the words, if they accurately describe how the child is feeling. We emphasize the importance of using language and tones that are strong and empowering, rather than polite and conciliatory, when expressing emotions like anger and frustration. A big "I" placed on the refrigerator can help family members stay on track with using the Power Lines. A contest can be held to see how many days the family team can go using healthier, more empowering ways of expressing emotion.

Jack walks in this week and announces, "I'm going to have fun today!" His tone is mechanical and singsong and his articulation is choppy and fragmented, but there is a newfound sense of meaning and investment embedded in his words. Billy walks in, says, "Hello, everybody!" and, rather than limiting himself to an isolated space in his own world, moves toward a group of children and looks to interact with them. AJ arrives soon after, places his supply of objects outside the door, enters the room smiling with arms outstretched and proclaims, "How about me?" We are not sure if he wants recognition for complying with the limit we set or if he's reacting to all of the happy greetings going on around him and wants to get in on that as well. We enthusiastically offer him a welcoming greeting as well as praise for leaving his toys outside. Jonathon follows Jack around, mirroring his singing. Rather than move away, Jack turns toward Jonathon and smiles as the rambling melodies become more in sync.

There is a shift in the room. Group members, some tentatively, some intensively, are venturing out of their worlds and finding other worlds to explore, engage and interact with. The different universes and isolated orbits occurring within the time and space of the group are slowly becoming more aligned. With interaction, excitement and alignment, though, comes noise, and sometimes that noise, especially when dealing with autistic children, can occur at a decibel level and frequency that surpasses what may be considered to be the norm. The noise is happy, reflecting deepening connections, yet some leaders in other settings may perceive it as unacceptable behavior and stifle an otherwise-important source of interactive energy that empowers social learning and development. The heightened frequency of noise and stimulation brought about by the playful interaction of autistic children needs to be tolerated on one hand and artfully managed on the other to maintain engaged levels of activity that are reasonably appropriate within the setting and situation. We give the two-minute warning and call for clean up.

At the red chairs, we ask the very open-ended question, "What are some ways that people can have power?" leading the discussion to the topic of identifying and expressing emotions and feelings. We talk about the importance of knowing about our individual opinions and then letting others know who we are and how we feel about things through strong and powerful words. We show a series of masks made from paper plates, Popsicle sticks and cut-out illustrations of children's faces representing mad, sad, scared, frustrated and happy expressions. We ask, "What might this boy/girl be feeling? What words could he/she say?" prompting the children to use full sentences to double what the masks appear to reflect, emphasizing the appropriateness and importance of expressing more difficult emotions like anger, frustration, fear and sadness with clear and forceful language. We indicate the Power Lines poster hanging in the room and go over all the phrases beginning with "I." Upon showing the mad face, Stevey says, "I am mad because the boy bullied me." Jason spontaneously says, "She feels sad" when we show the sad-girl face. When we hold up the scared face, Kenny spontaneously shares, "I get scared and I cry."

We read the original text written by Marianne, *I Have Feelings. How About You?*, identifying and expressing different emotions from a child's point of view (Chasen 2009). The children are attentive and engaged during the reading, spontaneously sharing and responding with statements like, "My brother makes me sad. I don't like when he takes my toys," and "I get scared of the dark." After reading the book, we explain how the locogram works, indicating five signs with either *Happy, Sad, Mad, Frustrated* or *Scared* printed on them with corresponding illustrations on different walls of the room. We used to merely write the words on paper with a stick figure face when we facilitated this activity in the early years, but our former intern, Heidi Landis, printed and laminated elaborate and colorful signs that we use to this day.

The children stand up and respond to questions that ask, "How do you feel about..." listing various situations, experiences and relationships such as school, brothers, reading, eating dinner, talking on the telephone, taking a bath or shower, computers, television, specific foods, parties, the playground, trains and Legos, by moving to the sign that best describes their feeling about the topic after each one is named. When the children arrive at the sign representing the emotion of their choosing, some spontaneously share their ideas with each other and the rest of the group as well. The leaders encourage everyone to take a minute and share their thoughts with other children who chose the same emotion for the particular topic. Ideas can be derived from intakes filled out in the beginning of the season to make sure everyone's interests are included, and the children can suggest criteria as well, as the activity unfolds.

The locogram activity prompts individual group members to identify and express, through pragmatic language, emotions and feelings relative to commonly experienced topics. It also builds the ensemble by assembling and disassembling a series of thematic sub-groups with which individuals can connect and move through, sharing similar feelings with each other in various formations relative to whole group identity. Group members simultaneously establish individual identity within the group and group identity in relation to their individuality, with each component mutually conducive to and supportive of the other, empowering both the individual and the group and deepening the connection between the two.

A leader calls out, "School!" and the group assembles around their choices. Walter, at *Scared*, says "I get nervous when I get a new teacher in the beginning of the year." Ian, at *Mad*, offers, "I get mad when I have to do my homework." Mike, from across the room at the *Happy* sign, adds, "I like going to school." Group members share, listen to and affirm each other's choices, finding common ground and perceiving different perspectives. A few of the children like Jack, Billy and a couple of others who are not as tuned-in today, are completely distracted and do not make purposeful choices. We coach them to respond to the activity and attempt to contain them within the movement of the room. Sarah, a five-year-old girl in the younger group, demonstrates our culturally ingrained prejudice and suspicion of expressing unpleasant emotions by going to the *Happy* sign for each criteria called out. Leaders can prompt the acceptance of a range of emotions as the children respond to the criteria with suggestive statements like, "Some of our friends might get mad about [topic] or feel scared when [topic]…"

We gather the group together and explain that they are going to "Pick a puppet and make a show about any emotion you feel sometimes." As they choose their puppets, we tell them, "Leave your puppets on stage, next to the puppet stage, and then take a seat at the red chairs." They each take a quick turn presenting their shows, some with one puppet that speaks one sentence, others with two or more for a more elaborate presentation. The audience is prompted to guess which emotion is being portrayed and acknowledge any personal connection by raising their hands or commenting on the enactment. AJ makes a "happy show" by having his puppets hug and kiss. Billy's puppet falls down, feeling "scared and upset." Jack's puppet sings, and the children guess, "Happy!" Hannah, after some coaxing, goes up with a peer model leader and enacts a "happy and excited" show about going to school. Timmy's puppet is "angry" because it got a poor grade on a test, and Walter's raccoon sprays a bunny with gas, yelling, "Die! Die! Die! I'm so mad!"

The children thoroughly enjoy creating and watching the puppet shows, evoking much laughter and excitement among the audience and the performers. All emotions and the situations they are presented within are accepted in the safe context and confines of the dramatic enactments. Along with developing pragmatic expressive language skills, the activity "encourages a process of personal investigation" (Salovey and Sluyter 1997, p.16), with no judgment or pressure to present only those emotions "geared toward the institutionally sanctioned requirement of behaving 'well' or 'nicely'" (p.15). The children are prompted to explore the full range of who they are within the context of the group process.

There are, of course, generally recognized limits with regard to how the emotion may be expressed. Curse words, language referring to sexual activity and verbally attacking others in the room are not allowed. But a judgmental or disciplinary stance against potentially unpleasant or taboo feelings such as anger or frustration is counterproductive to the teaching of emotional intelligence skills. After everyone has had a turn, we gather at the red chairs and ask the children to recall, "Who had a feeling like you?" as we record their ten points for the session. We add the skill *Expressing emotion* to our chart paper and say goodbye, reminding them that next week is prize week.

Session 5: Noticing Others

Session 5 uses games, enactment and costume to elicit a shift in perspective from self to other and support group members toward noticing and recalling details about the image and experience of another. This week's skill sheet asks parents to coach their children to notice and identify specific and familiar things about family members and the surrounding environment by asking younger children questions like, "What do you notice about Dad's face?" and, "What did you notice about dinner tonight?" and older or higher functioning children, "What's something you noticed in school today?" and "What do you notice about our playground...the town...the world?"

If any changes occur during the week, such as someone getting a haircut or new glasses, parents are encouraged to prompt their child to "notice something different." A game or contest can be made by keeping a running record of how many different things the child notices about the school day, the teacher, recess and any other routines or new experiences that occur during the week. The child can also practice noticing other people's moods and emotions while watching television, sitting in the park or waiting in line at the bank or supermarket. The parent can model this type of observation by saying something like, "Look at her frowning face. She looks mad!" or, "Look at those kids playing! They look happy!" and then, "What do you see? What can you notice?" Discretion obviously plays a part in this process so as not to insult or disrespect those who are being noticed. Parents can schedule a trip to the park or playground for precisely this purpose, allowing the child to earn points toward some special privilege as a result of noticing and making accurate and focused observations.

It is Halloween, a perfect day for working with costumes, and some of the children arrive already dressed up. Before we even introduce the skill, we hear them "noticing" each other in the waiting room with excited comments like, "Look! Timmy's an astronaut!" and, "Wow! Kenny is SpongeBob!" Jason, who has minimal language, is curled up and rocking back and forth in his father's lap in the waiting room, anxiously repeating, "No, thank you! No, thank you! No, thank you!" in urgently affected mechanical tones. He is fearful, his father tells us, of SpongeBob of all things.

We coax the hesitant Jason down the hall, reassuring him that it's just Kenny behind the yellow foam. Back in the group room, a leader who had seen Kenny's costume but was not aware of Jason's reaction starts playing a SpongeBob CD as the children come in the room, thinking it would be fun for them. It is not fun for Jason. He starts crying and wrenching his body around. We immediately turn off the music and coach Jason to "Use the power words," pointing toward the poster on the wall. We prompt, "I don't…!", and he says, "I don't like SpongeBob!" and then, "Put it away! Put it away! Sorry! No, thank you!" The words ground him, and luckily, Kenny is OK with taking off his SpongeBob mask. Jason is calm, but his anxiety is clearly heightened as he nervously lines up markers with the leader with whom he has built a connection.

Hannah, while remaining at the dollhouse, appears to be much more comfortable speaking and responding to other children around the room, turning to face them as she tells them she likes their costumes. Jonathon asks Jack if he can try on his Power Ranger mask and, surprisingly, Jack grants his request. Billy, who often plays in an idiosyncratic manner with a particular toy truck, moving it back and forth in the same pattern over and over again, all of a sudden blurts out, "He's frustrated he's stuck!" The truck moves more freely after Billy's containment and release of expressive energy through emotionally intelligent language. Six-year-old Glenn, whose father has recently been hospitalized, asks to hold on to the *Sad* sign as he comes into the room. He keeps it with him for the rest of the session. AJ, while continuing to keep his toys in the hall outside the room, has taken to kicking off his shoes and running around barefoot. Ritchie has had a couple of good and compliant weeks, but Walter has begun antagonizing Ian by purposely interrupting his play. The leaders ride through and respond to the behaviors, striving to keep interventions positive. It is helpful that it is prize week.

At the red chairs we ask the children, "What does it mean to 'notice' something?" and develop the conversation based on their responses. Depending on the age, functioning level and size of the group, there are a number of initial games and activities we may facilitate to engage the concept and skill. "Find the Leader," an activity also known as "Indian Chief," organizes the children in a circle, with one child leader initiating different patterns of activity, like clapping hands, stomping feet and tapping heads, from where they sit in the circle, while the rest of the group imitates the actions, paying close attention when the pattern changes. Another child who has been taken out of the room with an adult leader returns and guesses, by noticing the patterns of activity, who is leading the activity. With younger or lower functioning children, we create two lines of players facing each other and tell them to look at the person across from them and "notice the colors of your partners' pants, the shapes or pictures on their shirts, what they're wearing on their feet…" We then have them turn around and stand back to back. We prompt them to form a picture in their minds and recall what they noticed about their partner.

For the "Disappearing Child," we turn the show lights on and place a large play tent or appliance box on stage with a mat right beside it. We explain to the group that we are going to pretend to make a silly magician's show, in which each child has a turn to "disappear" by standing on the mat and then sneaking into the tent and out of sight when the magician waves the magic cape in front of the mat. When the first child comes up on stage and stands on the mat, the leaders playfully warn the group to "look closely and notice everything you can about [the child], because he/she may disappear…!" After about 15 seconds, the leader takes a large sheet—a bed sheet does the trick—waves it in front of the child, and says, in an affected and animated voice, something like, "Ladies and Gentlemen! Behold! I give you the *disappearing child*!" The child may have to be reminded in a loud whisper to sneak into the tent while the sheet is being waved in front, but that only adds to the farcical nature of the activity.

Once in the tent, the leader lowers the sheet and asks questions like "Who was here? What does she/he look like? What was he/she wearing?" with exaggerated affect. As the activity begins, Billy, from the audience, uneasily says, "He's in the tent." We support his inclination for reality testing and reiterate that we are just pretending. Each child takes a turn to "disappear," including Hannah, who finally comes up on stage. The older group may do a more classic version of choosing someone to stand on stage, step out the room, change something about their appearance and then return to see if the rest of the group can notice what changed.

We transition into working with the costumes, which all age groups enjoy. The leaders allow approximately four minutes for members to create costumes from the supply in the room. We then take another five to ten minutes, depending on the needs of the group, walking around the room and looking at each other. The children are instructed to walk up to as many people as they can and say, "I notice you [observation about the appearance of the child in costume]." We also, as always, encourage them to use names. The children usually create very noticeable conglomerations.

Except for a couple of children like Jack, Jason and Billy, group members are highly engaged and move excitedly from person to person, exchanging comments like, "I notice you are a white ghost, John!" and, "I notice you are wearing a clown nose, fire hat and hula skirt, Timmy!" Leaders shadow and coach the children who are likely to be distracted and off-task by the somewhat chaotic activity. After the ten-minute period, the children take off their costumes and we divide them into two or three teams that work amongst themselves to recall and list all the things they noticed about who was wearing what.

We squeeze whatever basic observations we can out of Jason and Jack, and Ian is able to reflect a sense of self, saying, "I noticed I am Mr. Incredible," a character he often fixates on and came dressed up as today. While these particular children are not yet able to perceive or articulate what they notice about others, they are encountering and engaging in an environment that consistently supports operations of shifting perspective from self to other and back to self again, in the ongoing process of social learning and development. For the rest of the children, the notion of exploring "Who am I?" is now supplemented by "Who is she or he?" and ultimately, "Who are we?" within the context of the group process and the ongoing construction of ensemble.

Even subtle shifts like Hannah's turning to face the people she speaks with creates ample opportunity for increasing embodied simulation activity in the mirror-neuron system, empowering relationship processing between perceptions of self and other, building empathy and generating intentional attunement among group members. Back at the red chairs, we ask the children, "What is something you noticed today?" tally up their points, let them pick prizes, add *Noticing others* to our chart list and say goodbye for the week.

Chapter 7

Character: Reflecting Goodness and Appropriateness

Session 6: Sharing My World

Session 6 uses improvisation, symbolic representation and narration to support group members toward constructing perceptions of self and then guiding movement between perspectives, connecting with others to identify and share meaningful aspects of self, and connecting with self to process meaningful information perceived from others. This week's skill sheet instructs parents to ask their children to identify and describe, in as much detail as they can, their favorite things to a person of their choosing. During the week, children can recall and describe particular interests, toys, activities or anything that makes them happy. Parents prompt the children to notice a full range of experiences, from the more obvious, such as the color of a toy, to the more complex, like how they feel when playing with the toy, and then to communicate their ideas to another person. If a child is fixated on a particular topic or object, we suggest the parent try and redirect the child to choose a different experience to describe, since such perseveration is more indicative of self-stimulation than connecting an aspect of self to another.

After the child describes the experience to a family member or friend, the family members or friends can then describe their own favorite experience or activity to the child. The child listens to, and then recalls and tells about the other person's experience in as much detail as possible. A list of question words like *Who...?*, *What...?*,

When did…?, Are you…?, How…?, Why…? and *Did you…?* written on a piece of paper for the child to refer to can prompt questions and interaction. The child can then notice if any similarities or connections exist between the two experiences. Parents are coached to manage resistance from their child due to developmental, behavioral or emotional challenges by making the activity fun and structuring it like a game or contest.

Ritchie enters the room and offers a cheery "Good morning," but he appears to be a bit "out of it," not as interactive as he usually is with other children and much less responsive to the day's activities as the session continues. At the end of group, his parents ask us how he had done, telling us that they started him on psycho-stimulant medication a couple of weeks ago and recently increased his dosage. We explain that he has certainly been compliant over the past few weeks, but his verbal participation and response to group activities has waned.

As the rest of the children from the five-and-six-year-old group enter the room today, we notice that instead of going off in their usual different directions, occasionally encountering each other for small periods of interactive play, the whole group, including Ritchie, has naturally gravitated toward sitting and playing in one area of the room, forming a loosely knit circle of interaction where they are simultaneously turned toward and tuned-in to each other.

Jason is there, too, but as the play becomes more involved through language and the exchanges of ideas, he breaks away from the group. He approaches the leader who often mirrors him as he lines up markers, and says, "Play dominoes, please." We are thrilled with his use of pragmatic language to reach out and connect with another. AJ has to leave the room and reflect with a leader because he is throwing toys around. Today, this appears to be more an issue of happy stimulation than anger or frustration. Meanwhile, Hannah has left the dollhouse to speak with other children and ask them what they are playing. She sits by Eddie and joins his dress-up activity for a little bit. Jack is playing with the Rescue Hero action figures, which is unusual for him. He plays alone, but we are happy to see him engaging in some form of projective, imaginative play instead of walking around the room singing and responding incoherently to random objects and thoughts. As leaders move to interact within the context of his play, he smiles, makes quick eye contact, and moves on.

Ian is going through a rough patch, throwing toys at Mike and Walter and aggressively aiming pretend guns at group members and leaders. We attempt to double his apparent frustration with Walter's antagonistic behavior the previous week, followed by a more sternly issued limit to expressing anger and frustration by pretending to shoot guns. Maneuvering through typically developing social connections is a challenge for anybody. For high-functioning autistic children, the combination of engaged but limited social awareness and lack of an intact social filter, along with fragmented operations of perception, perspective and communication, can make it especially difficult to navigate. They are tuned-in enough to feel the frustrations that come with social connection and compromise, but they are not ideally equipped to handle them in a manner that typically resolves conflict.

At the red chairs, we ask the children, "How might you describe what you like to do or play? What kinds of words would you use?" to begin the discussion by sharing our thoughts, interests and ideas with others. We explain that we're going to create and build examples of favorite things we like to play or do, using the tubes and the scarves, and then take turns showing and telling about them to our friends, recalling a similar activity we did at the beginning of the season. A leader models the activity, creating a symbolic representation of a personal favorite by using the materials to build a golf club, skis, or cooking utensils, for example, while providing further explanation as needed.

The room is divided in half by a line of masking tape across the floor. An equal number of mats are placed on either side, providing a "home base" for each child in the group. The children are directed to find and sit on a mat, think of what they will make to show what they like to do or play, and raise their hands to tell a leader and "get clearance" before going to get materials. If the children get their materials before deciding on a specific idea, they often get distracted by the materials and lost in play. Group members are given a few minutes to create representations of a favorite thing with the tubes and scarves at their mats.

The leader then explains that one side of the room is going to "visit" a friend on the other side of the room (divided by the tape) to hear about what they like to do or play. Depending on the age and functioning level of the group, the leaders can either assign friends to visit on the other side, or allow members to make their own choices. The leaders indicate a number of question words like *Who*, *What*, *Where*, *When*, *How* and *Why* written on large pieces of paper and placed on the walls around the room, to prompt the visitor to ask questions about their friend's favorite thing. After about five to ten minutes of asking questions and hearing about their friends' creations, the visitors are instructed to go back to their mats on the other side of the room. The friends they visited now come to visit them to hear about their favorite thing represented by the materials. As with all activities, leaders need to use judgment if visitors end up at someone else's mat they weren't assigned to, or if three people are visiting one person. If it's working and everybody has someone to interact with, it's probably fine.

The leaders walk around the room as the activity goes on all at once, with lots of movement and interaction occurring simultaneously. Jonathon visits AJ, who made a fishing pole. He studies the question words on the wall and carefully asks, "What fish did you catch?" The pragmatics of Jonathon's verbalization are just slightly off target, but they are fine for AJ, who happily answers, "A big one!" We praise them both and encourage them to think of "Who" and "Where" questions, and answers as well. Jack is reading the question words on the wall and does not answer Hannah's questions. Billy makes a hula-hoop but is also not able to answer his visitor's questions. We direct these visitors to other mats as leaders attempt to engage Jack and Billy. The majority of group members ask and answer pertinent questions like "What is your toy? How does it work?" and "Where do you play it?"

Back at the red chairs, we prompt the children to recall information they shared about themselves and learned from their friends during the day's activity. Along with the pragmatic exercise of constructing language and response relevant to the encounter, group members practice shifting perspective between self and other. The improvisation with the materials, creating a meaningful symbolic representation of a concrete object, along with the guided switch from sharing about self to asking about and perceiving another, provides an active template for the ongoing shifts in perspective that occur within the neurological function of social development and understanding. The activity also provides positive reflection and validation of the children as valuable individuals who engage in activities worthy of being shared. We ask,

"What did you tell your friend about what you like to do?" and "What did you find out about your friend?" and record their points on the chart. We add *Telling about what I like* to the skills list and walk them down to their parents.

Session 7: Finding Matches

Session 7 uses games, puppets, narration and mapping to engage and establish pathways of connection between perspectives of self and other. Personally meaningful choices representing self are affirmed, validated and empowered through positive mirrors reflecting similar choices made by others, while perceptions of others are further integrated through the reflection of choices that mirror self, engaging more accessible and interactive connections between the two. This week's skill sheet instructs parents to help their children come up with categories of interest, food or television shows, for example, and think about how many matches they can make with family members and friends. If the child loves chocolate ice cream or hates peas, who else do they know who also feels that way? Parents can make simple lists or colorful posters with their children about all the matches they can think of.

Children can then decide on a category and determine whom they will approach and ask opinions of in order to find new matches. They can present the activity as a homework assignment, saying something like, "I have to find people who I match with for a homework assignment. May I ask you some questions?" Parents can simplify the activity for younger or lower functioning children by prompting the child to find matches having to do with the colors of their clothing, hair, glasses and other more concrete and observable topics while at the bus stop, playground or store. Organization of the skill within the framework of a game or contest will likely increase the child's investment in the activity.

Jack is noticeably more interactive this week. He enters the room and says, or echoes, "How are you?" to a number of children, using their names, and then proceeds to have a conversation prompted by a leader about how he watches the news hour with his father, all the while maintaining eye contact with the leader. His speech and thought process is choppy and idiosyncratic, but he communicates in a manner that is sustained and relatively cohesive. AJ arrives a few minutes late as he frequently does, which cuts into his open playtime, but he is able to express and subsequently manage his frustration over not having much time to play. Hannah now moves freely around the room, telling Jack that she likes his singing, which he resumes after his conversation, and complimenting other children on what she notices about their activity. She tells Billy that she likes how he set up his toys, and he says, with intonations that are mechanical and echolalic, yet sincere, "Oh, thank you, Hannah! You saved the day!"

The children clean up the toys, puppets and costumes and we gather at the red chairs. We ask them, "What does it mean to 'make a match' with someone? What are some things we might match our friends with?" to begin a discussion around acknowledging similarities with other people. The children's responses are, as always, eclectic, with obscure notions like "We can match dinosaurs!" illuminating their sometimes fixated, self-referenced thought patterns mixed in with more typical ideas and notions. We attempt to re-phrase all responses toward contextual relevancy as needed, saying, for example, "Yes! We can see if our friends like the same kind of dinosaurs that we do!" and add, "But first we have to see if they even like dinosaurs."

We explain to the younger children that we are going to play a game called "Found a Match!" Here a leader will ask, "Find the friend who has the same favorite [topic] as you," completing the sentence with topics like food, restaurant, ice cream flavor, color, vacation spot, TV show and game. After each topic is called out, the children walk around, asking each other what their favorite is. When a match is made, the pair calls out, "Found a match!" and hold up their hands clasped together in a mutually engaged victorious gesture.

There is much opportunity for pragmatic coaching during the activity, as leaders encourage the children to look at each other and use names when asking friends the questions, to wait until the other friend finishes asking before asking questions, to wait to hear the answer to the question before moving on to someone else, and other practical matters of interaction. Pairs may turn into trios or small groups as children excitedly find matches with two, three or more children on a particular topic. Group members are encouraged to suggest topics for matching as well. For younger or lower functioning children, leaders can facilitate a more organized circle where children identify colors of clothes, for example, then find matches among the other group members. Objects like colored tubes or categories of puppets can be given out and leaders can ask, "Who's holding the same [object] as you?"

When we finish our list of topics, or cut it short due to restlessness and loss of focus, we place a large piece of paper, approximately ten feet by three feet (three meters by one meter) and cut from a roll, with some markers on the floor, and ask the children to draw pictures of the matches they made. After about five minutes, we hang the mural on the wall behind the stage and ask the children to come up, one at a time, show us the picture they made and tell us about who they matched with and what the match was. We coach them to use full sentences, such as "I like [the picture they drew]. I matched with [person]. We both like [match]," when it is their turn. Ritchie starts kicking and yelling when he isn't picked first. The leader tells him he will get picked when he raises his hand and shows that he can wait. He complies, and the leader calls on him three turns later. All of the children, including Hannah, are eager to get up on stage, show the chocolate ice cream cones and television cartoon characters they drew and tell about the matches they made with their friends. Billy tells us he made a match with Emily. We ask, "Who's Emily?" and he answers, "My sister!" While not exactly on target, he gets the gist of the activity.

If there is time, the younger groups can create quick puppet shows with a member or members they made matches with. Coached by the group leaders, the small groups develop shows about the matches they made, making connections between the matches and the pragmatic settings where the matches might be made, and language that might be used to make them. A leader could ask the ice cream flavor match group, for example, "Where is a place that you might make a match about favorite ice cream flavors with other kids?" Children can respond with settings such as birthday parties or ice cream parlors. The group can decide that the setting be used in the puppet show, and the leader can then ask, "What words can the puppets say to find out that they both like the same favorite ice cream flavor?" and the puppet show, in which a few lines of pragmatic language are exchanged, develops from there.

The nine-to-eleven-year-old group plays a game called "People Bingo" to facilitate matching among group members. Each child is given a paper formatted like a tic-tac-toe board attached to a clipboard and a pen or marker. The tic-tac-toe-style grid, containing four squares across, down and diagonal, each box containing a question or statement, such as, *A favorite TV show, What you want to be when you grow up?, A fun thing to play, A place you love to go, Something you want to change in your life, The kind of pet you have* and *Something you are good at.* Group members walk around, asking others their answers to the boxes. If a match is made, each person jots down the name or initials of the person they matched with in the corresponding box. They can try to find more matches with this person or move on to someone else.

When someone gets four in a row, across, down or diagonally, they shout "Bingo!" The group can keep playing until numerous people get bingo or fill up their whole sheets. After about 10 or 15 minutes, the group sits at the red chairs and the show lights are turned on. Group members come up on stage one by one, choose their color lights, tell whom they made the most matches with and share a personal opinion from any of the boxes. The audience acknowledges, with a show of hands, any other matches with the opinion, and, if there is time, the audience can ask a few questions of each person.

Another activity we have facilitated with the older groups involves sociometric mapping. While People Bingo takes up the entire session and it is the more fully interactive exercise, sociometric mapping has gotten a great response the couple of times we've done it. Pairs can be established through a quick, more age-appropriate version of Found a Match. Each team of two is given a large piece of white paper, approximately two feet by three feet (0.6 meters by one meter) cut from the roll, and markers with which to create a map. Each team creates their own legend icons for mapping experiences in the categories of *Home and Family, School, Activities, Interests* and other daily life functions. The teams represent these activities on their maps in any format they choose, placing colored sticky dots, which they are supplied with, wherever a match occurs between the two team mates. For example, if one group member attends dance and the other plays soccer but they each go to karate, corresponding icons can be created and mapped for all three activities, with a colored dot placed at the one indicating karate. At this age, the children are likely studying maps at school. Combined with their interest in mechanical and technical creativity and detail, the maps they come up with are usually very interesting.

Back at the red chairs, we ask, "Who did you make matches with?" and record their points on the chart. By making matches with others, individuals in the group are prompted to perceive aspects of self in the other and other in the self, generating a neurological as well as affective quality of familiarity and intentional attunement. A positive sense of personal and social identity reflecting goodness and appropriateness is asserted, empowering individuals in the group. We write *Making matches with our friends* on the list, say goodbye and express our excitement about getting closer to making our movies.

Chapter 8

Plot: Organizing Events

Session 8: Working and Playing Together

Session 8 uses improvisation, symbolic representation, cooperative engagement and collaborative storytelling to strengthen interaction among group members and empower group task mastering skills. With a foundation of connection between self and other more firmly established by activities from previous sessions, group members work with each other to organize and create one coordinated outcome from a variety of possibilities. This week's skill sheet instructs parents to ask their children to think about and decide on something they would like to create or make, like a cake, a building out of blocks, or a painting, together with another person—preferably someone who is a peer, more like a sibling or friend than an adult.

Once the activity and the partner have been decided upon, parents encourage their children to share ideas with their partner about how to proceed with the activity with questions like "Do you want to make a chocolate or vanilla cake?" or "What kind of building do you want to make?" or "What colors do you want to use for the picture?" The children say their ideas and are then prompted to listen to their partners' ideas and suggestions with the intention of working together toward a compromise. There will likely be times when both ideas can be incorporated, when the child's ideas will be used, and when the child will have to tolerate the partner's ideas in creating the one outcome together. The parent tells the partner about the nature of the activity beforehand in order to avoid the partner's being overly agreeable with the child. The parent can coach the child through the process with reflections and questions like "So, you want chocolate and [partner] wants vanilla. What do you think of [partner's] idea? How can we work it out together?" A list of questions and prompts for the child to refer to when communicating with the partner, such as "Do you want...?", "How about...?", "What do you think...?" and "Maybe we could..." can help keep the collaboration on track.

The group members enter the room, for the most part, happy and stimulated. It is the beginning of December, and we are immersed in the holiday season. Although the children do not have the best filters to sort through and process all the information and input the holidays bring, they are, like typical children, energetic sponges, reflecting their own excitement as well as the stressful agitation their parents are likely experiencing. The noise level is noticeably higher, indicating the excitement in the air as well as the deepening connection that is occurring among group members, as increased encounters and engagement lead to bursts of playful expression and minor flare-ups.

Hannah is part of this increase in decibel level; her previously almost inaudible voice can now be heard above the din, laughing and calling out the names of the children she plays with. Billy has moved from a completely isolated stance during open play to seeking out others to interact with on a more regular basis. Kenny is also transitioning toward more interactive play, while Jason and Jack remain close to their own worlds, occasionally peeking out to join the leaders who mirror their activity.

At the red chairs we ask, "What does it mean to work together?" to start the discussion on this session's theme. We continue with questions like "What's easy about working together? What's hard about it?" We tell them, "You all have such great ideas about how to do things. That can be an easy part, thinking of great ideas. The hard part can be when we need to work together, share our ideas with each other and compromise so we can include as many of the ideas as possible. Sometimes our ideas don't get used, and that can be really annoying. But we've got to practice working together so we can make our movies next week!"

We explain that we are going to play a game called "Make One Thing Together" using four stations, each containing a different material, like blocks, scarves, Legos and foam tubes, situated around the room. The children are divided into three or four teams of three or four children each, depending on the size of the group. The teams are put together beforehand by the leaders to construct an enjoyable working balance of personalities, expressive strengths and established relationships among the children. These teams will stay together for making the movies as well. Each team begins at one of the stations. The teams are instructed to create one assigned object out of the materials available to them at the station. After each round, the whole group reviews what each team created, reflecting on successes and difficulties with concepts like sharing ideas and cooperation. The teams then rotate to the next station of materials and create another object together.

We begin with a letter of the alphabet for the first round. The children are coached to share ideas before taking action and then decide together which letter to create and how they are going to create it with the available materials. If there is enough staff, a leader oversees the interaction at each of the four stations. After reviewing the results as a group, teams rotate to the next station of materials and create one tree together, then, after reviewing, rotate and create one house together, and, finally, a car. Teams can play with remaining materials at their stations after their task is complete while waiting for other teams to finish. The leader refers to large signs placed on the walls around the room with phrases like *Do you want to…?, How about if we…?, What do you think…?* and *How should we start…?* to provide pragmatic guidance for the children toward constructing language that fosters collaboration.

Working together in this manner is a difficult task for the children. There is usually almost no cooperation and much frustration during the first couple of rounds. Rather than making one thing together, the teams make three or four things at first. Higher functioning children can become agitated with the actions of children who aren't initially as focused on the goal of the task, especially if we increase investment in the activity by scoring the teams' results and making it a friendly competition. This needs to be done carefully, with clear indication that winning the "competition" brings no special benefits or awards, so as not to sabotage the intent of working together. The children usually, but not always, forget about the notion of competition once the activity is underway. It is used only to pique interest and excitement. If any of the children do pursue the idea of who "won," we try to stay genuine, fair-minded and supportive of all group members' abilities when coming up with a response, perhaps spontaneously creating a winning category for each team.

Kenny begins the activity oblivious to the ideas and choices of his teammates, and proceeds to do what he wants with the materials, causing Ritchie to scream. Jason, while not able or willing to actively engage in sharing his ideas and constructing the object, is aware and wary of others' agitation, and does not disrupt his team's undertakings. We place Jack on a team with more mild-mannered children who will not react so strongly if, and when, he becomes an obstacle to completing their task. Billy starts to do his own thing with the materials but is quickly brought back to cooperative focus by his teammates. Ian, Walter and Mike, after a few rough weeks of feeling out their potential connections with each other, do, like the rest of the groups, collaborate successfully by the third and fourth rounds.

We put away the materials and tell the children to remain sitting with their teams. We indicate the chart paper on which we have kept a running list of skills and concepts experienced throughout the season's activities. We add *Working together* to the list and announce that the children are going to meet in their teams to start planning for the movie. We explain that they can make any type of movie they like, but the team has to create one movie together that incorporates each of the eight skills listed: *Using our friends' names, Saying hello to our friends, Answering our friends' greetings, Expressing emotion, Noticing others, Telling about what I like, Making matches with our friends* and the newly added *Working together*. The teams meet with a leader for five to ten minutes, taking advantage of the freshly completed exercise in collaboration to brainstorm with each other and explore initial ideas for the movie.

Back at the to red chairs, we ask "What was easy about working together?" and "What was hard about working together?" and record their points on the chart. We pump them up and send them off with the anticipatory excitement of making movies next week, and then watching them with popcorn and prizes the week after.

Session 9: Lights! Camera! Action! Putting It All Together

Session 9 uses plot, scripting, set construction, costume, props, scenery, role-play, rehearsal and movie-making to consolidate, organize and reflect skills engaged and processed over the past eight weeks within collaborative stories created and enacted by group members and filmed by group leaders. The children work together to come up with a theme for the movie that can represent meaningful events in a manner that is cohesive and easily shared. This week's skill sheet informs parents that the children, divided into teams, will create and develop videos with the goal of incorporating all the concepts and skills the group has engaged in and practiced so far this season.

We tell the parents that the teams will apply the skills toward participating, cooperating and developing their video presentation, and then watch the videotapes next week, "movie style," using them as tools for self-assessment. We encourage the parents to show interest and ask their children about the movies they are making with questions like "Who are you in the movie? What happens in the story?" If parents feel especially motivated, they can ask about how the different skills are portrayed in the movie. We also ask the parents to please inform us if their child is allergic to or has problems with popcorn. We follow up by asking directly about popcorn allergies when we get the children from the lobby, and again when we bring them back after the session. During the session, a leader holds five-minute conferences with each parent and provides a formatted report on their child's progress regarding physical, language, play, behavior and social interaction skills.

As the children enter the room, some of them find their teammates during the open-play period and pick up where they left off the week before, discussing their ideas for the movie. Teammates Billy and Jonathon culminate a ritualistic engagement which began weeks ago when Jonathon began playfully "reeling in" Billy with the scarf. Their initial encounter, leading to playful interactions and shared jokes over the ensuing sessions, establishes a social bond celebrated by this joyful expression of connection. The boys hold hands, swinging back and forth in sync with each other's movements, repeating some indistinguishable rhythmic chant together, possibly including the name of a character from a popular cartoon, while looking into each other's eyes and laughing. They do this over and over again and continue to do it for the next three or four sessions.

While this behavior might be tolerated to a degree if the children were four years old, it would most likely be deemed inappropriate for seven-and-eight-year-old boys in most settings, and extinguished pretty quickly by many teachers, perhaps even those running social-skills programs. Although the repetition of the chanting can get a little grating after a while, we see how it empowers the social connection between the boys, as well as their general participation in the group, especially for Billy, who has moved from a mostly isolated and non-responsive frame of reference to one that consistently seeks out others to interact with. We also notice that Billy's pragmatic responses are becoming increasingly accurate with regard to content and sentence structure. The connections generated by the gibberish-sounding chant that teachers may be uncomfortable with seem to support, rather than discourage, enhanced ability with pragmatic language, at least for Billy.

We gather at the red chairs and take out the chart sheet that lists all of the skills we have worked on over the course of the season. We review the procedure for making the movies, emphasizing the importance of sharing ideas, working together and compromising to ensure a successful production. We explain how the children will decide together, in their teams and with a leader's help, on the theme of the movie, the setting, the characters, the plot and an outline of dialogue, giving examples for each, and for how to include all of the skills on the list. We tell them that once they decide on these things, they can collect any materials, set pieces, props, costumes and scenery they need, and start rehearsing their movies. Teams go to different unused rooms or areas in the center with their leaders to put their productions together. As the teams rehearse, one leader walks around with a video camera, checking in with the teams and getting a sense of who is ready to be filmed. The teams also prepare a title page that, along with the "clack" of a scene marker, begins their movie, as the leader announces the title and the names of the "stars."

If the leader filming the movie is also able to watch the final rehearsal before filming, it is a good idea to film the rehearsal as well. A number of times, we have seen teams successfully run through their movies in preparation for filming, only to have them fall apart once the camera is rolling. This has little, if anything, to do with stage fright or feelings of camera-shy anxiety, and everything to do with attention span and focusing ability. Kenny, after doing his part perfectly two or three times during rehearsal, launches into an unrelated and unstoppable monologue during filming that has nothing to do with his team's movie. His default system is not able to deactivate as the story in his head comes out of his mouth in louder and more deliberate tones as he states emphatically, "I need to finish the story!" Attempts are made to redirect him and get him back on track, which he eventually does. If a run-through and final version can be filmed, the leader can choose which one to show, or both versions can be shown so the children can compare the two. Otherwise, whatever is filmed and shown will serve as a useful tool. When showing Kenny's movie during Session 10, we prompt him to notice how he went off track, and he is able to reflect back on his participation.

The movies, performed for the most part with much joy and excitement, generally run two to eight minutes long. Ritchie's team creates a movie called *Dinosaurs and Rabbits Go Home* about a group of friends who are deciding what to play when another friend arrives and surprises them. Kenny plays the waiter in his team's movie, *The Jingle Bells Restaurant.* Jack follows the lead of his teammates in their movie, *Air Force Star Wars,* and is able to appropriately greet friends before singing one of his Sesame Street songs, saying, periodically through the verses, "It's karaoke!" Billy and Jonathon are part of the *Ghostbusters and Shadows* cast, where they find and explore a scary room. Hannah is part of an active group of friends in *Ice Age 4*, while Ian and Walter duel and then join forces in *Star Wars Episode VII: Attack of the Zombies.* The children, due to their lack of critical social filters, tend to be satisfied and happy with whatever they produce. After filming each team's movie, we return the costumes, props and materials to the racks, bins and baskets, and collect the group at the red chairs.

A myriad of mutually reinforcing and empowering factors are able to simultaneously occur within the process of making and then watching the movies. While making the movies, individuals establish cognitive and behavioral context by planning and enacting a specific set of process-oriented social skills with other group members. Teammates need to collaborate for organizing unity and cohesiveness of plot with a beginning, middle and end. They develop characters consistent and connected with other elements of the enactment, establishing incidents of recognition, reasoning and diction, empowering the ability to clearly and articulately say what is appropriate to the situation. Group members engage operations of memory, attention, processing and sequencing, neurological foundations of learning, through spontaneous and creative encounters as they shift perspective between self and other. The use of dramatic enactment integrates the array of skills, processes and operations within one child-friendly, creative, spontaneous, enjoyable activity. We ask each of the group members, "What skill did you show in your movie?" give them their points and say goodbye while building up excitement about next week's movie day.

Session 10: Movie Day

For Session 10, we roll in the big old television on top of the kitchen cart, both of which were donated, to a corner of the room before the children arrive, in preparation for simulating a movie theatre and viewing the videos. Along with functioning as a tool for self-modeling and self-assessment, the videos provide a mirror image through which individuals can see themselves performing positive actions and skills and successfully interacting with others, holding a mirror up to the mirror-neuron system to further empower embodied simulation of positive, self-initiated actions and intentions perceived in the video. This week's skill sheet informs the parents that our brains need to perceive, comprehend and process new concepts in this way: through numerous reflections and with much support before they become established within patterns of behavior.

We reiterate to the parents that our once-a-week sessions, while beneficial to their children's social and emotional growth, will only help their children reach full potential if they follow up at home with the skills and activities suggested throughout the season. We emphasize that a consistent and concrete management system that focuses on these skills, set up in a fun and positive manner, will help their children to reintegrate fragmented perceptions, "re-program" their neurological impulses, develop new responses and ultimately change social behaviors. We remind them that the process of neural development and adjustment occurs over a lifetime, and establishing routines for their children early on to keep them focused on these skills on a regular basis is an important part of a comprehensive strategy. Finally, we remind them that they are, and always will be, their children's most influential teachers.

We ask the parents again about any allergies to or problems with popcorn when we retrieve the children from the lobby. Some provide us with potato chips or other snacks for their child. The children enter the room, and a few of them express mild but fleeting disappointment about the size of the television. Guided by literal thought patterns, some group members envisioned an actual movie-sized screen when we talked about showing the movies in the group. The children play excitedly, periodically asking questions about watching the movies and eating the popcorn.

We sit at the red chairs, position the television in front of the audience and hook the camera up. We prop up the skills list next to the television for the children to refer to as they view their movies. We explain that we will watch the movies once without stopping, and then watch them a second time, pausing to comment when we see the skills portrayed. We tell them, "Raise your hand when you see someone doing one of the skills from the list!" Before we begin, we hand out brown lunch bags filled with popcorn to the children. We couldn't find more decorative and festive white bags or boxes with *Popcorn* printed on the sides in red like they have in movie theatres. No one seems to mind. We have small water bottles ready, if the children request them.

As we watch the movies, the children's wide smiling eyes are transfixed to the screen, and even though we told them we would watch through once and then comment during the second viewing, a few of them spontaneously call things out like "We noticed they came over!" and "I expressed myself!" on the first go around. We are so impressed with the level of observations that continue when we watch again, with the majority of children eagerly able to identify and describe how they and their fellow group members incorporated the skills into their movies, with statements like "We said 'hi' and used names!" and "We noticed who was in the room!" and "We were playing and pretending to be angry!"

Ritchie identifies that he "told them what I like." Hannah shyly points out, "We worked together," when she and her friends in the movie decide what to play. Jack exclaims, "Look, Dr. Lee! I'm on TV!" when we show his movie. We say, "Yes, Jack! What were you doing on TV?" He repeats, "Look, I'm on TV!" We try again with "What did you say to your friends?" He echoes the question, looking for further guidance, "What did you say to you friends?" We say, "Did you say hello to them?" He answers, in a singsong voice, "I said hello to my friends!" Billy has a similarly excited and general response, calling out, "I'm in the movie!" when he and his cast appears on the screen. We ask him what he's doing in the movie, and he says, "We made a movie!" We ask him how he felt in the movie, and he answers, "It was scary in the movie!" referring to the theme of their plot. We say, "Yes! You pretended to be scared and you expressed your emotion in the movie!" Walter proudly states, "We matched with our bravery," as he watches himself and his co-stars fending off the zombies. Jason was absent the previous week and did not participate in making a movie.

The myriad of mutually reinforcing and empowering factors that simultaneously occur when making the movies continues as the children watch their movies. The cognitive and behavioral context established when planning and enacting the movies the previous week can now be processed through visual observation and auditory perception, initiating another round of mirror-neuron activity. By watching themselves on video, individuals neurologically imitate and reenact what they perceive on the screen, further rehearsing and strengthening connections to neural centers that assist in generating appropriate and empowered behavioral action and response, established during the enactment. The activity also provides another "perspective" through which awareness of and movement between perspectives regarding perceptions of self and other can be further engaged. The integration of skills, processes and operations continue as the children watch and reflect upon their movies. We ask them for one final thought regarding the portrayal of skills, record the final ten points of the season, choose prizes and say goodbye for a few weeks until after the new year.

Chapter 9

Diction and Reasoning: Social Scripting, Facial Cues and Body Language

Session 11: Reunion and Reconnection

Session 11 uses familiar games, sociometry, puppetry and scripting to ease the children's return to the group environment after a three-week break for the holidays, and welcome new children who are beginning the group at the outset of the winter session. The sensory-driven difficulty and resulting anticipatory anxiety that occurs with transitioning back into group can be offset to some degree with activities that are comforting, predicable and provide opportunities for expression. This week's skill sheet reminds and informs returning and new parents of the importance of organizing a system at home to manage the acquisition of new skills and facilitate emotionally intelligent, expressive language.

We tell the parents that the children will be looking at specific language models that portray differences between greeting old friends and meeting new friends. We ask that parents start, if they haven't already, a routine in which their children tell them about an actual event, a "real life story" that occurred in the course of their day. Parents are coached to ask their children if the event made them feel happy, sad, mad, scared or frustrated. They are urged to refrain from judging or giving advice to "fix" the feeling if the child expresses emotion that may be difficult for the parent to hear about. We encourage parents to simply mirror back, empathize and show understanding of what the child says, with comments like, "So you were really upset! That makes sense. I would feel mad, too, if someone treated me like that!"

Depending on the age and functioning level of the child, the retelling may be very detailed or two sentences long. Of course, the parent may need to take some type of follow-up action based on what the child describes, but the initial response should be very measured in terms of reacting in a way that might censor the child from sharing in the future. Rather than extracting information from the child, the goal of the encounter is to support the child toward becoming connected to and comfortable with recalling, describing and reflecting on meaningful events using emotionally intelligent language, with parents acting as empathetic mirrors.

For a small number of the approximately 60 high-functioning autistic children who attend our social-skills group, returning to group, even after a relatively short break, seems like starting from square one. Kenny wanders around, talking to himself and echoing dialogue from television shows. He seems oblivious to the play and space of others, needing lots of prompts from the leaders just to keep him from stepping on people. Ritchie starts off the session demanding toys that other children are already playing with and refusing to back down from his threats to take the toys away from them. Hannah anchors herself back at the dollhouse, and Billy reverts back to more isolated activity, talking to himself and moving somewhat aimlessly around the room.

The majority of children, though, return with willing enthusiasm and their developing ability to connect and interact. They find their friends and their favorite objects and pick up right where they left off. We point to our list of skills from the fall session and prompt returning members to introduce themselves to any new children they notice, of which there are a few among the groups. After an enthusiastic "Hello, everybody!" AJ plays calmly and cooperatively with Timmy and Evan and the Rescue Hero action figures. Jason, after being prompted with "How can you say hello to the new friends?" approaches a new boy and surprises us by casually saying, "Hello, Luke," in tones that are more typical than mechanical and idiosyncratic. We give the two-minute warning and then call for clean up.

We gather the group at the red chairs and display the new points chart, which the children signed their name to during the open-play period. We describe how it works for purposes of review and introduction to any new group members. If there are new group members, we ask the children, "How can we say hello to the new friends who are here? What can we tell them about our playgroup?" Timmy says, "We should invite them into our room!" The children spontaneously take turns from where they sit or by getting up and going over to where new members are sitting, and greet them with waves, handshakes and welcoming language. They add comments like "We have fun!" and "We make movies!" to describe what goes on in our group.

We play Your Name in Lights, if there are new group members, and everyone takes a turn going onstage, introducing themselves and telling about what they like to do with the color spotlights of their choice. The group is encouraged to respond by calling out any matches, things they notice, self-expression and other relevant information and commentary derived from the previous fall session's skill list. Billy goes up, chooses blue and says, "Hi! I'm Billy! I like to watch *Attack of the Clones*!", eliciting excited responses of "Me, too!" from the new member Dan and some of the other children. Jack goes up, picks the orange lights and starts singing. We ask him to say his name and he repeats a leader's name over and over again. We prompt, "My name is..." and he fills in, "Jack." We continue with "...and I like to..." He echoes our statement, and we complete it with "Sing!" and ask him to say the entire phrase, "My name is Jack, and I like to sing!" which he does. Hannah won't go on stage, but tells us from her seat that she likes to draw and watch movies.

If there are no new group members, we begin the discussion by saying, "We haven't seen each other in a few weeks! Who remembers some of the fun things we did before the vacation? How can we connect with each other, now that we're back?" We indicate words and phrases such as *Did you...?*, *I remember that you...* and *How was...?* printed on large sheets of paper to prompt questions they can ask each other about the holidays. We ask who wants to try one, and the children take turns asking each other questions like "How was your vacation?" and "Did you get a lot of toys?" The children move through the procedure, asking each other, for the most part, about toys and video games they received for the holidays.

We start a locogram activity by saying, "We do a lot of different things over the vacation. What are some of the different things that people do to celebrate the holidays?" After hearing and reflecting the children's responses, we add, "Some of us like the different things that our families do and feel happy about them, and some of us might also feel scared, mad or sad about some of the things. We're going to see how we feel about the different holiday activities." We indicate the four signs on the wall, *Happy, Mad, Sad* and *Scared,* and call out criteria that includes "staying up late," "leaving school," "going back to school," "decorating the house," "not coming to group," "getting presents," "staying all day with brothers and sisters," "seeing cousins," "eating holiday food" and "going different places." We tell the children to strike a pose with their bodies and faces that show the emotion of the sign they choose. We encourage a range of response with suggestive statements like "Most of us are happy to get presents, but maybe we get sad if we don't get what we want, or scared that our new toy will break, or mad that we have to share..." Jason calls out, "I'm happy" as he moves toward the *Happy* sign when "going back to school" is called out. AJ goes to *Mad* for "going different places," folds his arms, scrunches up his face and declares, "I want to stay home!"

We play Found a Match with all age groups and start the game by explaining, "Some of us do things that are the same over the holidays, and some of us do different things. Let's see if any of us can find matches with some of the things we did over the holidays." The children walk around the room and question each other on criteria called out by the leader, shouting, "Found a match!" if they find someone who has the same response. The leader starts with, "Find a friend who..." and adds topics such as "...got the same toy as you," "...went to the same [holiday event or vacation] as you," "...watched the same [holiday TV shows] as you," "...ate the same [holiday foods] as you" and other holiday-related themes. We simplify the criteria for the younger groups, asking, "Who opened presents?" enabling Kenny to high-five Gary and triumphantly exclaim in his singsong voice, "We both opened presents! We made a match!" Ritchie has a tough time, yelling out, "I want to tell!" while other children share their matches with the group. Older and higher functioning group members can also suggest criteria for matching.

With the younger groups, we follow up with quick puppet shows reflecting and reiterating some of the holiday matches made during the game. The children may present their shows alone, in pairs or with three or four members. They may wish to present more fantastical rather than reality-based ideas, like a show about the bunnies who match because they all ate carrot pie for Christmas. This is fine as long as they develop and express their ideas using pragmatic language that depicts an encounter where matches are discovered, and, if the puppet group includes a new member, the different words used when encountering an old friend and meeting a new friend.

Group members, for the most part, are able to translate matches they made as themselves during the game into the roles and stories of the puppets. Some reflect the matching encounters verbatim in their puppet shows, while others utilize artistic license for their presentations. For lower functioning children like Jason, we look for simple enactment and expressive language through the role of the puppet. This in and of itself can be a difficult task. We ask Jason if he wants to have a turn in the puppet stage, and he enthusiastically says, "Yes!" He jumps up and heads for the stage. He chooses the puppet that the previous child used and thrusts it through the curtains. After a moment of silence, a leader asks, "What's your name, puppet?" No response. The leader prompts, "My name is…" and Jason echoes, "My name is…" and then adds, "Jason." We ask, "Who did you find a match with, Jason puppet?" He answers, "Games."

While Jason is not yet able to shift perspective in a manner that allows him to take on the role of another to represent self and coordinate and express information relative to the two states of being, we are encouraged that he is at least interested in this first spirited and creative step of putting a puppet on his hand and presenting it to the audience. By responding to the leader's prompts, he works to communicate and make himself understood to other people, engaging the process of representing aspects of himself and his ideas through a shared language that simultaneously considers others while thinking about self. We praise him and shape his response, saying, to the puppet, "Yes! You and other puppet friends played games over the holidays!" and then to Jason, "Great job, Jason!" He happily skips back to his seat.

It may be age-appropriate for the older groups to present puppet shows in this manner as well. If not, leaders can set up "partner chats" based on matches that were made during the game, where two individuals sit facing each other and spend a few minutes talking about something they liked about the holidays, and then something they did not like about the holidays. The group leader can turn it into a game, calling "Go!" timing the chats and then seeing how many things each partner remembers about the other, or how many matches were made between the two.

We gather around the chart and ask the children to recall whom they matched with as we played our games today. By facilitating reunion and connection among new and returning group members, we provide opportunities to construct and articulate pragmatic expressive language relative to the context of the interaction. When we get to Timmy, he asks, "Who made the match with me for playing Wii?" AJ says, "I did. I play Wii." Hannah says she "made a match with the new boy about drawing." Jack is only able to tell us something about what he did. Like Jason, he is not able to move from his own sense of self to the actions of another and communicate connections between the two. His emerging self-awareness and increasing ability to relate that to the group of others through language, though, establishes an important foundation toward the goal of shifting more freely between perspectives of self and other. We give out prizes if new members have joined, add *Reconnecting with friends* to the list and walk the children out to their parents.

Session 12: Interpreting and Responding to Nonverbal Cues

Session 12 uses games, improvisation and role-play to facilitate awareness, identification of and responses to body language, facial expressions and nonverbal cues. Group members take turns presenting, perceiving and interpreting meaningful intentions expressed without language through gesture and physical movement to develop deeper understanding of nonverbal social communication. This week's skill sheet asks parents to play a type of charades at home using physical expressions, gestures and body cues to communicate social messages such as "I want to play with you" and "I'm getting tired of this," and see if their children can guess what is being communicated. Parents can ask their children to describe a real or hypothetical social situation in which somebody might react or respond with those particular gestures.

Children then take a turn communicating a social message nonverbally, and parents guess what the child is trying to "say" and suggest a situation that might cause a person to react or respond that way. Making expressive facemasks from paper plates or leafing through magazines, cutting out pictures and identifying what the children think the person in the picture might be saying can also help them to practice reading and interpreting nonverbal cues, facial expressions and gestures. Parents can surprise their children with nonverbal expression when they are not expecting it, while they are playing something else, eating dinner or watching television, for example, to see if the child can spontaneously and appropriately respond. Facilitating the skill as a game or friendly competition where the children can earn a trip to the playground or special Sunday time with a parent makes it fun and interesting.

AJ enters the room and announces to the group, "Hi! I'm doing great today!" We acknowledge and reflect his positive greeting as he settles in to play with Timmy and Evan at the Rescue Hero action figures. Luke, wearing a football helmet and shoulder pads from the costume bins, comes over to a corner of the room where Jason sits with a leader. The leader playfully mirrors Luke's "tough" character with facial and body expressions. Jason looks up at Luke and smiles, while Billy and Jonathon walk around repeating their chant together. Jack is absent today. We hear Ritchie yelling, "Hey!" as Gary nears the body pillows that Ritchie has sandwiched himself between. We balance our response to the situation, coaching tolerance for Ritchie and respectful awareness of others' space for Gary. Gary references the Power Lines poster and says, "I need a pillow;" Ritchie, without further intervention, gives him one. We recognize and reflect both boys' successful actions.

We start the discussion at the red chairs by asking the children, "How do we tell each other things?" We affirm all their answers, which for the most part have to do with using language. A leader prompts more responses by making faces or gesturing with his or her body in an exaggerated manner, maybe by folding arms and scowling, asking, "What do you think I am telling you by looking this way?" The children gleefully shout, understanding that it's just pretend, "You're mad!" The leader responds, "Yes! What am I using to tell you that?" The leader strikes a couple of other expressive poses to elicit response from the children and prompt their identification of the use of hands, faces, arms and the rest of the body to communicate. The leader then retrieves the expressive facemasks used in Session 3. Holding the masks up one at a time, the leader asks, "What might this friend be saying?" The children are coached to use full, pragmatic sentences like "I am so sad that nobody's playing with me" to reflect what the face seems to be saying, rather than merely identifying the emotion expressed by the mask.

A leader holds up the sad face, and Kenny says, "This boy is scared because it's dark." We ask, "So what might his words be?" and he responds with, "I'm scared because it's dark." As an afterthought, Kenny adds, "I'm scared of the dark, too!" A murmur of agreement and response ripples through the group. We hold up the happy face and ask Jason, "What could her happy words be?" He responds, "She found a tooth." We prompt him to say, "I found a tooth," and ask him if he lost a tooth. He indicates the new gap in his row of teeth and says again, "I found a tooth!" Jonathon finds words for the sad girl's facemask, saying, "I'm sad because my big brother got a heart attack." His mother had informed us earlier that her brother, whom Jonathon is very close to, was in the hospital. Hannah says, "I won the game!" when the happy mask is shown, and AJ says, "I'm scared of monsters," as we hold up the scared mask. Jonathon adds, "I'm scared of fire drills." We ask Billy, who does not initiate any responses, what the boy's mad face might be saying. He says, "I lost the game," echoing what someone had just said.

After responding to the masks, the children are divided into two or three teams with a leader in each to play "What Were They Thinking?", a game that coordinates connection between facial expression and pragmatic expressive language. Each team receives a large poster board laminated with six different photos of children's expressive faces cut from magazines. The leader explains that team members will look closely at the faces in the photographs and write what they might be thinking on sticky notes, and then stick them in thought bubbles drawn above each face on the poster. Again, as with the facemasks, the children are constructing full, pragmatic sentences on the notes, as if the child in the photo were saying them, rather than just identifying the feeling of the face. We found sticky note pads with large quotation marks on each side of the note that emphasizes this point.

We place the posters on the floor and the teams gather around them. The children work diligently and collaboratively, exchanging comments like "I think he's angry," and "Maybe he's more frustrated," as they figure out what to write on the sticky notes. A leader asks about a particular photo, and AJ says, "Surprised. Her got presents! I got presents, too!" The leader attempts to inconspicuously coach AJ toward correcting his grammar by saying, "She got presents? What do you think she got presents for?" He says, "She got presents for Christmas!" Billy continues to echo "Games" for every response to every photo. Other responses coordinated with the faces and recorded by the teams include "Someone was nice to me," and "My Legos broke."

When all of the six bubbles corresponding to the six expressive face photos are filled with a sticky note, the team takes the sticky notes out of the bubbles and places them in a row on top of the poster. Teams then switch posters to see if they can place the sticky-note thoughts back in the bubbles that the first team had originally put them in. The leaders emphasize, when the whole group is going over all the sticky placements, that a number of answers may be possible and there are no definitive rights and wrongs, but it will be fun to see how many sticky-note thoughts are placed back in the same bubbles by the different teams.

We usually facilitate another activity before the teams switch posters, in between filling out the thought bubbles and figuring where the other teams placed them, since coming up with and articulating possible corresponding language to place in each thought bubble can be arduous work for the children. They seem to enjoy the activity and approach it enthusiastically, but scrutinizing the faces in the photos and constructing corresponding pragmatic language wears on their attention after a while, even when there is a team of three and each child is responsible for coming up with captions for only two photos. A quick break in the middle of the poster activity that moves group members around a bit while working with the theme, helps to hold their interest. With the younger groups, we do a quick version of a Simon-Says mirroring activity, where leaders, and then children, take turns reflecting emotion and feeling through gesture, facial expression and body language while the rest of the group mimics the movements and guesses what the initiator is trying to say.

With the older groups, we play a version of charades in which the children take turns getting up on stage after conferring out of earshot with another leader, and expressing through gesture and body language a phrase such as "This gets me so mad!", "We won!", "Hey, I was here first!", "Leave me alone!", "That is so cool!", "It's my turn!", "I don't want to do this anymore.", "I don't like that!", "What's your problem?", "Come with me!", "Get out of the way!", "There's no room!" and "You wrecked my game!" from a prepared list. The children are welcome to make up their own phrase to enact, as long as they run it by the conferring leader to make sure ideas are cohesive, clear, able to be communicated and universally understood.

Timmy jumps up and down with a big smile on his face and tells the group his phrase, "I'm happy! I won!" after a few guesses. Jonathon comes on stage with a sad face and slumped shoulders, saying, after the group makes guesses about sad feelings and possible situations, "My brother got hurt." AJ stomps up on stage with his fists clenched, eventually telling everyone that his face and body say, "She took my toy away!" Ian tells us, "This is from the horror genre," and grabs his open-mouthed face as he cowers in fear. Walter and Mike are close enough, with their guesses of "Help! The monsters are attacking me!" Both of Walter's presentations are similarly loud and explosive, even though he says completely different things with each turn. We successfully coach him to focus more and take charge of how his body moves in order to communicate what he is trying to say. After everyone has a turn or two on stage, we get back into teams and switch posters.

When there is time, we divide the whole group in half and brainstorm elaborate hypothetical social situations, such as "a child gets picked on for messing up the kickball game and someone on the team comes to his or her defense," or "someone in a group of friends leaves another friend out of an activity, leading to a confrontation between the two while the others look on." Each group, out of earshot from the other, decides upon a specific situation and practices telling the story using only gesture, body language, facial expression and no words. The groups can prepare their stories in the hallway or another unused room, so the other half doesn't see or hear them, and then return to the group room to perform their story. The other half, as audience, sees what they can understand and pick up about the situation from watching the mimed event.

Kenny has an unusual response when he finds out that his team put some of the sticky notes in different thought bubbles than where the original team placed them. He starts crying that he "lost the game." We reassure him that there is no losing or winning, and we go over how his team's choice of where to place the sticky notes fit in just fine with the faces. Through his tears, which are very out of character for him, he repeats what we say as a way of soothing himself and adds, in his singsong and mechanical tones, "I'm crying, but I'll feel better soon. It's OK. I didn't lose the game. I'll do better next time." He continues to speak with us and continues to cry, as if the two experiences are completely separate from each other. We ask the children what they remember about what the faces were saying, or what they used to convey their messages, record their points, add *Seeing how we use our bodies and face expressions to communicate* to our skill list and say goodbye.

We speak to Kenny's mother after group, and she tells us that he has been reacting in this unpredictable and emotional way lately. We suggest that Kenny's reaction reflects a new and deeper way of connecting and interacting, as the idea of winning or losing in relation to others had never before been part of his consciousness or perspective. Kenny's upset feelings about "not winning" meant that he was invested in the interaction in a way that he had never experienced.

His mother agrees, telling us that along with his more emotional reactions, Kenny has been much more verbal and engaged with others at home and at school.

Session 13: On the Right Track—Building Conversation

Session 13 uses symbolic representation, set-building and simulation to create a railroad and train-ride theme, an extremely popular subject among many of our group members, to facilitate shifting of perspective between self and other while promoting connection through composition, construction and articulation of conversation. Children choose topics of interest, find travel partners and move along the track together, stopping at a number of station houses along the way that guide them with questions and prompts for building and sustaining conversation. This week's skill sheet asks parents to work on conversation skills with their children at home by exchanging ideas using the question words *who, what, where, when, why, which* and *how.*

Parents can choose a question word for each day, asking *who* questions on Monday, for example, like "Who is your best friend?" and "Who is your favorite teacher?" and "Who do you like to watch on television?" The children answer, and then ask parents similar questions as a springboard for finding common interests and developing conversation. *What* questions can be asked on Tuesday, *Why* on Wednesday and so on. Or, a particular topic can be chosen for the day and all the questions can be applied; for example, "Who is your best friend at school? What do you like to play together? Where is the most fun place to be together? When do you get to play? Why do you like him/her? How do you act together?"

It is important that the children establish and express an opinion or perspective on some meaningful topic, ask others about their perspective on the same topic, and then relate their own personal perspective to the other person's response through an ongoing exchange of ideas and language that builds conversation. Parents can keep track of how many times the child and family member or friend can go back and forth, taking turns to respond to each other's perspective while staying on the same topic. Parents are told that it is fine and natural to transition to another topic during the conversation, but the key word is transition, rather than awkwardly or haphazardly jumping to another topic. The parent can make a list of "bridge words" and phrases such as *That makes me think of…, Did you ever…?* and *What do you think about…?* for the child to refer to that can bridge one conversation topic to the next.

We have no open-play period this week, as the room is set up for the train theme and the activity will take up the entire session. We blow a train whistle in the hallway where the children can't see us, before we get them from the lobby. We hear their excited voices around the corner saying things like, "Whoa! What was *that?*" and, "It's a train! A train is coming!" A couple of the higher functioning Asperger's children, prompted by their tendencies for literal thought, are a bit disheartened as we step into the lobby and blow the whistle again in full view. Sammy turns to his friends and says, with a mildly disappointed affect, "Its not a train, guys, its just Dr. Lee." We tell them, in the lobby, that the room is going to look different today to prepare them for the change in routine.

The children enter the room and take in the set up. The show and pretend lights are on, and the red chairs are assembled in rows by a makeshift booth labeled *Tickets*. There are a number of large cutouts of station houses made from colored poster board hanging on the walls around the room. Train tracks drawn on long pieces of paper cut from the paper roll lay on the floor, connecting one station house to another. Traffic and street signs bearing phrases like *Make an effort, Ask questions, Stop and listen, Respect others, Plan ahead, Teamwork Avenue* and *Honesty Street* purchased from a local educational supplies store are taped on the walls in between the station houses. A cardboard cutout of a train set with tracks also purchased at the store is taped to another wall.

The children gather at the red chairs set up by the ticket booth at their station of departure. One of the station house cutouts is positioned behind the ticket booth, with a big square drawn in the middle, the word *Destinations* heading the top and *Something you like* printed right underneath. Under that are a number of conversation topics the children can choose from, such as *Pets, Television, School, Games* and *Vacations*. Children can request that the ticket seller, played by an intern or volunteer, add other topics of interest to the list of destinations. We ask the children what a conversation is and discuss how we can participate in conversations. We explain that they will use the train ride to choose a topic and find a partner or partners to travel with through the stations, visiting each station house and opening the doors, where information will prompt them what to do. We try to limit traveling groups to three for logistical purposes and to make sure everybody is participating verbally…but if an excited and enthusiastic bunch of four or five ask to go through together because they want to talk about a particular topic, we certainly won't turn them down.

Two leaders demonstrate the procedure of asking and choosing each other to travel with and agreeing on a topic with which to move through the stations. They tell the ticket seller what their topic is, and the ticket seller writes it on the ticket, created and printed six to a page from a computer so the word *Ticket* and a train icon are printed on each and cut out for distribution to the children. The travelers start their journey, follow the track and arrive at Station House #1. They open the cardboard door held to the house with colored duct tape and a brass paper fastener and read the directions printed on the other side, which say, *Ask your friends a* what *or* where *question about your topic. After everybody answers, each of the other friends asks a* what *or* where *question about the topic, and everybody answers.* They follow the instructions, asking and answering each other's questions.

After exchanging their ideas, they travel along the track to Station House #2, open the door and follow the directions, which state, *Ask your friends a* who *or* when *or* which *question about your topic. After everybody answers, each of the other friends asks a* who *or* when *or* which *question about the topic, and everybody answers.* At Station House #3, the friends ask each other and answer *why* and *how* questions, and Station House #4 instructs them to ask and answer a variety of *who, what, where, why, how, when* and *which* questions of each other. For some Asperger's children who have a more natural flow of verbal expression, the procedure can seem a bit stilted at first, but for most children in the program, the back and forth exchange of questions and answers warms them up to verbal interaction that becomes more smooth and consistent as they travel to and from the stations.

We encourage all the children to use the questions and answers as a starting point for building conversation, and they don't have to worry about sticking to the exact instructions at the station houses if they add more words and ideas to their conversations than what the instructions tell them to say. This way, the children with more verbal ability can develop their conversations at a quicker pace, while children like Jason, Kenny, Jack, and Billy, who need more support, can rely on the procedures listed at the station houses. After moving through the station houses, the travelers return round trip to the ticket booth waiting area, get their tickets stamped and see how long they can continue their conversation while waiting for the others to arrive back at the starting point. When everyone returns, we take a few minutes to reflect on the process as a group and then we begin another journey. Group members can pick new partners and topics if they choose. We usually take three trips around the tracks.

While the other children, with a little guidance, pick partners and excitedly line up at the ticket booth, Jason, Jack and Kenny wander around, unable to follow this part of the procedure. The leaders usher them to the ticket line, partner with them to choose a topic and escort them through the process. Other leaders walk around, check in with traveling groups, offer support and make comments like "You looked at each other's eyes when you asked and answered the questions! That was great!" We help them structure and reform their questions, which at times can sound a little awkward. When taking about pets, Timmy asks his fellow travelers, "Why are they called *pets?*" which pretty much stops the conversation. A leader suggests, "Try a 'how' question, Timmy," and he bounces back with, "How do you take care of pets?" Individuals in the group answer the more pragmatically accessible question.

Billy is making an extended high-pitched sound that sounds something like "heee heee" or "veee veee." He repeats it over and over, walking up to children, standing in front of them and making the sounds. He focuses on Jonathon, finally offering a clue as to why he had been vocalizing this for the past ten minutes. He asks Jonathon, "Cars? Cars?" and then the more complete, "Do you want to talk about cars with me?" We assume he is talking about the popular Disney movie, since he tends to fixate on them, and perhaps he was echoing the sound of an engine or siren heard in the movie. The leaders slowly and methodically work with the younger and lower functioning children to piece together questions and answers relevant to their topics, while the older boys, including Walter, Ian and Mike, speed along the tracks, deep in conversation about Star Wars, video games and Legos.

Along with the metaphor of keeping the conversation "on track" with the train activity, we have also used the metaphor of building a conversation using the foam tubes and scarves to actually build a conversation on the infrequent occasions when the train activity seems too young for certain older groups. The children are split into two teams and prompted to "build" a conversation by choosing a predetermined or brainstormed topic, asking questions and exchanging ideas about the topic among teammates and adding a tube or scarf to a structure they create each time an exchange is made that remains on topic or smoothly bridges to another topic. The different colored tubes can represent different types of questions. When someone connects with an answer, the team adds a connector piece to the tube. Related comments can connect the tubes together or drape them with a scarf. Certain tubes can represent bridges to other conversation topics. The longer the teams keep their conversation going, the bigger their conversation building structures gets.

Before we leave, we ask the children whom they talked with, what topics they talked about and record their points for the day. We happily reflect on their ability to stay on topic and articulate their ideas clearly with appropriate language, singling out every individual with an example of success we noticed during the activity. We add *Asking and answering questions to build conversation* to the skill list, and the children walk down the hall, checking out all their stamped tickets that they excitedly show their parents.

Chapter 10

Complication and Resolution: Interactive Language Skills

Session 14: The Right Words in the Right Place at the Right Time

Session 14 uses games, symbolic representation and improvisation to support group members toward building and sustaining conversation while attending to variations in the setting for modulating volume, pragmatic content and other elements prompted by differences in the environment. Children work in teams, improvising with objects and exchanging thoughts and ideas based on a suggested thematic settings to empower shifts in perspective and coordinate context for interactive language response. The information sheet asks the parents to continue working on conversation skills at home by applying question and response exchanges using *who, what, where, why, when* and *how* in different locations such as the bank, the library, the supermarket or any other place visited in the course of the day, and focusing the conversation on the environment they are in at the moment.

Along with asking questions about the different places, parents and children can also make statements about things they notice in the environment as a way of starting the conversation. Attention can be paid to the differences in volume that are appropriate for diverse places such as a library and the playground. Parents monitor sudden shifts in topic while accounting for the natural flow of conversation. If, for instance, parent and child are in the supermarket and the parent asks, "What's your favorite snack?" and the child says, "Chocolate chip cookies," and then adds, "When are we going to Jimmy's house again?" it may seem like the child is impulsively switching to another topic in an unfocused manner. But if the child can explain his or her thought process within the context of the conversation, as in, "We had chocolate chip cookies at Jimmy's house," then it counts as a score or a point if the skill is organized in a game or contest format.

Jason enters the room and, instead of anchoring himself to one of his two or three regular spots, starts moving around the space in back and forth patterns. He is also verbalizing more than usual, echoing some dialogue that we can't quite understand, but they are words and phrases rather than the random sounds he sometimes vocalizes, or the one-, two- or occasionally three-word responses he gives during activities. As the leader playfully mirrors his actions, he laughs and says, "Play!" to her as they move around the room, perhaps as a request to engage her further, or maybe a happy acknowledgment of their activity. Kenny, who was so connected last week, seems lost this week. He plays alone and talks to himself, rolling around the cushions like he did at the beginning of the year.

AJ is playing cooperatively with a group of children, and he uses power words, instead of lashing out when Timmy, who's having a very rare bad day, hits him on the arm after AJ accidentally knocks over his set-up rescue action heroes. Timmy uncharacteristically keeps to himself for the rest of the play period. Hannah, while initially situated at the dollhouse, turns to watch and talk with the children around her. She inches toward the areas where some of the other children are playing. Jack is absent again today. His father left a message saying that he's had recurring ear infections. Walter, Ian and Mike continue their epic battles, finding ways to share the Darth Vader mask and coordinate the stories that each of them want to enact.

Jonathon looks to play with Billy, who is walking up to everybody in the group saying, with the exact same intonation each time, "What's your name again?" He doesn't wait for an answer, leading us to believe that he is echoing dialogue from a television show or movie. He also calls out a long and loud "Yeeaahh!" as he moves from individual to individual. Jonathon is getting frustrated as he follows Billy around, asserting, "I want to play with you!" Billy finally breaks his solo routine, sees Jonathon, and engages him with their ritualistic chanting and hand movements. His behavior is still stereotypical and idiosyncratic, but he is clearly more connected, responsive and socially attuned when he interacts this way with Jonathon. We end the open-play period with the two-minute clean up warning.

Our discussion at the red chairs considers the challenge of having a conversation and staying focused on one thing at a time, as well as figuring out and knowing what to say about a topic. Group members are divided into three teams situated in three separate spaces in the room with a leader at each team. A leader explains, "I'm going to show you a picture of a place. After you see what the place is, your team is going to use the tubes and the scarves to make some things that could be used or found in that place. Like if I show you a picture of a restaurant, you might use the tubes to do this..." The leader pretends to eat using a tube as a utensil, prompting the children to guess, and then drapes a scarf over a couple of tubes pretending to read it as a menu, again prompting the children to guess what the leader's actions portray. The leader reiterates, especially with the younger group, "Is this *really* a [fork, menu, or whatever was improvised]?" and continues, after the group responds, "No!" with, "Right, we just *pretended* that it was."

The leader continues to explain "After two minutes of making the things out of the tubes and scarves, you're going to put the tubes down and one of your teammates is going to start a conversation with a *who, what, where, when, how* or *why* question (indicating the words printed colorfully on large paper posted around the room) about the place I showed you in the picture. Another teammate will answer, and then someone will ask another connected question or give another answer on the same topic. Your team captain [the leaders, interns, volunteers] will keep score with how many connected pieces of the conversation your team can put together."

The leader then shows a series of pictures, purchased at a local educational supplies store, depicting familiar places, such as a playground, classroom, supermarket and library. After each picture is shown, the teams take two minutes to build their objects and quickly show the other teams what they made. They then get another five minutes or so to see how many on-topic conversational exchanges the team can make while the team leader keeps score. We hear how many connected exchanges were made from each team leader, and the next picture is shown.

The tubes and materials are distracting to the children, and it is difficult for many of them at first to transition from the building to the talking, but that is part of the process. Ritchie has an especially tough time with this, causing Gary to become extremely frustrated. He attempts to leave the room twice. We coach him to use power words, and he says, "I don't like what Ritchie's doing! We won't get our points!" We reassure him, along with the rest of the children who are trying to cooperate with the activity and have to deal with distracted teammates, that everyone who tries will get prize points on the chart, even if one team gets more conversation points in the game than another team.

While we don't want to breed disharmony among group members by placing activities in the context of competition, it is a strong motivating factor that keeps most of the children focused and connected in a way that is fun and exciting for them. A few of the children like Gary may get frustrated with the level of participation from their teammates, but coping with that frustration, which also reflects connection with others, is part of the process as well. After the first couple of rounds, the teams settle into engaged and collaborative units, chalking up 10, 15, 20 exchanges of on-topic questions, comments and ideas pertaining to each of the settings they were shown. Billy, AJ and Kenny, with the support of their team leaders, do very well with the activity, offering relevant input and responding appropriately to others. Jason watches, occasionally responding when a leader asks him a direct question.

The process and adjustment toward building connection seems to operate like tectonic plates for many of the children. As experience mounts and pushes through blocked or partially disconnected pathways, connection can be sudden and tumultuous, like initially chaotic seismic activity that ultimately results in a more balanced and adjusted relationship between two plates previously pushing against each other. Aftershocks and uncertainty abound for a time after the plates have adjusted. One week Kenny is as connected and interactive as he has ever been, and the next week he is isolated and disconnected once again. Billy makes such strong strides with social interaction and then regresses, repeatedly making loud and unintelligible sounds that have little if anything to do with others in the environment. The developmental, hormonal and chemical shifts that naturally occur in all humans, most notably during adolescence, are that much more pronounced when neurological makeup and atypical wiring amplify the experience. We take two steps forward and three steps back, but we know we will be taking five steps forward and only two steps back in the near future. We ask the children about their topics of conversation, give them their points, add *Staying focused on the conversation topic* to our list, say goodbye and walk them to their parents.

Session 15: Stay to Play or Walk Away?

Session 15 uses set-building, simulation and role-play to explore and construct empowered language-based responses that address challenges of attempting to join in with others. Children take turns role-playing situations where they ask to play with others and deal with the possibility of being turned away. This week's information sheet asks the parents to assist their children with finding comfortable language they can use when looking to connect to a social situation, and what they might do if others choose not to include them.

Parents encourage their children to try out different words and phrases to use when engaging others and see what might be a good fit for his or her unique personality. Parents can help their children practice these approaches using improvised scenarios at home, in which family members involve themselves in an activity the child could connect to, as well as real-life situations resulting from play dates and visits to social settings where other children are playing. In the improvised scenarios, parents can prepare their children for the possibility of social rejection from other children by role-playing incidents where family members and friends turn them away when they attempt to connect.

This will likely bring up feelings and reactions that will need to be sorted out through further enactment and discussion. If, for example, the child is on a play date at someone's house and is being ignored and left out, then it is appropriate for the child to get the help of an adult who can address the other child's behavior. If, on the other hand, the child approaches another child he or she does not know at a playground or while on vacation and is turned away from joining in, it is more appropriate, perhaps, to move on and try to join in or play with someone else. These situations can be very confusing, especially for someone who has difficulty reading and responding to social situations. We remind the parents that the only way to gain more competence with navigating tricky social situations such as these is by practicing, and even adults still learn after decades of experience.

Jason enters the room this week and moves more freely and comfortably around the space. We are excited to see him settle by an area of Legos, where he parallel plays with Gary and Stevey. He moves away after a few minutes and a leader tries to coach him back, asking him if he can find a certain color and build a certain object, but he is done. The leaders acknowledge amongst themselves that it was a big, successful move for Jason, even if it only lasted a couple of minutes. Kenny seems to be back to his newly more connected self as he talks to leaders and seeks out other children to interact with. AJ continues his streak of cooperative behavior and interactive play with the other children. Timmy is back to his happy and cheery self. Jack is absent again.

Hannah goes right to the dollhouse and seems to want to crawl inside and hide. A leader tries to engage her, pointing out some of the things her friends are doing around the room, since she usually likes to talk about what she notices, but she does not look around or even up at the leader sitting next to her. The leader gently references the emotion posters around the room to see if Hannah can express what is going on with her today. Finally, she tells the leader that she feels "shy" about her hair. Her beautiful, full curly blonde locks had been straightened to a new and sophisticated style for the day, and the change was apparently making her very uncomfortable. The leader stays by her, reflecting authentic and positive support, as they play.

In general, the feel of the room during the open-play period has moved from isolated and mechanical, at the beginning of the year, to engaged and interactive, through imaginary and expressive play. Groups of two or three children are laughing with each other and their puppets at the puppet stage. Another bunch play with the action figures, talking and enacting with each other through the projected roles. Evan has set up a pretend lemonade stand with a play booth, some scarves and other improvised materials and is trying to drum up business. He approaches potential customers and asks them if they are thirsty. Some politely decline, while others visit his stand, make the appropriate inquiries and pay with pretend money they pull out of their pockets. Walter, Ian and Mike take turns playing the pirate who steals the treasure and needs to be apprehended by the others. Typical minor problems are addressed with power words and a little help from a leader, if needed.

We meet at the red chairs and talk about how to invite others to play and how to join in with groups of children, and what we can do and say if others don't let us play and leave us out. We play a round of "Correct the Leader," where two leaders improvise a number of scenarios on stage that has one looking to join the play of the other. The approaching leader first grabs the toy out of the other's hand and demands a turn, then asks the children sitting in the audience what the problem was. They usually identify the nasty affect of the approaching leader. Each time the group corrects the behavior (with much laughing) the leader replaces it with a new inappropriate behavior, until the last approach, which finally incorporates all their corrections. After being corrected about the nastiness and demanding tone, the leader approaches politely, but still grabs. Then, without grabbing, the leader asks too loudly, then too soft, then spaced out, then invading the other's space, and so on, each time playfully imploring the audience, "I'm doing what you say, but she/he still won't play with me!"

With the younger children, we bring out two or three play tents or large appliance boxes that have been decorated and cut for doors and windows and set them up around the room. We explain that three friends are going to start the "come out and play" game by choosing a toy to bring inside one of the boxes, so there is a child with toys in each of the "houses." We explain to the group, "Three more friends are going to pick other toys and call on the friends in the houses to come out and play with their toys. The friends in the houses might say yes, or they might say no. They might ask you to play with their toys instead, or they might just go back inside. You can decide if you want to stay and play if they say yes or ask you to play with them, or walk away and try to find someone else to play."

During the first round, the six children remain engaged for five or so minutes while the rest watch from the audience and narrate what they see. A range of possibilities can play out, from two "callers" ending up playing together, to all six playing together in one house. Each child needs to interact in some way with at least one other child among the six. If a child is attempting to join in but is being left out for some reason, the audience can be prompted to verbally support his or her efforts. A child who isolates with the toy and does not interact will have to return the toy and sit back in the audience, providing good incentive to remain engaged.

After the first six have worked through and settled into their choices on what to play and who to play with, the rest of the group can attempt to join them in any configuration, working through the same process of approaching the groups, asking to play and managing responses, or a new round can begin. Eventually, the last round will engage all children in some manner at the same time. For lower functioning group members like Jack and Jason, the goal is merely to approach another child or children and use language to initiate play. Sustained, interactive play would be the icing on the cake. For others, it is to approach and then sort through the various responses and possible rejections from the other children, make choices about what they want to do, and follow through with appropriate actions and language to engage sustained, interactive play.

We enact more specific scenarios to role-play on stage with the older children. We tell them, "We're going to see if we can figure out ways to handle it when we want to play with people, but they don't want to play with us." We explain that sometimes it might be appropriate to stay and stick up for ourselves if someone doesn't let us play, and other times it might be better to just walk away. We begin by asking who will be comfortable acting as the people who say, "No!" when the children approach them to play in the scene. In the past, children have volunteered to play the part of the kid who says, "No!" and then felt uncomfortable and a little confused with the role once they were onstage, instead graciously accepting the child who approaches them, insisting that they'd never do that, and undermining the intent of the role-play in a very endearing manner.

We now take extra time to initially emphasize that the scenes are only pretend and we know the children acting those parts aren't saying "no" for real, and that they are nice kids who would not be mean to anybody like that in real life, and they don't have to play those parts if they don't want to. But if they do want to try playing those parts, they have to say, "No!" when the other children ask to play with them in the scene. We usually get a core of three or four children who thoroughly get it and can move comfortably into and then out of this role. The rest of the children take turns role-playing in the scenes as the children who attempt to join the play. For each child, we assign a different setting and situation: at a playground, at a friend's house, with cousins during a holiday, on vacation, at an amusement park, at recess, a birthday party and so on, sometimes enrolling the kids who say "No!" as strangers, sometimes as siblings, and sometimes as friends or family.

After the child in role approaches the group on stage, asks to play, and receives the "no," the audience, along with the child playing the role, considers if they should stay to play or walk away. We look at the circumstances in the role-play that might warrant either taking a stand and pursuing inclusion, or leaving it alone and moving on. We ask the children, "Does [person in role] know these people? Did they come together? Are there other people to play with nearby? Are they just being mean and would be no fun to play with, anyway? Are they shy and need time to warm up?" The child who is being rejected strategizes an approach and enacts a comfortable and empowering response guided by the leader and the support of the group and then returns to the audience as the next child is prepared to take a turn by changing the setting and circumstances.

The children are excited to choose toys and go inside the boxes, and they do well with the pragmatic language called for by the role-plays. Some of them bring extra complications to the scenarios, though, challenging the group to consider a wider range of possible resolutions. Kenny knocks on Stevey's door and takes the toy out of Stevey's hand before asking if he wants to play. Mark asks if he can use the toy he bought from home that waits outside the door with AJ's toys for the activity. We allow him to, and then deal with the consequences as a number of children knock on his door and he refuses to come out or let anybody in to play with it. Surprisingly, AJ does not ask to bring his toys in. The group decides to resolve the situation by leaving all toys from home outside the door. The older group deals with the complications in the more specific role-plays, staying to play or walking away, rehearsing and generating pragmatic responses and resolutions to the potentially confusing encounters. We ask the groups who they played with and how they resolved the problems, record their points on the chart, give out prizes, and add *Joining in with friends* to the list of skills.

Sessions 16 and 17: Director's Chair— Asserting Social Language and Solving Problems

Sessions 16 and 17 use sociometry and the Director's Chair technique to support individuals toward constructing empowered language-based responses to specific challenging social situations. Group members take turns sharing complications from their personal lives and exploring potential resolutions by directing scenes reflecting related and meaningful real-life events. Individuals cast and then observe others in the role of self, mirroring neurological operations necessary for development of intentional attunement. The skill and information sheets for the two weeks it takes to complete this activity ask parents to help their children identify and express emotionally intelligent language regarding challenging social encounters, and then use the power words to build satisfying and empowering responses.

Parents are reminded not to react by immediately attempting to "fix" the problems that it is hoped their children are telling them about, as this may make the children less likely to share their experiences. We explain that the goal is to get the children interested and invested in talking about situations they are involved in; "grilling" them for answers might cause them to withdraw or become distracted when asked about their day. Parents are encouraged to mirror their children and empathize as much as possible when responding. Even if the child committed a wrong act or behavior in the situation he or she is talking about, it is important for parents to first understand (but not condone) the child's perspective without judgment, saying, for example, "Then you hit him? He must have made you *so mad!*" Rules and consequences can be calmly enforced later if needed, after this initial period of non-confrontational interaction that builds trust, safety and alliance.

Parents are then instructed to use the Power Lines with their children, words and phrases beginning with "I am…", "I feel…", "I think…", "I know…", "I want…", "I need…", "I don't…", "I can…" and "I will…" to construct strong and empowering responses to challenging social situations. Posters with these words prominently printed on them can serve as a reminder for the children as well as everybody in the family to use the language when dealing with problems. Along with thinking about events that happen in their own lives, children can practice the Power Lines while watching television, identifying conflicts between characters during commercials and suggesting possible words they could say. We reiterate to the parents that powerful responses used to address challenging situations shouldn't necessarily sound conciliatory or polite, but they should, while expressing loud and clear opinions in strong tones, remain respectful.

Jason enters the room and before the leaders are able to greet him, he initiates a cheery "Hello" without any prompting. We say hello back and tell him what a good job he did saying hello to us first. Ritchie comes in, tells a group of leaders and children about some sea creatures he has been researching and goes to lay on the pillows. He sees Gary looking his way and says, with an air of resignation, "Here," pulling one of the pillows out from under him and pushing it in Gary's direction. We bring out one of the boxes from the previous week's activity, causing a buzz of excitement among the children. Ritchie leaves the pillows to go inside. A few other children join him. We are pleasantly surprised, to put it mildly, when Jason walks over to the box and asks, "I play?" We try to contain ourselves while saying, "Sure, Jason, you can go in!" He goes inside and spends a few minutes with the other children before happily exiting and returning to his other, more mechanical stereotypical activity.

Jack is back, and his sporadic attendance over the past month has taken its toll. He is withdrawn and distracted, and he is not singing. His illness and medication have no doubt had an impact as well. The subtle effects of antibiotics and decongestants on behavior and temperament that we all experience are often magnified for people with sensitive neurological makeup like those on the spectrum. His easygoing demeanor is replaced, for the time being, with an agitated and reactionary affect. Jonathon and Billy walk around the room together, talking about the different shows they like and pretending to be some of the characters. AJ, Eddie and Evan play together in the box. Hannah is absent today.

We hear Walter from down the hall. He is crying and screaming that he doesn't want to play today. He makes it into the room with help from a leader, but he continues his relentlessly piercing tirade, yelling that he is not playing and saying something about being mad at his father through his torrent of tears. Another leader takes a walk with him down the hall to the Reflections area, where he is able to speak about how angry he is that his father was late getting him to group today. Even though it was only a few minutes or so, it was hard for Walter that the group was brought down to the playroom before he arrived. He is obsessively fixated on time and schedules. The leader empathizes and guides him through the different reflection blackboards painted on the wall, writing Walter's power words in chalk as he speaks them. When he is calmer and somewhat "vented," he is ready to return to group and participate.

At the red chairs, we talk with the children about how we can use words to solve problems and avoid getting in trouble. We use the sociometry emotion signs with the younger group and ask, "What happens to our face and body when we get mad/sad/scared/ frustrated?" and "What are some things we do when we're mad/sad/ scared/frustrated/even happy that could get us into trouble? How can we use words to say what's making us so mad/sad/scared/frustrated so the grownups will hear us and help us to solve the problem without getting us into trouble?" Kenny, back on track with his newly tuned-in frequency and ability for connected verbal response, asks, in his singsong affect, "You got in trouble when you were a little boy, Dr. Lee?" We affirm and process the group's responses and indicate the Power Lines poster if they haven't already done so during the discussion. We go over the words and phrases listed colorfully on the wall and ask the children to come up with ways to complete the sentences that begin with "I am...", "I feel...", "I think...", "I know...", "I want...", "I need...", "I don't...", "I can..." and "I will..." The children make their proclamations.

If a group has more than eight members, we go right to the Director's Chair activity to ensure that all group members will have a turn over the course of the two sessions it takes to complete the activity. Four children per week will allow for a comfortable pace that takes up the whole session after the open-play period. If there are fewer children in the group, the leaders can initiate some related warm-up activities as well. Rather than sitting at the red chairs and completing the power phrases, children can take turns saying them on stage with the microphone and their choice of colored lights. A sociometric locogram determined by the five emotion signs on the wall can warm up response to familiar social situations, settings and encounters with criteria such as *birthday parties, kids playing with your toys, playing with cousins, waiting your turn, being left out, not going first, sleepovers, going to a restaurant, playing at the playground, going to the movies* and *going bowling,* moving the children to share with others at the emotion signs of their choice, as the leader calls out each topic.

For the Director's Chair activity, the leaders turn on the show lights, set up a director's style folding chair facing the stage with a megaphone and a television remote (with batteries in it, so the red light turns on when the buttons are pushed) placed in the seat or on a stool next to it. We explain: "When it's your turn, you are going to sit in the director's chair, take the director's megaphone, and tell us about a time from your *real life* when you were with friends or other people and you were so mad, sad, scared or frustrated." We emphasize *real life* because we want to build pragmatic responses to real-life situations, and many of the children are prone to getting caught up in more fantastical thought and "television talk." The construction of reality-based language compliments, for some children in the program, is an important exercise in reality-based orientation and thought, as discussed previously with Ian.

We continue explaining: "Then, after you tell the story about something that happened in your real life, you will pick people from the audience to be the actors who will perform your show on stage. So, if I was going first, I would tell the story about the time I [leader uses an example from a real-life childhood argument or problem with a friend]. Then I would pick someone to be me, someone to be my [friend, brother, classmate, or whatever the story calls for], someone to be [other characters from the story just told] and the actors would go on stage. I'd tell you what to say and what to do, and then I'd call, 'ACTION!' (into the megaphone) or 'Play!' (pointing the remote at the stage) and you'd do the show. If something happens that's not supposed to be in the show, or if someone forgets a line, I can call, 'CUT!' (into the megaphone) or 'Pause' with the remote, fix it and then 'ACTION' to start the show again."

When the director is ready to cast the show, he or she is usually confronted with a sea of waving hands from the audience and calls of "Ooh! Ooh! Pick me!" for each role. We remind the children that the director gets to choose who to cast, and not everybody is going to be in every show. Some of the children may be uncomfortable acting in certain roles. We reassure them that we're all just pretending and if anybody is uncomfortable with a certain role, they don't have to play it. Sometimes, an initially enthusiastic volunteer may balk at a certain role, once on stage. We support them with "We know you are a really nice boy/girl, and you're just *pretending* to be the [mean or other uncomfortable characteristic] in the show," and allow them to opt out if they wish. For the most part, everyone is excited to be in the shows in any capacity.

After the scene is played and the director calls "CUT!", the leader asks the actors and audience, "Who knows what it's like to be [name of director in chair] when this is happening?" Rather than having the children retell the story or share extended stories from their own life, which they tend to do, the leader prompts them to respond with a word or two, an emotion that describes what it might feel like to be in the director's situation. After hearing the group's empathetic responses, the leader guides the director to rework the scene by choosing power words from the Power Lines poster that the actor, playing his or her role, can say at some point in the scene, explaining, "What power words could [the actor playing the director's role] say to maybe help things work out a little better?" The actors play the scene with the power word response scripted by the director to engage a meaningful exchange of thoughts and feelings, rather than an imposed cliché that could superficially "fix" the situation.

During each scene, another leader fills out a paper artistically formatted as a scene marker with *Title of My Show, Where I was, What it felt like* and *Power words I can say* laid out and printed in theatrical-style fonts in the center. Blank lines underneath or alongside these headings provide space for the leader to write in relevant information based on the child's show. A "Power Lines Menu," listing all the power word phrases, along with icons of a megaphone, movie camera and director's chair, complete the document of the child's experience. They are handed out to the children who had a turn at the end of the session to take home.

Stevey sits in the chair and tells about the time when his father hit him, and then he bit his father. When his father got even madder at him for biting, Stevey said, "Well, you hit me!" causing his father to say, "I can do whatever I want!" We tell Stevey that we are so happy he is doing this show, because we do not like it and do not think it's fair when parents hit the children, no matter what. There is a murmur of agreement in the audience. The content of Stevey's show also prompts us to talk about stage fighting, the rule that any show portraying physical aggression needs to be acted so that the actors do not actually touch each other but only pretend to hit and get hurt. Two leaders demonstrate a physical altercation where no physical contact is made, and each pretends to get hurt. We explain that this is how all actors do it in any shows they see that have fighting in them.

Stevey picks Kenny to play his father. We silently wonder if Kenny will be able to handle playing a role, but he does a great job as the father, pretending to hit Luke, who is playing Stevey, reacting in pain when Luke pretends to bite him, and then stomping his foot down and declaring, "I can do whatever I want!" right on cue after Luke says his line. We prompt Stevey to call, "CUT!" and ask the audience, "What do you think it's like to be Stevey when that happens?" The children respond with "Mad!" and "Sad!" and "Not nice!" Stevey takes it in and looks at the Power Lines poster. He decides that Luke should say, "I feel so mad! I don't want to get hit!" instead of biting. The actors take their places, the leader clacks the scene marker, saying, "Lights, camera…" or, "Quiet on the set," for effect, and points toward Stevey who calls, "ACTION!" The scene plays out with Luke as Stevey, speaking the power words loud and clear. The director calls the final "CUT!" and the cast returns to the audience.

The children may need pragmatic support when constructing and sharing their stories from the director's chair. The leader facilitating the shows can begin by asking the director, "Where did your story take place? At school? At home? On the playground?" and then, "Who was there?" and finally, "What did they say? What happened?" That is usually enough to warm up the director, if needed, to share the story in a way that the audience can follow. We also remind the audience to "Listen closely to the story and the different parts, because you may get picked to be in the show!" The actors on stage also need a good deal of prompting, as they may become distracted, over-stimulated or unfocused during the show. Kenny is also picked for a role in the next show, directed by Ritchie. When it comes time to say his line, he stomps his foot and says, "I can do whatever I want!" We remind him that he is in a different show now and give him his new lines again.

During Ritchie's show, Gary tries to leave the room because he hasn't had a turn yet. We usher him back in and point out that six other children haven't had turns yet either, and if he can sit through a couple more, he'll be able to have a turn this week. If he tries to leave again, he'll have to wait until next week. He holds it together and is eventually called to sit in the chair. He starts talking about what happened when he ran out of the room before, and we try to focus him on his story. It then dawns on us that he wants to do the story about running out of the room as his Director's Chair show. He picks Matt to play himself, Ritchie to play Ritchie, and Jason to play the leader, who says, "Ritchie's next!" Like Kenny, Jason does a great job with the role, saying his line as soon as it's given to him, and then again during the show when the leader prompts him to.

For children who tend to communicate by echoing and repeating dialogue, acting in the directors' shows gives them an opportunity to successfully participate using language. In some of the season's other activities that seek to generate spontaneous dialogue, children like Jason, Jack, Kenny and Billy have a tougher time interacting. In Director's Chair, they reproduce lines and dialogue scripted for them, and, because of their tendency to echo, they are usually quite animated and expressive, adding a dramatic flair to the scenes. Their fellow group members view them being successful, and the children perceive and experience that affirmation from the group either directly, by people appropriately laughing and positively commenting on their performance, or indirectly, by sensing people energetically tuning in to the scene. While Jason doesn't quite seem to grasp the full concept of his line or the larger picture of why he says it, he purposefully connects himself to the process by delivering it with enthusiastic energy when cued to do so.

After Jason, as the leader, gives his line, Matt, as Gary, runs off the stage toward the door, as he was directed to do. The leader prompts Gary to call "CUT!" and asks the audience, "Who knows what it's like to be Gary, when you don't get picked to be next or you don't get what you want?" The children offer their reflections. Kenny calls out, as life imitates art imitating life, "What about me?" because the leader hadn't gotten to him just yet. The fact that Kenny is even paying attention to what is going on and showing an interest in responding is a significant change from the beginning of the year. We say, "Yes,

Kenny! We want to hear from you!" He offers, "Frustrated!" Gary is having a bit of a tough time finding the power words he wants Matt to say. The leader prompts, "I feel…" and he completes the phrase, saying, "…so sad." We say, "I need…" and he finishes with, "…to sit in the chair." We play the scene with the power words and prepare for the next show.

During the second week of shows, Jason quickly raises his hand and says, "I do a show!" when the leader asks who wants to start the shows for the week. He skips over to the director's chair and hops up onto it. He's happy to sit in the director's chair, but he can't conceptualize and articulate what he wants to say or do. The leader suggests that maybe he can do a show about his fear of SpongeBob, which has come up periodically since the time around Halloween, when one of the children wore the costume and the leader played the music. If a child comes in wearing a t-shirt with a SpongeBob character, or someone says a popular phrase from the show, Jason becomes anxious and agitated. He shows no sign of protest or anxiety at the suggestion to make his show about that, though, so we proceed.

The leader prompts much of the casting and structure of the show for Jason. We give him choices like "Should we make the show about what happens at your house, or what happens at school?" and "Should we get scared because we hear SpongeBob on TV, or see a picture of him in a store?" He is, for the most part, able to indicate his choices. All of the children are very eager to play SpongeBob, and some ask Jason why he doesn't like the character. Jason is not able to answer and gets a little uncomfortable with the questions. We prompt his power words: "I know SpongeBob is pretend and can't hurt me," and ask him to say them before seeing and hearing Ritchie, who is playing Jason, say them in the show. Kenny resists directing a reality-based story, but the leader eventually gets him there. Jack, like Billy, has a hard time coming up with a show but is attentive and responsive to the leader who helps them put simple ones together.

The children complete their shows over the course of two sessions and receive their scene-marker story outlines documenting the content of their shows and their power word choices. Along with rehearsing empowered pragmatic responses to challenging situations, and generating opportunities for developing empathy and intentional attunement, children who direct as well as act also benefit from personal disclosure and structured cathartic release that occur in the shows. Timmy directs the story of when his parents got a phone call from school, informing them that he had hit another student because he wasn't allowed to sit next to a mutual friend. Hannah, along with volunteering to be in a number of other shows on stage, does her own show about how she anxiously picks paint off the walls in the rooms of her house, chip by chip, throughout the night, until the walls are stripped bare. Her beleaguered parents confirm the story at the end of the session. Jonathon, in the role of AJ, enacts AJ's story of frustration at his mother with focused intensity and emotional release, appearing contentedly exhausted after his performance. Walter chooses to direct a show about what made him so angry and frustrated that morning, scripting the power words, "I need to be at Kid Esteem. I am OK if I'm a little late."

For autistic children, everyday frustrations and complications are made even more complicated by atypical neurological makeup and sensitivities. The Director's Chair activity supports participants by organizing and sequencing operations and concepts to contain and resolve challenging social and emotional events. Empathetic actors and audiences collaborate with the director in a rehearsal process to script strong, self-aware pragmatic language responses that address real situations. Participants see themselves and their personal situations enacted by others, prompting them to perceive others as another self. The working mirror that Director's Chair reflects, the template that simulates the neurological process of intentional attunement, ideally empowers more spontaneous generation of intentional attunement while facilitating clearer perceptions of and smoother transitions between perspectives of self and other.

In the past, when groups were small and there was time left over after all the children had directed a show, we sometimes used popular television shows to promote the use of the power words for problem-solving. We split the group into two or three teams based on the choice of a favorite television show they wanted to work with. The teams would choose characters from their shows to play, prepare costumes and props and come up with a scene to enact a social conflict portrayed or prompted by the theme of the show. The teams would script their scenes using the power words. With younger or lower functioning children, the leaders would model and act out problems that occur in social situations, such as grabbing, hitting, crowding, taking turns and going first, while another leader calls, "Oh, no! We need the problem solvers!" Teams of children take turns being problem solvers and suggest appropriate language and power words to apply to the situation.

Before we leave, we ask the children to tell us which Director's Chair show reminded them the most about a situation in their life, record their points on the chart, add *Using power words to solve problems* to the skills list and wish them a great weekend.

Chapter 11

Comedy and Plot: Broadening Perspectives and Constructing Solutions

Session 18: What's So Funny?

Session 18 simulates an "open mic" format, using jokes, comedy and humor to facilitate understanding of double meanings and a more conceptual shifting of perspectives. Children take turns getting up on stage with the microphone and telling jokes to explore how words can represent different meanings and perspectives. This week's information sheet asks parents to use jokes and humor to help their children navigate between perspectives, by borrowing a joke book from the library or asking a family member or friend to tell some jokes and see if the child can decipher the different meanings, play on words or ironies embedded in the context of the joke.

We explain to the parents that many of our activities focus on helping the children respond to shifts in the social perspective that constantly occur in the course of the day. We describe to the parents how a simple question from a classmate requires their children to leave their own thoughts for the moment, perceive and search for understanding of the other child's perspective—represented by language and gesture, to name but a few of the dynamics in the exchange—relate it back to their own perspective, and then construct a response with the other person's question in mind that can relate the two perspectives.

We remind the parents that for most people, this is a natural, automatic and relatively smooth process. For children on the spectrum, it is as tedious and labored as the description in the above paragraph, laden with much opportunity for confusion and loss of focus. Telling jokes is a simple and fun way to practice shifting between perspectives, as humor is often based on a silly or unusual intersect between meanings. So a joke such as "Where do good little engines wash themselves? Behind their engine-ears..." prompts us to perceive and shift between two perspectives: the engineer as the driver of the train, and the silly suggestion that the engine of the train has ears it can wash behind, within the single context of the joke that simultaneously supports both meanings and perspectives. Parents are encouraged to explore these multiple meanings and perspectives with their children, playfully asking them to specify what kinds of different meanings make the joke funny.

The playful, less-rigid side of Jason continues to emerge as he arrives this week. He runs around the room skipping and laughing, stopping suddenly in front of various leaders and then scooting away, squealing with laughter, as the leader reaches out to catch him. The game is typically joyful, conscious and not at all mechanical or idiosyncratic. Kenny pleasantly says hello to everyone and starts playing with Sarah at the dollhouse. Hannah moves more freely around the room, playing with friends at the costume bins and the puppet stage. Some of the children, especially the boys in the older group, are perusing the joke books we've put out around the stage. They quietly try out some of the material on the leaders and each other, in eager anticipation of our upcoming comedy extravaganza.

AJ, on the other hand, arrives today in a foul mood. He takes off his shoes and throws them around, which he hasn't done in a long time, and starts calling people "stupid." He tells some leaders that he hates them, punches the walls, rocks back and forth, crashing into things when a leader tries to sit with him and settle him down, and then starts banging his head against the walls. We take him out into the hallway and enlist the help of his mother, who, as with our previous encounter, anxiously tiptoes around the situation, working too hard to rescue AJ and make it better for him, pleading with him to behave. She tells us, while attempting to contain him, that AJ has been sick, is on medication, her husband is away on business and AJ's two brothers had been torturing him all morning.

The leader, in an attempt to more appropriately align with AJ and jolt him out of his meltdown, gasps dramatically and says, "*What? What were those brothers doing?* AJ! Were your brothers being *mean* to you?" He looks up from his writhing around on the floor and says, "Yes." The leader asks again with exaggerated but authentic indignation, "What were they *doing* to you?" He answers, "They took my (some toy we couldn't comprehend) and hid it under the couch!" The leader turns to AJ's mother and asks, "Is this true?" She answers, "Yes it is." The leader turns back to AJ and says, "Well, you know, it's joke day on stage with the microphone, and they are *not* allowed in! I think we should find some jokes about mean brothers and get up on stage and tell them to all the kids!" His face breaks into a big smile as he says, "Yeah!" and heads back into the room. We don't find jokes about brothers, but AJ is fine during the rest of the session.

We gather at the red chairs and ask the children, "Why are jokes funny?" leading to a discussion and explanation of how jokes often mean two different things at the same time. We use examples like "How do you get a baby astronaut to go to sleep? You rock it (rocket)!" and "Why did the lion spit out the clown? Because it tasted funny!" and ask the children, "What two things did that joke mean?" We explain that we are going to have an open mic day, where the children take turns on stage with the lights, telling jokes into the microphone. After each joke, the audience playfully analyzes why it was funny with regard to the different meanings and perspectives it contains. Group members can also tell funny stories about something that happened to them.

Some of the children take the joke books on stage with them when it is their turn, while others attempt to come up with their own jokes. For obvious reasons, those who come up with their own jokes often butcher the material, and we tactfully try to help them piece together the more familiar jokes we are able to recognize and inconspicuously help them restructure. "Why did the chicken cross the road?" for example, might be delivered as, "Why did the chicken have to go to the other side?" A leader would then chime in with, "Oh, that's a great one about why the chicken crossed the road! Go ahead—start again! I love that one." A subtle prompt like that is usually enough to put the joke back on its pragmatic track.

Everyone gets on stage, including Hannah. Jason goes up with a leader, who whispers the joke into his ear. He echoes it into the mic and out to the audience. Jack grabs the mic and launches into an unintelligible two-minute stand-up routine. The children good-naturedly laugh at anything and everything, thoroughly enjoying the relatively loose and easy activity of taking turns on stage, under the lights, telling jokes into the microphone. Sometimes, the leaders have no clue what the joke is about or how the child is trying to say it. For jokes and stories that don't make any sense at all, we navigate a fine line between sticking to our process of analyzing what makes the joke funny and glossing over the confusion, to make sure we don't dampen anyone's spirits.

The children meet in predetermined movie groups with a leader for the last ten or so minutes of the session. We review the winter session's skills, adding *Telling jokes and noticing funny things* to the list that includes *Reconnecting with friends, Seeing how we use our bodies and face expressions to communicate, Asking and answering questions to build conversation, Staying focused on the conversation topic, Joining in with friends* and *Using power words to solve problems*. We ask them what their favorite joke of the day was, give them their points and say goodbye.

Session 19: Lights! Camera! Action! Putting It All Together Again

Session 19 follows the format of Session 9, using plot, scripting, set construction, costume, props, scenery, role-play, rehearsal and movie-making to incorporate skills and concepts engaged and processed over the past eight weeks within collaborative stories created and enacted by group members and filmed by group leaders. This week's skill sheet informs parents that the children will be creating videos to reflect these skills and then watching them during Session 20 for purposes of self-modeling and self-assessment. We again ask them to notify us of any allergies or problems with popcorn. During the session, a leader holds five-minute conferences with each parent and provides a formatted report on their child's progress with physical, language, play, behavior and social interaction skills.

The children are excited to make their movies. Jason again greets us with unprompted hellos and plays cheerfully and comfortably with various toys and materials around the room. Although he plays alone or with a particular group leader, and his pragmatic expressive language remains very limited, his mechanical and idiosyncratic style of playing, methodically lining up the markers in rows, taking items out of a bin in order to put them back in again, has transformed dramatically during the winter session. Ritchie comes in and starts chatting about a new video game coming out in May. Soon enough, he and Gary are haggling over the body pillows, but they manage their ongoing conflict with little, if any, intervention from a leader.

Billy continues to perseverate on asking everyone he sees what his or her name is. Today, he retrieves a toy magic wand from the props bin, walks up to Timmy and abruptly says, "Hi, what's your name? I'm going to change you into a bear! Hocus-pocus!" He waves the wand and starts to move away toward the next group member to repeat the same words, before receiving any response or reaction from Timmy. Billy's actions and words are apparently the result of echolalic regurgitation rather than an invitation for interaction. He stops and takes notice, though, because Timmy has turned into a bear, stalking and roaring around the room. Billy moves back to Timmy and says, "I'm going to change you into a penguin! Hocus-pocus!" Timmy becomes a waddling penguin. They go a few more rounds, transforming into a couple more animals. Higher functioning Timmy seeks to transition with Billy to a new activity, asking, "You want to play with me?" but lower functioning Billy has moved on, standing in front of Sammy, saying, "Hi, what's your name? I'm going to change you into a bear! Hocus-pocus!"

We gather at the red chairs with our list of skills from the fall and winter sessions to talk about making the movies. For most group members, this is a review of the activity they participated in during the fall session. The new members who joined at Session 11 take in the excitement and enthusiasm expressed by the children who made and watched their movies during Sessions 9 and 10. We go over how the teams, each working with a leader, will decide together on the plot, characters, setting and dialogue of the movie, and how to include the Session 2 skills. After the teams organize their productions, they collect materials, set pieces, props and costumes, rehearse and create a title page and prepare for filming.

In *The Playground*, Gary, Kenny and Luke meet at the monkey bars and ask to play with each other. Someone gets hurt, they help each other out and Kenny tells a knock-knock joke. *Uh, Oh, It's Time to go to Kid Esteem* portrays Ritchie, Jason and Stevey lounging around playing video games and eating breakfast, until they see that it's late, prompting Jason to say, "Time to go to Kid Esteem!" Ritchie wants to keep playing his game but the other boys want to leave. He agrees to finish his game in the car. Leaders often need to prompt the actors with lines and staging directions to keep the story on track during filming. While we try to keep verbal cues from the leaders off-camera as much as possible, most of the movies, especially the ones made by the younger groups, include some type of intervention from the leaders that hampers the flow of the action. This is, I'm sure, much more bothersome to the artistic sensibilities of the drama therapist than it is to the group members, who do not seem to mind at all.

Billy, AJ, Jonathon and Timmy can't agree on what to play when they arrive at Timmy's house in *Hello! Let's Play the Incredibles and Puppets!* They use power words to find a compromise. In *Hannah Montana's Rescue*, Eddie asks Hannah, played by a group member, to attend a concert given by the popular singer, played by Meghan, with Jack on lead guitar and vocal accompaniment. Meghan, as Hannah Montana, chokes during one of her songs and Eddie and Hannah save her, prompting her to ask them to go on tour with her. The intergalactic confrontation between good and evil continues in *Star Wars VIII: The Big War* starring Marcus, Mike T., Mike F. and Dan. Fortunately, power words save the universe. In *Basement Wars*, Ian, Walter, Mike K. and Sean are trying to have a play date in the basement playroom, but Sean's little sister keeps turning the lights out on them.

As with the previous movie-making session, group members establish cognitive and behavioral context for the skills by organizing and enacting unified and cohesive elements of plot and character in collaboration with other group members. Memory, attention, processing and sequencing are engaged through spontaneous and creative encounters as the actors' perspectives shift between self and other within a number of dynamics, including self and self in role as other, self and other cast member, self in role and other cast member in role, and a host of corresponding relationships involving self, other and environment. Pragmatic expressive language, interactive play and conflict resolution among group members is rehearsed and the resulting successes are documented on film to be viewed and processed during the next session. Everybody returns to the group room after all the movies are filmed. Back at the red chairs, we ask each group member "Which skill did you show in your movie?" prompting them as needed. We record their points and share excitement about next week before leaving.

Session 20: Movie Day, The Sequel

For Session 20, we roll that big old television on top of the kitchen cart back into the room and get our bags of popcorn ready. Like in Session 10, we watch the movies made by the children for self-modeling, self-assessment and as a pragmatic tool for perceiving self-initiated images of social actions performed intentionally, collectively and collaboratively by group members. Individuals neurologically mirror the video images of self, successfully interacting with others in a meaningful manner through the process of embodied simulation, generating further opportunities for intentional attunement within the ensemble. This week's skill sheet again reminds the parents of the importance of establishing and organizing routines at home to facilitate skills in a fun and enjoyable way that can capitalize on the brain's neuroplasticity and their child's potential for growth and development.

This week, when Jason comes into the room, the leaders must have been engaged with other children or tasks and not noticed his entrance, because we suddenly hear him from the middle of the room giving a loud, drawn out "Helloooo…" in a more typical-sounding, teasing, singsong tone uncharacteristic for him that could almost be described as sarcastic, as if to say, "I'm here, but no one is noticing…" He plays happily with a leader, at one point standing in front of her and holding out his hands. When she asks, "What do you want to do?" he answers, "Jump, please!" and they hold hands and jump. Kenny notices another child who is wearing a striped shirt like his and says, in his affected but tuned-in voice, "Look at us! We're twins!"

Billy continues with his "Hi, what's your name again?" repetition, to which a leader good-naturedly says, "Billy, I like how you're asking for your friend's names, but I think you know their names—and if you're going to ask, you can at least wait for an answer! Do you know his name?" referring to the boy Billy just asked. He answers matter-of-factly in his sweet, stilted and choppy speech, "Yes, that's Timmy." The leader says, "Timmy and the other kids may not like it if you keep asking them what their name is over and over again." Timmy chimes in with, "Oh, I don't mind." We have to chuckle. Who are we to judge? Jack, seeming to taking some kind of cue from this exchange, starts walking up to all the children and leaders in the room, using their names and saying hi to them.

Hannah shyly walks up to Eddie, who is playing at the castle and says, "Hi, Eddie." After having their first "date" in their movie last week at the Hannah Montana concert, they seem quite taken with each other. They play for a while together at the castle, and then Eddie takes her gently by the hand and leads her to the puppet stage, where they play and laugh a little more. When we give the two-minute warning for clean up, Hannah returns to the dollhouse. She takes a boy figure and a girl figure, outstretches their arms into a hugging position and pushes them as close together as they can possibly get.

We gather at the red chairs, dole out the popcorn and watch the shows with our skills list propped up next to the television for the children to refer to. We watch the movies once through without stopping, and then watch a second time, pausing to comment at the end of each show or when someone raises their hand because they notice a skill being enacted. As we watch the movies the first time through and hear the narrator, a leader, in the video say, "...starring Kenny..." to introduce his team's film, Kenny excitedly calls out, "That's me!" from the audience. When we watch a second time, Kenny calls out, at the same point of narration, "That's us!"

The children are engaged and attentive while watching the movies. Their hands pop up during the second viewing, offering observations like "We joined in!" and "I used power words!" Kenny adds, after viewing *The Playground*, "I told a funny joke!" We try to get Jason to make an independent, unprompted observation with the more open-ended question, "What did you see in the movie, Jason?" but he is unable to respond and just smiles back at us. We ask the more specific

"What words did you say in the movie?" and he repeats, "Time to go to Kid Esteem," with the same intonation he used in the movie.

Hannah speaks out and says, "We worked together to solve the problem of Hannah Montana choking," after viewing her movie. We ask Billy, "What skill did you show in the movie, Billy?" He thinks for a minute and answers, "We played Mr. Incredible." We press a little, with "What skill did that show?" He does not know how to answer. We prompt, "Did you join in with friends?" and he answers/echoes, "I joined in with friends." Jack happily points out that he played the guitar in the movie, and we prompt him, after highlighting the part of his movie where someone got sick, to say that he worked together to solve a problem. With characteristically deadpan delivery, highly intellectual Marcus points out, "We used power words to save the universe."

The visual and auditory stimuli emanating from the images on the screen and perceived by the children initiate another round of mirror-neuron activity reinforcing the cognitive and behavioral context established when planning and enacting the movies the previous week. The neurological rehearsal process is further empowered by virtue of the fact that individuals are neurologically mirroring actions and intentions performed by themselves, strengthening pathways to neural centers that generate self-awareness, connection to other, interaction and purposeful movement between perspectives of self and other. It's also a fun and enjoyable activity that builds and tightens the ensemble and the sense of connectedness among group members. We ask the children for one final thought regarding their movies in order to continue their integration of skills, processes and operations, record the final ten points of the season, choose prizes and say goodbye for a few weeks until after the spring holidays.

We are saddened to hear from Jason's father that Jason may not be able to attend the spring session, as the father's new job might require him to work on Saturdays and Jason's mother doesn't drive. His father says he is "just sick about it" and has tried every which way to see how he can get Jason to group, but it wasn't looking too promising.

Chapter 12

Actions and Life: Simulating Events

Session 21: My Story

Session 21 uses sociometry, story-making and narration to help group members reconnect after a two- or three-week absence for the spring holidays, and to practice the new chart structure for acquiring skills and earning points. Children create and share storyboards, comic-strip style, about their lives and experiences, prompting other group members to respond using skills covered in the fall and winter sessions, including noticing details, finding matches, stating opinions and expressing emotions with regard to what is being shared. This week's skill sheet informs the parents that there will not be regular skill sheets handed out during the spring session. Instead, periodic assessment guides, checklists and requests for feedback will be made available to support the activities and themes of certain weeks.

We explain to the parents that a number of activities for the spring session, including a game day, telephone day, bowling day and restaurant day, will provide opportunities for the children to apply their skills in thematic environments simulating social encounters that occur within the community. There will also be a number of weeks during which individuals will make Power Videos about particular challenging situations from their personal lives. In addition, we tell them that each week the children will have the opportunity to bring in something of interest from home that has some significant meaning in their lives. The children can bring in objects such as photographs, trophies, toys, certificates, personal creations, awards, baseball caps or souvenirs—anything that reflects a positive aspect of their personality and accomplishments. As they share their objects, the rest of the group will be coached to tune in and connect to the experience by asking questions, expressing opinions and sharing their own related personal experiences.

We also provide the parents with a formatted "How am I doing?" checklist to fill out with their children at home and to use as a tool for working on skills as they interact within their communities. The checklist has five columns, headed, from left to right with *Tasks, I do this a lot, I do this sometimes, I do this a little* and *I don't do this yet.* Underneath the *Tasks* column are nine tasks labeled in rows, including *I look in people's eyes when I talk to them, I say hello to people with waves and words, I remember and use people's names when I talk to them, I control how my body moves when I play with my friends, I notice and respond to what others say and do, I stay connected by finding matches with other people, I stay connected by using words to join in with friends, I stay connected by saying my opinions and ideas* and *I use power words to say what I feel and to help solve problems.* Parents and children can work together to check the boxes next to the tasks to indicate if the child does it a lot, sometimes, a little or not at all yet, and use the list as a guide for practicing the skills that are more challenging.

Some of the children return from the break a little disjointed. Jason does not show up, which makes the leaders feel a bit disjointed as well. Kenny is unfocused and non-responsive as he wanders around the room, echoing dialogue from popular television shows rather than engaging with others as he was doing during the winter session. Ritchie walks out of the room to find his father without telling anybody. We catch up with him in the hallway and steer him back to the group room. Walter clumsily runs around the room, loudly yelling, "Earthquake! Earthquake!" His demeanor is playful, but the volume and level of activity starts to get to some of the group members, especially Ian. We coach him, a number of times, to lower the volume and calm the energy level. Some children are rolling around the floor, crawling under cushions and responding to each other in mildly agitated tones. We theorize that the mild difficulty with re-entering the space and process is in part developmental and sensory, and partly due to withdrawal from the chocolate and candy laden with sugar, chemicals and food dyes the kids were likely indulging in all week for the holidays.

The children also return with their skills noticeably intact. Kenny takes a moment out of his self-absorbed wandering to stop in front of a new intern and say, "Hello, my name is Kenny. What's your name?" The leaders ring bells and excitedly say, "Kenny! You said 'Hello' to a new friend! You told her your name and asked what her name is! You get a point!" We go to the new chart on the floor where the children are signing their names and put a tally mark in one of the boxes. Kenny goes back inside his head but brings the experience with him, narrating, in his singsong voice that echoes the leader's excited intonation, "I said 'Hello'! I told her my name! I get a point!"

The other children are intrigued by the leaders' reactions and scope out the situation to see what all the bell-ringing is about. They don't have to wait long, as Jonathon says, "I'm really upset Billy's not here. I like singing with him." We ring our bells, exclaiming, "Jonathon! You expressed your emotions with words! You get a point!" Jack walks in a few minutes late, looks at a leader he connects with, and says, "Hi, Lili!" Our bells ring once again as we say, "Jack! You looked at Lili's eyes and said hello. You get a point!" We give the two-minute warning and then call for clean up.

We settle in at the red chairs, welcome everybody back and go over the new chart to which the children were introduced during the open-play period. We indicate the heading *Ring that bell!* on top of the chart, and ask the group what just happened when someone showed one of our skills from the list. We explain that whenever group leaders notice a child enacting any one of the following skills, the bells will ring and a check will be put in their row for that particular skill. We review the skills written on top of the columns across the chart where the session numbers had previously been listed. We read, "I stay connected by looking at people's eyes," "I stay connected by saying 'Hello' with waves, names and words," "I stay connected by noticing what others are saying and doing," "I stay connected by expressing my ideas, opinions and emotions with words," "I stay connected by finding matches with other people," "I stay connected by asking and answering questions," "I stay connected by joining in with other people," "I stay connected by working together" and "I stay strong and connected by using power words to solve problems," and we go over each one, asking the children to provide examples of what they mean.

When a group member asks or answers a question about the chart as we discuss it, we jump up very dramatically, take the bells out of our pockets and start ringing as we put a tally in the *Asking and answering questions* column in the child's row, emphatically stating, "You stayed connected by asking/answering a question!" When Timmy spontaneously recites all the power word phrases after going over the corresponding skill on the chart, we ring the bells and give him points for *Joining in*. The children are very entertained by this, of course, and start laughingly asking questions and making comments to engage the skills listed across the chart so they can earn tally marks and watch us react—and we, of course, gladly comply, with bells on.

We also get them excited about our upcoming activities, including game week, bowling week and restaurant week. If the group is small and time allows, we may do a quick locogram with criteria about the holiday break to facilitate reconnection and familiarity among group members. Otherwise, we show the children a booklet made from a piece of legal-size paper, folded in half, with a sequence of eight boxes set in two rows of four labeled 1 through 8 from left to right on the inside of the fold. On what becomes the front cover after the paper is folded, we format *My Story* in a stylized font on top of the page with lines underneath for writing in a title, and then *A story about when I feel mad, sad, scared or happy* under the blank lines for the title. We include decorations and icons showing a range of emotion on the front cover, like a smiley-faced sun and cartoonish caveman looking scared.

We tell the children, "Make a story using these boxes to tell us something about your life. You can tell about a time when you were happy, mad, sad or scared. It can be from a time at school, a time when you were on vacation, a time when you had to do something you didn't want to, or a time when you were having fun playing. You can draw pictures or write words in the boxes." Evan says, "It's like the comics!" We ring bells and tally points in Evan's row for noticing and saying his idea. We ask them, "Which box do you think the story should start in?" They answer, "One!" and again we ring bells and tally points as needed. We tell them, "You can use as many or as few of the boxes you want to make your story."

Upon finishing their stories, the children take turns sitting in the author's chair, choosing colors for the lights and sharing their stories with the rest of the group by reading and/or showing the pictures. The audience group is encouraged to earn points by practicing the skills listed and responding to the stories with relevant comments about things they notice, opinions, ideas, questions, matches and feelings. As the children take their turns, most of the audience is fully engaged and invested, responding in a manner that gets bells ringing and points tallied. Jack has trouble keeping his hands to himself, though, as he sits in the audience. These new behaviors have him touching, poking and pinching the arms and sides of the person sitting next to him. Even though the children are understandably agitated at his actions and express their displeasure with appropriate faces, gestures and words, Jack smiles longingly back at them, as he continues what appears to be an attempt to connect rather than an act of aggression. He is, as previously discussed, perhaps adjusting to a neurological seismic shift resulting in a newfound ability to connect on a deeper level. These behaviors comprise, in part, the aftershocks of that adjustment.

We switch places with the children sitting next to Jack, placing a leader on either side of him who later report that Jack was also passing gas, seemingly intentionally, and looking for reactions from the leaders. While these actions are obviously socially inappropriate, he does them with others in mind, trying to get their attention rather than sitting in socially oblivious isolation, comprising, as odd as it may seem, a step forward developmentally. That doesn't mean we allow these behaviors to continue, but we respond and attempt to modify them in the context of the larger positive picture in which he seeks out others to notice and pay attention to him, a new dynamic in his otherwise disconnected, echolalic way of relating.

In the author's chair, the children share happy, mad, sad and scared stories about baseball teams, video games, siblings, vacations and other meaningful events and experiences from their lives. The audience is taking full advantage of the opportunity to ring bells and earn points by noticing, commenting on and finding personal matches for every possible detail about what they hear from other group members. This is exactly how we want them to react. Kenny shares about a television show he likes to watch, and Gary practically leaps out of his seat, exclaiming, "I watch that show, too!" Ritchie talks about his trip to the aquarium, and Stevey bursts forth, proclaiming, "I went there!" We ring those bells and tally up their points.

Hannah, as usual after a break, initially balks at placing herself in the center of attention sometimes called for by the activity. She looks down and shakes her head when the leader suggests that it can be her turn to sit in the chair and share her story. Eddie comes to the rescue, gently offering to go up with her and sit by her to make her feel better. Hannah looks up with a big smile and is able to take her turn, without Eddie's escort, after a few more children go.

Jack is eager to have a turn. His story is random but cohesive, illustrating some of the things he likes to do, like singing and watching television. Walter is unusually quiet and attentive as he and the other children share and react to each other's stories. A leader takes photographs of the children as they participate and will continue to do so for the next seven weeks in preparation for a yearbook project we will be putting together for Sessions 29 and 30. We get the children excited for next session's game week and tell them to have a great weekend.

Session 22: How to Be a Real Winner

Session 22 uses sociometry, board games and self-assessment scales to facilitate pragmatic skills and procedures of interactive play, such as taking turns and considering others' ideas. Children are provided with an alternative, more inclusive context for what it means to be a "winner" and coached to play games with each other in order to practice shifting perspectives between self and other. This week's information sheet, titled *The Way to be a Real Winner* informs parents that we will be working on interactive play skills by exploring the following ten criteria with the children, using basic board games and play objects:

1. Know that you are good enough to play with. What makes you a good friend?

2. Make a play choice. What do you feel like playing? Do you know how to play it?

3. Find a friend. Who do you want to play with? Who can play with you?

4. Ask the friend if he or she wants to play with you. What are the words you can use?

5. Share your ideas for playing. Tell your friend what you want to play.

6. Hear what your friend wants to play. Let your friend say his or her ideas for playing.

7. See if you can agree on what and how to play together. Come up with a plan, a compromise that is fair to your ideas and your friend's ideas, or find another friend to play with.

8. Find and share a good place to play. Make sure both of you have enough room to play the game and arms, legs, etc., will not be in each other's way.

9. Decide together when to finish. Try not to leave in the middle of a game if you don't want to play anymore. Find out if your friend feels the same way you do. You can say, "Do you want to keep playing this?" If he or she wants to finish, try to be fair and finish the game, unless you have a better idea that your friend likes. Stay focused on the game, in the space you are playing in.

10. Clean up together. Work together to put your playthings and pieces back where they belong.

We tell the parents that the children's challenge will be to maintain focus, connection and interaction within the boundaries of the board games, while adhering to the criteria that we will be discussing with them. The children will be coming out of group with a self-assessment rating scale that measures how easy or hard it was for them to follow and integrate the criteria. We ask the parents to please review the scale with their children and use it as a tool during the week to help them practice the concepts that were harder for them.

The children enter the room and say hello to each other, prompting the leaders to start ringing the bells with urgent exclamations like "You looked at your friend and said hello! That's a point for you!" and "You noticed the games! That's a point for you!" They become very invested in this process, eagerly running up to the leaders with comments like "I notice Stevey has a picture of a fish on his shirt!" and "I joined in with Luke!" Gary, after the usual verbal tussle with Ritchie over the pillows, says, "I can use them later." He is so excited with his response that he needs to go out to the waiting room and tell his mother, "I'm solving problems with power words!" We honor and tally points for all their relevant responses and comments.

Billy enters the room after last week's absence and announces, "Hi! I'm Billy. I went to Disney!" as if we were meeting him for the first time. His speech and language is awkwardly idiosyncratic, but, within his fragmented thought patterns, he apparently attempts to apply the skills we have been practicing in order to remain connected with others. We smile and say, "We know who you are, Billy! How was Disney?" He answers, "Great!" and starts talking about some event or experience that we have no context for following or understanding. He is extremely stimulated, most likely due to his change in routine and all of the sensory input from his trip. He stomps and jumps around the room, speaking fast and furiously about something that we can't comprehend. He eventually gets so worked up that he hits Timmy. It isn't intentional, but it isn't accidental, either. Timmy, unfortunately for him, was merely serving as an object through which Billy could expend some energy and soothe his sensory overload. It isn't a hard hit, and Timmy says, "Hey! That hurts! I don't like that!" Billy catches himself, perceives Timmy as another person, an objective self that can feel pain, and quickly says, "Sorry! Sorry, Timmy!" We ring bells and give points to both boys. We give the two-minute warning, clean up and meet at the red chairs. Eddie rushes over to save a seat for Hannah next to his.

Some of the children have brought in objects to show and talk about. Ritchie brings in his plastic sea animals and gives us an interesting lesson in marine biology. AJ brings in his armload and proceeds with his narration of how all the objects connect to his life. The rest of the children watching the presentations are attentive, making observations, comments and connections with their own lives and interests. We ring the bells and tally the points.

Our discussion looks at what it means to be a winner. We ask the children, "What does it mean to 'win'?" Some respond with comments about getting the most points or beating the other players, but others add ideas like, "playing fair" and "being a good sport," which is the direction we want the conversation to go in. We take out our *The Way to be a Real Winner* banner and go over the ten concepts listed above in the parent information sheet. We tell the children, "Some friends think that the only way to be a winner is to get the most points, get to the finish line first, or get to the next level, but here are ideas that can make you a real winner whenever you play a game, even if you don't come in first." We explain and give examples for each of the concepts, eliciting response from the children as well.

Tommy says, in a voice that is one part moan and one part whine, "But I hate to lose!" For the children who have difficulty in this area, we ask the group which baseball team is the best in the world, and, being from New York, most of the children who know about baseball say, "The Yankees!" We ask them how many games the Yankees have to win to be the best team in the world, and impress them with our answer of, "About 100 games!" More important, we ask them how many games the Yankees lose when they are the best team in the world. Guesses include "none" and "ten." We slowly and dramatically tell them, "In order to be the best baseball team in the world, the Yankees have to be OK with losing about *70* games!" We ask, "What do you think would happen if they got so mad each time they lost a game?" and answer, "They would be too upset to win the next time! So if they are going to be the best baseball team in the world, they have to get used to losing almost as many times as they win!"

We tell the group that they will be choosing and playing the board games with their friends, practicing the ways to be real winners, and then looking at and thinking about how they did. Before we start, though, each group member needs to address the first and perhaps most important concept on the list: Why he or she is a good friend to play with. Most of the children respond fairly easily, with statements like "I'm nice" and "I play fair," and we tell them to go choose a game and find a friend. For some of the children with receptive-expressive language challenges, like Billy and Jack, or self-esteem and anxiety issues, like Hannah, the procedure is a little more difficult. We hold them to the task of coming up with their self-affirming statement, though, and with prompting and support from the leaders as well as other group members, everyone is eventually able to positively proclaim a reason why others should like them.

We may do a sociometric exercise different than the locogram, depending on the functioning level and size of the group, to facilitate choosing each other to play board games with. If so, we tell the children, "Before we play with the board games, we're going to play a choosing game where you walk around and pick the person who fits the idea that I say. Pick the person you want to choose by pointing to their shoulder. Don't touch them—just point. You can pick a different person each time I say a new idea." Criteria for group members choosing each other include: "Pick the person you think is funny," "Pick the person who is nice," "Pick the person who is a good friend," "Pick the person you like playing with," "Pick the person you have fun with," "Pick the person who helps you," "Pick the person who you think is cool," "Pick the person you would like to get to know better" and "Pick the person you want to play a game with." We prompt second and third choices if we see children getting upset about not being chosen, which is rare for this population, but we remain vigilant during the activity, making sure everyone is recognized and supported.

The children choose from a variety of age-appropriate board games, including Candy Land, Yahtzee and Battleship. They may switch partners and/or games, or stay with the same ones throughout the session, as long as they try to adhere to the ten criteria discussed. Leaders intervene as needed, explaining how a particular game works, coaching the children through an impasse, and often ending up as primary play partners for lower functioning children like Jack and Billy, although both boys are able to play appropriately with groups of children for a good bit of the session. Kenny does well at Rebound, a shuffleboard-like game where marbles are rolled for points, saying, "I'll be red, and you can be blue," and Stevey agrees. Eddie and Hannah play together, but the game is secondary to their innocently flirtatious exchanges. Walter, Ian and the older boys are all over the elaborate Pokémon Trainer game, successfully making up and executing their own rules for playing. As the children play, a leader observes the interaction and fills out some or all of the criteria organized on a sheet formatted as a checklist, based on age and ability of individuals in the group. Another leader takes photos of the children engaged in their games.

The leader calls for clean up, and the group assembles back at the red chairs after playing for about 20 to 30 minutes. We hand out the checklists placed on clipboards, headed in a playful font with *The Way to be a Real Winner*, and pens, explaining that the children will be identifying things about playing that were harder for them and things that were easier during the session. Running down the page are ten rows: *I know I am a good friend to play with!*; *I can choose what I want to play; I can find a friend; I can ask a friend to play with me; I can say what I want to play; I can listen to what my friend wants to play; We can agree on ideas and rules for playing; We can find a good place to play; I can stay focused on our game, in the space we are playing, until we decide together when to finish;* and *We can clean up together* listed down the left column creating ten rows. Across the top are three columns, headed with, from left to right, *This is HARD for me, In the middle* and *This is EASY for me.*

We read through the concepts listed on the checklist, phrased to reiterate and affirm the criteria from the banner discussed at the beginning of the session and explain to the children that they will check either the *hard, middle* or *easy* box, whichever they think is most true, for each concept. The leader explains that placing all the checks in the easy column is not indicative of a higher score; the "best scores" are when there are checks in all different columns, because that helps us know more about how we are doing with all the different parts of playing. The leaders fill out most of the form with the children in the youngest groups, while the oldest group members are able to fill them out on their own or with minimal support. Groups in between need varying degrees of support.

With the advent of video games, the social interaction unique to board games has almost become a lost art. The children have fun with the games, switching perspective between self and other literally, as they wait to take their turn and respond to whatever move the other player has made, and figuratively, as mirror neurons fire for actions taken by self and other within the encounter, coordinating and sorting perceptions between the two. The children take their checklists out to their parents, where, in the spirit of the session, we reiterate the importance of "winning" by having checks in all the categories, rather than just the *easy* column.

Session 23: Calling All Friends!

Session 23 uses simulation to facilitate pragmatic skills and procedures around using the telephone for making social plans and conversation. Children "call" each other, using the intercom mode on wireless handsets in the different rooms of the center, or leaders' cell phones. The information sheet informs parents that the children will be looking at proper phone etiquette by using telephone extensions to call each other, practice conversation skills and invite their friends to upcoming group activities. Each child will make and receive a phone call and be coached to effectively hold the phone and speak and interact appropriately with the person on the other end.

Parents are told that the children will also be exchanging phone numbers and email addresses with each other, using phone books that we create for them. Parents can encourage their children to make a call and/or send an email, under their supervision, to another group member during the week. Parents can coach their children to use language and conversation skills such as noticing, finding matches, stating opinions and feelings, and asking who, what, where, why, when and how questions that we worked on in the fall and winter sessions.

We ask parents to ask other parents in the waiting room if they would like to exchange phone numbers and email addresses for their children to practice with during the week, especially if they think their child will not be able to retrieve and record group members' phone numbers during the session. Even a simple "hello" over the phone and the use of a friend's name would be a good step for children who are not used to talking on the phone. We reassure parents that they and their children do not have to participate if they are uncomfortable giving out their numbers. We also let parents know that we will be simulating a restaurant and serving food next week and to please let us know about any food allergies. We post a menu for review in the waiting room.

Kenny enters the room a little disconnected today. Rather than greeting us and seeking out others to interact with, which he has been doing on a more regular basis, he mumbles to himself and lies down on the cushions. Attempts to engage him are mostly ignored. Ritchie seems to be highly interested in the new intern, talking with her in animated tones and looking to sit in her lap. The intern looks to the leaders for direction on how to handle his affectionate overtures. Issues of physical contact and affection between leaders and children in the groups are determined on an individual basis. For children like Jason, hugging, holding hands and occasional sitting on laps are an important part of building trust, comfort and connection. Children like Ritchie, on the other hand, may use affectionate contact as a way of avoiding or manipulating a situation, and it might be best to modify the contact by suggesting something like "How about sitting next to [leader] instead of in her lap?" If the child points out that other children are able to sit on laps, we address the behavioral issue at hand very directly by saying, for example, "Yes, but when its time to get off [leader's] lap and sit in the red chairs [or clean up, transition or follow directions] and pay attention to what we're doing, [the child allowed in lap] is able to listen." We have never had a child point out any such discrepancies, however. We give the two-minute warning and call for clean up.

Timmy shows and tells about his new Ironman toy, and then Gary proudly presents his soccer trophy, once we are gathered at the red chairs. The children respond and connect, causing bells to ring and points to accumulate. Our discussion is about using the telephone. We hold up a wireless handset and ask the children, "What do you do with it? How do you hold it? What might you say during a phone call?" We model the basic protocols of holding the phone appropriately to speak and hear clearly, saying hello, identifying yourself and asking to speak with the person you are calling for. We review the question words for building conversations and talk about making matches with others. We tell the children that our activities over the next two weeks will include setting up a restaurant with real food so we can have lunch together, and then going bowling together in the playroom. We suggest that the children invite their friends from group to those activities as part of the telephone conversation.

We divide the group and take half of the children to another room with some games and toys. We also give them phone books we created with the computer for coloring and exchanging numbers. On the cover of the phone book, made by folding paper, the title *My Friends' Phone Numbers and Email Addresses* are printed in a playful font with an illustration of a hand holding a receiver and a place for group members to write their names. The inside of the cover is printed with suggestions and prompts for what to say:

> When someone answers the phone, say: "Hello, this is [your name]." Ask to speak with the friend you are calling for: "Is [your friend's name] there?" Tell your friend why you are calling: "I want to invite you to…" or, "I wanted to see if…" or, "I just wanted to say hi…"

Ask your friend a question about something you like to do: "What are you watching on TV tonight?" or, "Did you go out for recess today?" Say your opinion and try to find matches: "I like watching…" or, "We didn't go out today. I was mad." When you are ready, say goodbye: "Goodbye. I'll see you on Saturday."

An inside page printed with *Name, Phone number* and *Email address* with blank lines next to each, copied and pasted to fill both sides of the page, is stapled into the cover page. A fun icon of a phone ringing off the hook is printed on the last page. A total of eight pages are created in the phone booklet by folding the two pieces of paper and stapling them together.

The children settle into playing while the leader in one room dials the extension in the other room and then hands the phone to the child who is taking their turn to call someone. The group member asks to speak with whomever they want. The leader, who answers the phone in the other room, calls out in typical fashion, for example, "Timmy! Phone call for you!" After the children have a brief conversation, say their goodbyes and hang up, the leader in the room that received the call asks the children, "Who's ready to call someone? Who do you want to speak with?" and dials the other extension. The leaders go back and forth in this manner until everyone has had a turn making and receiving a call. Another leader takes pictures of the children as they make and receive their calls.

Many of the children, lower as well as higher functioning, need a good deal of coaching with regard to proper use of the telephone, even after our demonstration. They hold it too far away from their faces or turn it upside down. They launch into unrelated monologues without knowing whom they are speaking with. They end conversations abruptly and hang up. It's as if the lack of visual support, not being able to see whom they are speaking with, significantly hampers their ability to pragmatically organize and appropriately respond to the experience. Leaders keep group members on track, coaching them to stay focused by visualizing an image of the friend they are talking to.

The children have fun with the activity, although a few are somewhat resistant to getting on the phone. Some of the resistant children express anxiety about using a telephone, while others just don't want to interrupt their playing. Jonathon is excited to call Billy, though, and AJ has a good conversation with Evan about an animal show they both saw. Eddie paces back and forth, eager to have a turn so that he can call Hannah. We allow Ian to make a "prank" call about a running refrigerator and an extra large pepperoni pizza, after he calls Mike and has a conversation about the upcoming bowling and restaurant activities. Kenny decorates his phone book and fills it up with names and made up numbers of celebrities and people we've never heard of. Jack continues to talk on a toy phone he finds in the room after he has a turn making his call. We wonder how much of a difference he perceives between the two experiences.

We all return to the playroom and reflect on the experience. Eddie makes sure he gets Hannah's home number. We ask the children, "What was hard about speaking on the phone? What was easy?" The children respond with observations like "It was hard to hear," and "I liked talking about stuff." Before we leave, we get the children excited about next week's restaurant, which they are understandably confused about. They question whether we will be pretending with plastic food, or if we will be going out to a real restaurant. We tell them that it's somewhere in between. We'll be pretending that our playroom is a restaurant, but we'll be serving real food. We also say a few words about the type of behavior we'll be expecting at our "restaurant." Since we will use real food, we will all act as if we are at a real restaurant and practice good restaurant behavior, which the children identify as sitting in your seat, waiting for your food and "being nice." This conversation is meant especially for the boys in the older group, who have a tendency to be playfully loud and wild. We tell them to come hungry, and we'll see them next week. We again make the announcement about next week's restaurant to the parents and ask about any food allergies.

Session 24: Out to Lunch

Session 24 simulates a restaurant to provide opportunity for applying learned skills and practicing pragmatic procedures and social etiquette of visiting a restaurant. Children are seated at tables, receive menus and play money, place their orders with a waiter, participate in table conversation while they wait for their food, eat and then pay for their meal.

In the waiting room, we remind the children that it's restaurant week. We tell them the room is going to look very different and there won't be any toys out. We make sure to ask parents directly about any food allergies before we take the children down to Café Kid Esteem. In the hallway just outside the entrance of the playroom, a blackboard easel borrowed from another room announces the specials of the day. A leader acting as the maître d', or host, greets the children at the door and hands them a menu.

The menu, made on a computer with a fancy font, is headed with *Café Kid Esteem* and then *Brunch with your friends* on the cover. There is an illustration of happy children seated around a table with the prompts *Look at your friends' eyes when you talk to them; Speak clearly when ordering from the waiter; Notice what is going on around you and what your friends are saying; Think of topics to talk about with your friends at the table; Find matches between you and your friends;* and *Stay connected by using power words to ask questions, say your ideas and solve problems* playfully printed underneath.

The menu, created by folding a piece of paper in half, opens up to a selection of "entrées" including Bagel with Butter or Cream Cheese, Peanut Butter and Jelly Sandwich, Crackers and Cheese Plate, American Cheese Sandwich and Rice Cakes with Jelly. "Side Dishes" include Yogurt Cup, Bag of Chips, Cheese Stick, Applesauce, Pineapple Cup, Carrots, Cucumbers and Dip and Grapes. For "dessert" there are Chocolate Chip Cookies and Fig Bars, and a choice of Berry Juice Box or Water Bottle for "drinks." The entrées are priced at two dollars each, and everything else is one dollar. We used to be much more ambitious with food choices, including chicken nuggets, french fries and other things that needed to be cooked in a toaster oven or microwave. We learned from that experience, however, and recommend simpler fare that is easy to put together. All food is free of chemicals, dyes and preservatives, and when possible, organically grown and gluten free.

The children are ushered into the room and seated at one of three tables decorated with tablecloths, six place settings and flower centerpieces. The show lights are on, and soft music plays to create an atmosphere that is simultaneously formal and soothing. Each place setting has a decorative paper plate, napkin, fork and spoon, along with seven dollars of play money in one and two dollar bills, a fake credit card collected over the year from promotional mailings, and a couple of crayons with which to color the menus.

The children rise to the occasion and manage the abrupt change in routine. As they settle in to their seats and look over their menus, Gary turns to Luke and says, "Excuse me, Luke, but that movie on your shirt is my favorite movie." Gary loves to hear those bells ring. AJ politely thanks a leader for getting him a chair and emphasizes "please" when asking for his juice box. Two leaders acting as waiters take the orders and tell the customers that they'll be right back with their drinks. Kenny and Stevey initially have an tough time staying seated after they order, but we remind them that it's prize week, and that helps them return to the table. Ritchie asks for more paper and crayons to help him wait and not "get out of hand." More bells ring.

We talk with the children about table conversation and topics we all have in common, like the emergence of spring and the approaching summer vacation, as we wait for our food. Billy is engaged today, looking directly at his friends as he speaks and responds. Jonathon wonders, "Where does the waitress cook the food?" Walter is calm and quiet. He answers Mike's question about his favorite video game, which starts a conversation between the two. Ian momentarily turns from a conversation he is participating in at the other side of the table to chime in as well. A leader takes pictures of the children eating and enjoying each other at the restaurant.

Jack, who asked the waiter for chocolate milk, is upset when the food arrives and there is no chocolate milk, even though we told him when he ordered that we didn't have any chocolate milk. He repeats a choppy, mechanical mantra of "Chocolate milk, please" and "Can I have chocolate milk?" over and over again. We point out the juice box we brought him, ask him if he'd like water and try to get him interested in his potato chips, but he is fixated on chocolate milk. As the session continues and the children eat and pleasantly interact, Jack becomes more distraught, eventually laying his head on the table while continuing to ask, echoing in the same intonation he has likely been taught to use to get what he needs, for chocolate milk. It does not get through to him, no matter how much we gently and clearly try to explain it, that we have no chocolate milk. He is able to contain himself, though, and the situation does not escalate.

As we clear the tables and hand out the checks, Jack perks up when a leader, in excited and triumphant tones, says, "Jack! You did it! You made it through the restaurant without chocolate milk!" He smiles and echoes, "I made it!" Stevey walks up to the leader acting as a server and says, "Here you go," tipping her with a play dollar bill. The older children, for the most part, are able to figure out and pay their bills, while the leaders work more closely with the younger children to sort out their money. AJ becomes agitated when its time to pay and we're not sure why, but it quickly passes.

Before we leave, we reflect on the experience with the children, what was hard about it, what they liked about it and tell them to keep their menus as a memento of Café Kid Esteem. They select their prizes and we take them down to their parents. Hannah's mother is thrilled to hear that she ate a bagel with cream cheese, as they had been having some eating difficulties lately. We tell Jack's father about the chocolate milk. He rolls his eyes and says, "Oh, yeah, we can't go to a restaurant if there's no chocolate milk." We respond, "Well, he did today!"

Session 25: Roll with It

Session 25 simulates a bowling alley with plastic pin and ball sets to provide opportunity for applying learned skills and practicing pragmatic procedures and social etiquette of bowling with friends. Children take turns bowling in three lanes, shifting perspective between self and other by listening for and responding when it's their turn, attending to spatial perceptions, managing physical boundaries and cheering on their friends.

Parents are given a notice about next week's Power Videos activity and asked to respond with pertinent information in order to help us prepare. We tell them that during the following three weeks, the children will be working on improving their individual responses to particular social challenges. Each week, three or four children will take turns presenting a specific, personally challenging situation to the group. The group will then brainstorm appropriate and effective responses, suggesting empowering body postures, voice and language (power words) that can potentially resolve the situation. We will videotape re-enactments of each situation, highlighting the child's attempt at a more successful response. We will then review the videos for commentary and assessment. Each child receives a "Certificate of Success" describing the situation and the power words used after taking their turn. We ask the parents to please write down on the sheet provided any specific situation or experience that would be beneficial for their child to work on.

This week, though, we bowl. The children enter the room set up with three bowling lanes made from plastic pin-and-ball sets and long pool noodles placed end to end, attached with masking tape. We set a table up at the other end of the lanes opposite from the pins, where leaders and/or group members can sit and keep score with score sheets made on the computer. The leaders steer the children onto the stage as they arrive, since the lanes take up the space where the red chairs and toys usually are. When we are all together on the stage, we have a discussion around bowling etiquette, how to play, listening for when it's your turn, not walking across the lanes or in front of others preparing to bowl, waiting for the person in the next lane to go and cheering teammates on.

We put some of the toys used during the open-play period on the stage along, with some games. We reiterate that as they play with the toys and games in between frames, they will need to pay attention when their turn comes up. We tell them, "If you hear your name called and it's your turn, you have to stop what you're doing and take your turn. Then you can go back to whatever your were playing after you bowl." This back-and-forth activity between turns, in and of itself, gives the children quite a workout with shifting perspective and attending to the environment.

We give the children individual score sheets made on the computer to color on while they bowl and to record their final score at the end of the game. The formatted sheet, titled *Bowling With My Friends!*, is printed in a playful font and bordered by rows of stars. There is a big illustration of a bowling ball crashing into some pins, a place to fill in the child's name and final score, and prompts, also printed in a playful font, reminding the children to *Look in your friends' eyes when you speak to them; Notice when it is your turn and which lane you are bowling in; Cheer your friends on when they bowl;* and *Stay connected by using power words to ask questions, say your ideas and solve problems.*

Kenny is happy to play with Ritchie and Sarah in between frames, but he is confused when Ritchie gets upset with him for running onto the lane and kicking over the last two pins standing after Ritchie's first ball. We explain to Kenny that Ritchie gets another turn to knock his pins down, and we remind him of the bowling courtesy rule we discussed before we started about not running onto the lanes. He insists, for a while, that he has to help knock the pins down, but he eventually relents and expresses an understanding that the friends may become upset with him if he continues to do so. We tell him he can knock the pins down a few times with his feet or hands at the end of group, if he leaves them alone while we are all playing; he agrees, although he forgets about it by the time group is over.

One hour later, during the next group, AJ eagerly waits for his turn to bowl and jumps up and down in excitement when he knocks some pins down on his first ball. His happy demeanor quickly turns to anger and frustration as Billy, who seems to have that same sensory urge that Kenny has, runs onto the lane and kicks the rest of the pins over. We slowly re-explain the game and the rules to Billy, and ask him to look at AJ's face and body. We ask him what he sees, and he says, "AJ's mad!" We ask him why, and he answers, "I knocked his pins down. Sorry, AJ!" We set up AJ's pins for his second ball, and he is back to smiling. With reminders, the children pay attention to moving carefully from the stage to the lanes, taking care not to get in the way of other bowlers or kicking the noodles that define the lanes out of place. Some need more reminding and guidance than others.

The children enjoy playing with each other in between frames. AJ puts on a puppet show while he waits for his next turn, attracting a small audience. Jack starts talking to his hand as if it is a puppet and then responds with his index finger as if it is talking back to him. We do not know if his activity is spontaneous and creative, or if he is merely echoing something he saw on television. Either way, it seems to have been inspired by his perception of AJ's puppet show. Hannah interacts with the other children and dances to Jack's singing in between frames. She jumps up and down and cheers for her friends when they knock a lot of pins down.

Ritchie and a couple of other children lose interest in the bowling game after a while and we let them be, as long as they take a number of turns and play appropriately with others. The leaders take shifts, setting up the pins after each turn, which can be exhausting, but the older children can set up their own pins, and some of the younger children, like Billy, enjoy setting up the pins as well. Doreen keeps telling me, in between setting up pins and taking pictures of the children bowling, that she's going to make a ball-return out of a long cardboard cylinder used for packaging rolled-up carpet.

As we finish up, Tommy gets a little upset about his score. We remind him about being a real winner, and tell him that, on average, "You knocked down more than half the pins *every time* you bowled!" Kenny, on the other hand, is thrilled with his 23 and proudly tells everybody he sees about his score. The children manage the general chaos and sensory assault of navigating spatial boundaries while being surrounded by sharp and sudden sounds, just as they would in a real bowling alley. They practice repeated transitioning and shifting perspective while staying focused and tending to the extended activity. We take them down to their parents, excitedly waving their score sheets.

Chapter 13

Reversal: Individualized Scripting

Sessions 26–28: Power Videos

Sessions 26, 27 and 28 use narration, simulation and video-modeling to empower effective pragmatic response to personally challenging situations. Individuals envision, script, rehearse and enact alternative responses to specific and meaningful real-life events, which are videotaped. Group members then watch their videos and perceive images of themselves being successful with the difficult task or encounter. Neurological mirroring and embodied simulation generated in the individual while viewing the video reinforces the cognitive and behavioral reorganization that occurred when initially conceptualizing and enacting the new response to the situation. The potential for transforming and reversing the individual's otherwise limited and/or ineffective role response to the challenging situation is further synergized, as the now-observing individual perceives and neurologically mirrors self-initiated actions and intentions purposefully performed by the same individual on-screen, in a sense holding a mirror of a mirror up to the mirror.

When we go to the waiting room to bring the children down to group, we collect any information the parents have to offer regarding challenging situations their children face. We prefer the children to come up with their own situations, but parental input serves as a good backup if some of the lower functioning children are unable to share a scenario, or if a group member gets stuck and can't think of anything. As we gather the papers from the parents, we overhear Kenny ask Sarah how old she is. When Sarah answers, "Six," Kenny bursts out, in highly affected but genuinely enthusiastic tones, "I'm six, too! We made a match!"

The children enter the room and get to the business of playing. Luke notices that Gary is wearing a witch hat from the costume bin and says, "It's like you're at a Halloween party!" We start ringing bells. Ever since the *Calling all Friends!* activity of Session 23, Jack has been playing with the toy telephone, camera and bullhorn, which he calls "the microphone." It's as if he's symbolically using the toys as tools to amplify his social functions of being able to see, speak and connect with others. He walks around, looking through the camera lens, asking other group members to "Say cheese!" and greeting them with the (nonworking) bullhorn, using the toys to respond to what is going on around him. At one point, he seems to think of something in particular and starts urgently scanning the room with the camera. After a while, he comes up to a leader and says, "Uh, oh! Lili [another leader who isn't here today] is missing!"

The children, for the most part, play cooperatively and imaginatively with each other during the last remaining open-play periods of the program. Ritchie and Luke draw side by side, talking about Super Mario something or other. Billy and Jonathon walk around the room together, inviting children to joke and sing with them. AJ puts on costumes and giggles with a bunch of children, while Hannah skips and dances freely around the room, sometimes laughing loud enough to be heard above the concerto of happy noises orchestrated by the children. Walter, Ian and Mike, like all of the children in the groups and everybody else in the world, have their good days and their not-so-good days. The children have found their way though to a more joyous, less mechanical play that celebrates the ongoing liberation of their creativity and spontaneity.

We clean up, meet at the red chairs and take some time during each session of the three-week period to show and tell about some objects—a dinosaur, Batman, a dance outfit, a karate belt—before we get started with the videos. The group responds and connects to their friends' presentations, causing bells to ring and points to rack up. We begin our discussion around the session's theme by asking, "What do people do to get better at things?" The children respond with ideas like "practice" and "try." We ask group members to think about what they would like to get better at. Their responses are, at first, typically limited to things like video games, physical activities and academic pursuits. We expand the concept and explain that we will be making Power Videos to practice and show us getting better at doing or handling a hard thing or situation with our behavior and the way we act.

We prepare the children by telling them that only three or four group members will be able to take a turn each week. We explain that this will give us enough time to make the videos and then watch them together, and we reassure the kids that everybody will get to go over the next three weeks. Individuals will take turns sitting in the director's chair, facing the group, and telling about something they want to get better at. Group members sitting in the audience will assist with brainstorming power words and responses that can help the person making the video to be more successful with the challenging task or situation they are describing. The children describing their challenging situations then cast group members in supporting roles, but play themselves in the videos. After the three or four videos are taped for the session, the group watches them together, with the individuals who made the videos moving back into the director's chair for a front-row seat when their particular video plays. A leader takes photos of the children as they watch themselves.

As the children view the videos, another leader fills out a "Certificate of Success" for each group member who directed a video that session. Made with the computer and blank certificates purchased from the local office-supply store, the documents are headed with *Certificate of Success* in a fancy, underlined bold font, with blank lines underneath to write in the individual's name. Printed under the line for the name, again in a fancy or playful font, is *Was Able to Get Better At.* Three blank lines are centered below that for writing in the situation the individual took on in the video, and any power words that were used to make it better. Printed on the bottom left of the document is the word *Signed* with a line next to it for an official signature by the group leader in charge. *Date* is printed on the right next to a line for writing in the date. We give out the certificates to the three or four children who went that week at the end of the session with a bit of pomp and circumstance.

The ensemble works together, creating the videos to support individuals as they take on their challenges. Ritchie tells the group that he wants to get better at "not having a fit" when he plays a game with his father and doesn't win. The group collaborates on the situation and makes suggestions for empowered response. Ritchie casts Stevey in the role of his father, and the two enact losing a game. Within the scene, he says with strong affect and gesture, "I feel upset that I didn't win!" and then, "I know I am still smart." The leader filling out the certificates writes *Ritchie* was able to get better at *knowing he is still smart even if he doesn't win a game.* Gary gets upset and disruptive because he is not chosen to go first. He rolls around on the floor and makes distracting noises. We tell him that we know it's hard for him when he doesn't get to go first, but if he continues, he will have to wait until next week or the week after to make his video.

Kenny's mother writes that while Kenny has made tremendous strides in greeting others and communicating on the playground, he does not sustain the connection and play with the other children. The leader helps Kenny to construct a situation where he meets some children at a playground and then plays with them on the equipment. While he watches, Kenny says, in his singsong affect, "I'm playing on the slide! I'm going on the swings!" His certificate reads that he was able to get better at *asking to play with kids and then staying with them to play.* Eddie's video is about controlling his anger at school, which periodically gets him in trouble. He casts his teacher and classmates, and, as the pressure to comply with the demands of the classroom start to mount, he says, "I feel angry! I can turn it around! I know how!" His certificate reflects his triumph.

A number of children, including Gary, Timmy and Mike, use the videos to address their frustration with losing video games. Jonathon presents a situation in which he gets "yelled at" by his teacher because he gets "too silly" with a particular boy in his class. He enacts the scenario, sticking out his tongue and speaking gibberish to Billy, who plays the role of his classmate. As the teacher, played by Meghan, starts to get annoyed at him, he looks to the Power Lines poster on the wall, and proclaims, "I know I can stop!" The leader writes that he was able to get better at *stopping himself from being too silly in class by saying, "I know I can stop!"* AJ's video is about not wanting to leave his house and go somewhere with his mom. He says, instead of his usual response of growling and throwing things, "I feel mad! I don't want to go!" and then, "I know I will come back soon." We write the words on his certificate.

Billy's father reports that he wants Billy to get better at knowing what to say when the family is at a store or public place, instead of talking to strangers in random detail about a Disney show. We start his video with Jonathon, in the role of store clerk, asking him what his name is; Billy replies, "Dash!", a character from a Disney movie. Take two. We prompt Billy to respond with his real name and a more realistic reason for why he's at the store, when the clerk asks, "How can I help you?" He answers appropriately and directs his power words, which we write on his certificate, to his father, played by Evan, saying, "I know I can talk about real things to people in stores." Hannah's video is about asking children to play at her school during recess, and Jack, for the most part, echoes a situation reported by his father and constructed by the leaders in which he follows some simple directions at home.

Walter starts complaining and crying, loudly, when he realizes that we are not serving popcorn with the viewing of these videos. He does find his power words before it gets out of hand, though, saying, or yelling, "I am frustrated about the popcorn!" We empathize with him and he is able to settle down. He tells us in the director's chair that he gets very upset if he thinks he will be late when his family goes to see a movie. His mother, played by one of the leaders, delivers the line, scripted by Walter, "I don't think we can go yet. Your brother made a mess in the bathroom." Walter gets worked up, tightening his fists, breathing heavily and scrunching up his face. Through clenched teeth, he asks, "What did he do?" and the leader replies, as directed, "He stuffed up the toilet." Walter's face turns red with rage and he spits out, "He *WHAT?*" The leader repeats, "He stuffed up the toilet. I don't think we'll make the 12:30 show." At that point, his rage dissolves into laughter, and he finishes the video with, "I feel so frustrated! I want to go now! But I know it's OK if we go at 2:30 instead."

Ian's mother writes that she wants him to be more discriminating when he gets mad at somebody, and not to say mean words that hurt other people's feelings. He recently told another boy who wasn't purposely bothering Ian, she continues, that he was irritating, and Ian didn't understand why that was wrong to say to him. We balance our group concepts of staying grounded in reality-based thought and using clear, empowering language to express how we feel with this more subtle and seemingly contradictory issue of accessing one's social filter in certain situations. Ian reenacts the situation, casting a leader as his mother and Mike as the irritating boy. He whispers in his mother's ear, likely utilizing a strategy suggested by his mother, and then says to the camera, "I feel mad at him, but I don't want to say it out loud because it will make him feel sad."

As individuals talk about their situations and make their videos, the rest of the group becomes very involved, making comments and suggesting power words while empathizing and supporting their fellow group members. There are, of course, typical distractions and loss of focus that disrupt the process from time to time, but these are addressed, and everyone is able to stay on task to the best of his or her ability. Like in the movies of Sessions 10 and 20, the leaders often prompt the children to help them remember lines and actions, and much of that prompting is caught on film; however, it does not detract from the experience, which group members proudly absorb, watching intently with wide eyes and smiles as they view themselves triumphantly managing their challenging situations.

Making Jack's video seems, at times, like a futile effort. He basically echoes the leader's scripted responses after numerous prompts, and doesn't appear to be connected at all to the plot, supplied by his father, during enactment. His mind, thoughts and attention during the process seem to be anywhere and everywhere else they possibly could be. As he watches himself on the video, though, his eyes are glued to the screen. He calls out, "Look! I'm on the TV!" A leader asks, "What are you doing on the TV, Jack?" He repeats, "I'm on the TV!" We ask again, "What are you doing on the TV? What story are you showing us? What are you getting better at?" He answers, "Listening to Daddy!" as he continues to watch with a big smile.

We can't say whether this experience of holding a mirror of a mirror up to the mirror through enactment and video viewing will have a long-term impact on cognitive and behavioral change in participating group members. We can say, though, that there is impact in the moment. The children speak and act in a significantly meaningful manner that has a positive effect on a personally challenging situation. The approach is structured, as much as possible, to empower the children toward self-initiated actions and intentions, rather than imposing a more superficial or adult perspective of right and wrong. The children experience the momentary shift in cognitive and behavioral perspective experientially, initiating a number of sensory avenues through which information can be perceived and processed, including visually and kinetically, as well as neurologically. For some group members like Walter, cathartic release adds an extra dynamic and benefit to the experience. The Power Videos comprise a part of the process, another piece to fit in to the neuroplastic puzzle. We say goodbye to the children, reminding them that there are only two sessions left.

Chapter 14

Episodic Outline: Tools for Reflection and Celebration

Session 29: Yearbooks

Session 29 uses narration, reflective storytelling and photographs of individuals participating in group activities to outline, organize and create a visual documentation of the group experience for each individual. The room is set up with the usual toys and materials available during the open-play period, along with a table piled with photographs and supplies, including construction paper, stickers, stamps, markers, sequins, glue sticks and staplers. The children are drawn to the busy and colorful table as they enter the room and start looking through some of the materials. When all or most of the children have arrived, and the chorus of "What is this for?" and "What are we doing?" reaches a crescendo, we sit them down at the red chairs and explain the procedure for the day.

We tell them that we will be making yearbooks reflecting some of the fun things we've done during the year. We show the children some of the pictures that were taken of them during show-and-tell sharing, storytelling, game week, telephone week, bowling, the restaurant and the Power Videos, organized with paper clips into individual piles for each group member. We hold up a copy of a page onto which they will glue the pictures, formatted with a box that takes up the top two-thirds of the page to border the photo glued inside, and four blank lines underneath with quotation marks on each side, where they or a leader will record their response to the photo.

Leaders are instructed beforehand to capture and document language expressed by group members when describing the photo in order to give the yearbook an authentic, pragmatic narrative. They prompt, when necessary, by asking the children what they were doing in the photo, who they were with and how they felt about the experience. Grammatical and syntactical corrections should be made sparingly when recording their responses on the page in order to balance the promotion of pragmatic clarity with an attempt to capture, portray and reflect the unique personality of each particular child.

We explain that the toys will be out for half of the session, during which time group members can either play or get started on their yearbooks. After we put the toys away, all group members will either begin or continue working on their projects. Extra and double photos are printed for group members to look through and choose to include in their yearbooks if they wish. After the children glue their photos onto the pages and write their narrative responses, they choose construction paper colors for the front and back covers, along with a couple of other formatted sheets to be stapled together with their pages of photos and narratives. The children come up with a title and decorate their yearbooks.

One of the formatted sheets comprising the first page of the yearbook reads as follows:

> Hello! You did a great job this year! We had a lot of fun playing and learning together! Over the summer, stay connected by remembering to look at people's eyes when you talk with them, noticing things about other people, making matches with your own ideas, and asking questions! Don't forget to use your power words when you get upset, frustrated, mad, sad, scared, worried or anything else you are feeling! Here are some of the power words you can teach to your parents and practice using with them: "I am... I feel... I can't... I want... I need... I don't... I think... I know... I can... I will..." Thanks for playing and working with us this year! We hope to see you again! Your Friends, [leaders' names]

We may also include a printed, individualized letter for each group member, formatted with an illustration of a trophy or prize ribbon on top, to be stapled in as the last page of the yearbook. The following is an example of one such letter:

> Hi, Mike! You were a great friend to have in group this year! Even though it seemed to get a little tough for you during the Spring Session, you always had a lot of good and important things to say! You responded to situations brought up by the other kids with maturity and caring. You listened, paid attention and focused on whatever we were talking about or doing. Your creative ideas and good acting made a lot of the videos and stories really cool! We also liked seeing your shows and hearing you use power words to express your frustration and solve problems. You are a good and well-behaved friend to everyone, and an important and cooperative member of our group! Hope to see you soon! Sincerely, [leaders' names]

Kenny, a few minutes after group starts, bursts into the room and announces, "Guess what, everybody! I did it! I used the hand dryer!" His mother follows him in and tells us that he just had "a big sensory breakthrough" by using one of those loud blowing hand dryers he had always been afraid of, for the first time, in the Kid Esteem bathroom right before group. We excitedly reflect and celebrate his triumph. Kenny continues to talk quietly to himself about his experience. Jack is not interested in making his yearbook just yet and sets out to find his tools. One of the other children is using the bullhorn, and he gets a little agitated when he realizes this. Instead of his usual shutting down in a corner, though, he approaches a leader and says, in his choppy, idiosyncratic speech, "I want the microphone, please" and then, with a smile, "I used my power words." We praise him for such a great response and reassure him that he will have a turn with it in just a few minutes.

Most of the children enjoy working on their yearbooks. Some, like Gary, have a tough time at first putting away the toys and switching gears. Ritchie, displaying the range of neurological challenges that exist even among the higher functioning, intellectually on-task members of the group, needs to ask a leader, after 30 weeks of working and playing together, the names of some of the children from his group who are in the photos with him. The group members work to create another mirror, a tool for documenting and reflecting visual images and expressive language that symbolizes their meaningful experiences and developing connections between self and others. When the session is over, we say goodbye and tell them they can finish the yearbooks next week, the last week of the program.

Session 30: Sharing Memories

During Session 30, the children complete and share their yearbooks with each other, recall positive and empowering events that occurred during the year and say their final goodbyes for the season. The children are excited with the end results as they finish their colorful and creative reflections. Kenny mirrors a leader who, while looking at his yearbook, proclaims, "I love this book!" Kenny echoes back, "I love this book!"

Ritchie's game-week page, reflecting step one from the "real winner" criteria, reads, *I was good enough to play with Meghan and Stevey.* He may not have remembered the names of the people he was playing with at first, but a more important concept instilled weeks ago apparently stayed with him. A page from Stevey's book reads, *I did good. I always felt good at Kid Esteem.* Kenny's bowling page exclaims, *That's me! I was having fun! I was bowling with Sarah and Ritchie!* Jack's restaurant page reads, *I am eating at the Kid Esteem Diner! It's me and Krista! I'm saying "Hello!"* He approaches a leader and says, "I'm proud of you! I did the sticker and made the book all by myself!" The syntax and word usage is a little confused, but his meaning is clear and sincere. AJ's Power Video page with the photo of him watching his video reads, *I am doing my power words movie. See that? It's a picture of me! I was excited! I got better at going places without fighting.* Timmy stamps an *F* on the cover of his yearbook and says, "The *F* stands for fun!"

The children walk around, showing each other their books. Some of the older group members exchange books and sign their names on each other's back covers. We sit together toward the end of the session, sharing memories and reflecting on some of the fun things we've done over the year. The children take turns naming, if they want, their favorite activities, what was hard for them, what they've learned and anything else they might need to say to anyone they might need to say it to. We talk about the different ways the children may feel, since it's the last day. We wonder if they may feel sad because they'll miss their friends, or maybe happy because they'll get to do different things on Saturday mornings, or they may feel a mix of emotions. We go around the group and hear from all the children. Most are sad, some are happy and some express mixed feelings. We remind the groups that some of the children may come to the summer fun program, some may return next year and some may be moving on. On past occasions, a couple of the children who seemed the least likely candidates to do so, have cried. We simultaneously console and praise them for being able to feel so deeply.

In our "goodbye circle," the final activity of the group, one of the group members starts by saying goodbye to any of the children or leaders in the group. They pick a particular way to say goodbye, with language and gestures, and tell us why they chose that person to say goodbye to. That person then picks the next person to say goodbye to, and so it goes, until all group members have received a goodbye from someone and offered one to someone else. The children take their yearbooks, and we walk them down to their parents. We hand a final progress report to the parents and thank everybody for participating.

Chapter 15

Reflections: I See You

A number of years ago, while working on a research project that measured the impact of integrating emotional intelligence skills with literacy instruction on the reading and writing scores of first and second graders (Chasen 2003, 2009), an advisor wondered, with a hint of skepticism in his voice, whether the students' significantly increased test scores were more the result of the objective instructional program or the positive effect of the facilitator's engaging and animated personality. It was an important question, since much of traditional psychotherapeutic and pedagogical theory and practice, aside from the humanistic movement in the 1960s, has been and continues to be anchored in a more measurable, personally detached, "scientific" approach. The program, not the facilitator, is what we are allegedly interested in reproducing and distributing.

The discovery of the mirror-neuron system, though, brings a whole new meaning to the notion of objective scientific approach and the elements that comprise it. Based on recent observations and measurements made by neurobiologists and neuroscientists, it turns out that the positive effect of the facilitator's engaging and animated personality is a critical, essential and inseparable component of neurological development and learning, just as the negative effect of a dismissive or controlling personality would be. Individuals, from the day they are born, neurologically imitate and reenact what they perceive in others, constituting the primary developmental operation for understanding self, others and the relationship between the two. We viscerally experience, through embodied simulation, what others reflect, and others experience what we reflect, initiating, for better or worse, neural pathways that determine how we might respond to and neurologically process the encounter at hand.

For social-skills clinicians and group leaders, the discovery of the mirror-neuron system is nothing short of profound. The affect and personality of people in positions of leadership, including classroom teachers who inadvertently teach social skills every day, has always been a consideration in terms of how children and group members learn and interact, but affective factors have typically been thought of as separate from cognitive functions that promote the acquisition of skills. We now see that this is not the case. Cognitive actions and affective intentions perceived and interpreted by members of any group have a clear and measurable impact on neurological systems and the ongoing development of our neuroplastic brains. People in positions of leadership, especially with groups of children, therefore, have a fundamental responsibility to question and consider what we reflect when engaging our populations. How do we perceive and reflect upon the individuals in our groups? How do they perceive us perceiving them? What do they perceive in their encounters with us?

In James Cameron's 2009 film *Avatar*, the Na'vi are a race of fictitious beings whose lifestyle is ravaged by human extortion and the sociopathic need for immediate gratification. Cameron creates a social custom for the Na'vi, a people deeply connected spiritually and neurologically to their natural environment, of saying, "I see you," when they encounter each other. This response transcends mere visual scanning, alluding instead to a deep understanding and meaningful connection among individuals that perceives the best in the other person on all levels of encounter: personal, social and metaphysical. We see the children who come to Kid Esteem. They see us seeing them, reflecting deep understanding of their highest functioning selves. They see us seeing, no matter what their functioning level, a whole person rather than a fragmented series of disabilities and dysfunctions. We strive to fully mirror and engage their greatest potential.

Just as leaders of social-skills programs need to mirror the potential of whole individuals participating in their groups, the approach and activities of the group need to mirror the whole experience of the social encounter, including social engagement and social learning. Drama and theatre have classically functioned as mirrors of our human and social condition. It is perhaps the cultural art form most concretely reflective of our whole experience, reflecting what we look like, what we sound like, what we think, what we feel and what we do, while purposefully encouraging, through specifically tailored images and experiences, questions and exploration around how and why we do it. In this light, drama contains a natural, "built-in" psychotherapeutic structure that promotes human development, prompting children to initiate spontaneous symbolic activity that facilitates whole, empowered functioning and effective management of life's encounters.

As an applied therapeutic modality, drama provides an approach that harnesses and aligns these naturally-occurring operational functions, providing autistic children with a jumpstart for reconnecting processes and pathways that may be out of sync. Participants gain guidance and experience with shifting perspective between self and other, a primary component of dramatic enactment and a defining challenge for people on the autism spectrum. In a Process Reflective Enactment model of group drama therapy for high-functioning autistic children, techniques and approaches mirror neurological and developmental processes, providing a template for empowered functioning. Clinicians and leaders facilitate and engage the ensemble to perceive and reflect the best of each whole individual, while simultaneously holding individuals responsible and accountable for perceiving and actualizing the best in themselves through the reflective ensemble experience.

The 30-session social-skills program utilizes Process Reflective Enactment techniques of drama therapy to reflect a social learning process that is whole, rather than fragmented. Sessions build upon skills and experiences from previous sessions with an eye toward integrating operations and processes in future sessions. Basic perspective shifting between self and other prompted by dramatic enactment deepens awareness and understanding of each, and then moves group members toward connecting through meaningful encounter within the ensemble, generating spontaneous, interactive play. Individuals are also empowered to address personal and social challenges through improvisation and scripted role-play experiences, rehearsed to prompt effective pragmatic language responses.

Group members become more fluent with perceiving themselves, perceiving others, perceiving themselves as others and perceiving others as themselves. The full range of engagement, from the initial encounter to the learned social skill, allows individuals to plug in to the process on the level at which they are able. Jack and Jason participate to build a sense of self-awareness, while Kenny and Billy explore initial connections with others. Mike and Ritchie, meanwhile, gain experience navigating more nuanced relationships between self and other, all within the same activity. These children are not, by any means "cured" as a result of their participation, but their ability to imaginatively and symbolically play, the foundation of cognitive and affective development, is enhanced and integrated within their ability to socially interact. Parents have helped to build a body of "circumstantial evidence" of the program's effectiveness over the years, with anecdotes on how their children mirror and reflect our approach to social encounters, engagement and learned skills outside of the Kid Esteem environment, in their schools, on playgrounds, at family functions and other social areas of their lives.

A Process Reflective Enactment approach to drama therapy, like the concept of neurodiversity, reveres what is outside the box and does not automatically pathologize differences among individuals. Treatment is seen as expanding roles and possibilities rather than limiting behaviors. While behavior modification is certainly part of the process, especially when working with autistic children, there is no room for judgment or criticism when the goal is empowering individuals through connection to the ensemble. This atmosphere allows children who have been suspended or expelled from other group settings due to destructive and violent behavior toward peers and authority to function in the Kid Esteem environment as respectful and compliant participants. A leader may express authentic frustration (using power words, of course) toward a group member's actions with the proactive intent of improving the situation, but this differs from a reactionary display of anger that seeks to censor and negate the individual. A Process Reflective Enactment approach recognizes that many of our institutionalized systems for disseminating health, well-being and nurturance don't work in the way they were intended to, and may actually be leading us to our own demise.

A Process Reflective Enactment approach to drama therapy strives to be liberating, healing and empowering. Leaders reach in with playful, joyous experience so that autistic children may reach out, causing a neuroplastic domino effect, initiating neural connections that prompt acquisition of social skills and enhance social interaction, which initiates more neural connections, that prompt acquisition of more social skills. Finally, while it may appear that a model of drama therapy grounded in neuroscience might drain the mystery, intrigue and dramatic tension from the process, it has been my experience that finding such a clear framework for understanding the function and operation of drama as a neurological healing agent actually frees up all that is aesthetic, spiritual, mystical, fun, silly and whimsical about drama, making these elements more accessible. The words in this text are a mirror. You are holding a mirror up to the mirror. Do you see me? Am I seeing you? May my actions and intentions inspire you in our collective efforts to heal.

References

Akshoomoff, N., Carper, R. and Courchesne, E. (2003) "Evidence of brain overgrowth in the first year of life in autism." *Journal of the American Medical Association 290*, 337–344.

Altschuler E., Hubbard E., McCleery, J., Oberman L., *et al.* (2005) "EEG evidence for mirror neuron dysfunction in autism spectrum disorders." *Cognitive Brain Research 24*, 2, 190–198.

American Psychiatric Association (1952) *Diagnostic and Statistical Manual of Mental Disorders* (1st edition). Washington, DC: APA.

American Psychiatric Association (1994) *Diagnostic and Statistical Manual of Mental Disorders* (4th edition). Washington, DC: APA.

American Psychiatric Association (2000) *Diagnostic and Statistical Manual of Mental Disorders* (4th edition revised). Washington, DC: APA.

Aristotle (1920) *On the Art of Poetry.* Trans. I. Bywater. Oxford: Clarendon Press.

Aristotle (1996) *Poetics.* Trans. M. Heath. London: Penguin Books.

Baker, J. (2003) *Social Skills Training.* Shawnee Mission, KS: Autism Asperger Publishing Company.

Belli, B. (2010) "The search for Autism's missing piece: Autism research slowly turns its Focus to Environmental Toxicity." Available at www.emagazine.com/view/?4984, accessed on May 12, 2010.

Bettleheim, B. (1972) *The Empty Fortress.* New York, NY: The Free Press.

Bettleheim, B. (1981) *Surviving and Other Essays.* New York, NY: Knopf.

Boal, A. (2005) "A Democracy Now War and Peace Report." National Public Radio, June 3, 2005.

Bolton, G. (1979) *Towards a Theory of Drama in Education.* Harlow: Longman Group.

Bradstreet, J. and Rossingol, D. (2008) "Evidence of mitochondrial dysfunction in autism and implications for treatment." *American Journal of Biochemistry and Biotechnology 4*, 2, 208–217.

Brecht, B. (1964) "A short organum for the theatre." Trans. J. Willett. In *Brecht on Theatre: The Development of an Aesthetic.* London: Methuen.

Breur, J. and Freud, S. (2000) *Studies in Hysteria.* New York, NY: Basic Books

Centers for Disease Control (2007) "Prevalence of autism spectrum disorders: Autism and developmental disabilities monitoring network, 14 sites, United States, 2002." *MMWR Surveillance Summaries 56*, 1, 12–28.

Centers for Disease Control (2009) "Prevalence of autism spectrum disorders: Autism and developmental disabilities monitoring network, United States, 2006." *MMWR Surveillance Summaries 58*, 10, 1–20.

Chasen, L. (2003) "Linking emotional intelligence and literacy development through educational drama for a group of first and second graders." (PhD dissertation, New York University of Chicago).

Chasen, L. (2005) "Spectacle and Ensemble in Group Drama Therapy Treatment for Children with ADHD and Related Neurological Symptoms." In C. Haen and A. Webers (eds) *Clinical Applications of Drama Therapy in Child and Adolescent Treatment.* New York, NY: Brunner-Routledge.

Chasen, L. (2009) *Surpassing Standards in the Elementary Classroom: Emotional Intelligence and Academic Achievement through Educational Drama.* New York, NY: Peter Lang.

Chiu, P., Kayali, A., Kishida, K., Tomlin, D., *et al.* (2008) "Self responses along cingulate cortex reveal quantitative neural phenotype for high-functioning autism." *Neuron 57*, 3, 463–473.

Cody-Hazlett, H., Gerig G., Gimpel-Smith R., Mosconi M., *et al.* (2009) "Longitudinal study of amygdala volume and joint attention in 2- to 4-year-old children with autism." *Archives of General Psychiatry 66*, 5, 509–516.

Courtney, R. (1980) *The Dramatic Curriculum.* London: Heinemann Educational Books.

Courtney, R. (1989) *Play, Drama and Thought* (4th edition revised). Toronto: Simon & Pierre Publishing.

Courtney, R. (1995) *Drama and Feeling: An Aesthetic Theory.* Montreal: McGill-Queen's University Press.

Damasio, A. (1994) *Descartes' Error: Emotion, Reason and the Human Brain.* New York, NY: Putnam.

Damasio, A. (1999) *The Feeling of What Happens: Body and Emotion in the Making of Consciousness.* San Diego, CA: Harcourt Brace.

Dapretto, M. and Iacoboni, M. (2006) "The mirror neuron system and the consequences of its dysfunction." *Nature Reviews Neuroscience 7*, 942–951.

Dawson, G. and Fernald, M. (1987) "Perspective-taking ability and its relationship to the social behaviour of autistic children." *Journal of Autism and Developmental Disorders 17*, 4, 487–498.

Dintino, C., Forester A., James M., Johnson D., *et al.* (1996) "Towards a poor drama therapy." *Arts in Psychotherapy 23*, 293–308.

Duffy, T. and Jonassen, D. (eds) (1992) *Constructivism and the Technology of Instruction: A Conversation.* Hillsdale, NJ: Lawrence Erlbaum Associates.

Emunah, R. (1994) *Acting for Real.* New York, NY: Routledge.

Erikson, E. (1950) *Childhood and Society.* New York, NY: W. W. Norton.

Erikson, E. (1968) *Identity: Youth and Crisis.* New York, NY: W. W. Norton.

Food and Drug Administration (2010) "Drug approved to treat two psychiatric conditions in children and adolescents." Available at www.fda.gov/ForConsumers/ConsumerUpdates/ucm048733. htm, accessed on November 2, 2010.

Fox, J. (ed.) (1999) *Gathering Voices: Essays on Playback Theatre.* New Paltz, NY: Tusitala.

Freud, S. (1914) *On Narcissism.* In B. Fine and B. Moore (eds) (1995) *Psychoanalysis: The Major Concepts.* New Haven, CT: Yale University Press.

Freud, S. (1965) *The Interpretation of Dreams.* New York, NY: Avon Books.

Gallese V. (2006) "Intentional attunement: A neurophysiological perspective on social cognition and its disruption in autism." *Brain Research 1079*, 24, 15–24. Accessed on April 12, 2010 at www. unipr.it/arpa/mirror/pubs/pdffiles/Intentional%20Attunement.pdf.

Gallese, V., Keysers, C. and Rizzolatti, R. (2004) "A unifying view of the basis of social cognition." *Trends in Cognitive Sciences 8*, 9, 396–403.

Galway, K., Hurd, K. and Johnson D. (2003) "Developmental Transformations in Group Therapy with Homeless People with a Mental Illness." In L. Oxford and D. Weiner (eds) *Action Therapy with Families and Groups Using Creative Arts Improvisation in Clinical Practice.* Washington, DC: American Psychological Association.

Goleman, D. (2006) *Social Intelligence.* New York, NY: Bantam Dell Books.

Greenspan, S. and Wieder, S. (2001) "The DIR (Developmental, Individual-Difference, Relationship-Based) Approach to assessment and intervention planning." *Zero To Three National Center for Infants, Toddlers and Families 21*, 4, 11–19.

Gutstein, S. (2009) *The RDI Book: Forging New Pathways for Autism, Asperger's and PDD with the Relationship Development Intervention Program.* Houston, TX: Connections Center.

Hadjikhani, N., Joseph, R., Snyder, J. and Tager-Flusberg, H. (2006) "Anatomical differences in the mirror neuron system and social cognition network in autism." *Cerebral Cortex 9*, 1276–1282.

Healing Thresholds (2009) "Applied behavior analysis for children with Autism." Available at http://autism.healingthresholds.com/therapy/applied-behavior-analysis-aba, accessed on May 14, 2010.

Helliker, K. (1983) "'Day After' yields a grim evening." *Kansas City Times,* November 21, 1983.

Herbert, M. (2005) "Large brains in autism: The challenge of pervasive abnormality." *Neuroscientist 11,* 5, 417–40.

Horvath, K., Papadimitriou, J.C., Rabsztyn, A., Drachenberg, C. and Tildon, J.T. *et al.* (1999) "Gastrointestinal abnormalities in children with Autistic Disorder." *Journal of Pediatrics 135,* 5, 559–563.

Iacoboni, M. (2006) "Failure to deactivate in autism: The co-constitution of self and other." *Trends in Cognitive Science 10,* 431–433.

Iacoboni, M. (2008) *Mirroring People.* New York, NY: Farrar, Straus and Giroux.

Ingersoll, B., Screibman, L. and Tran, Q. (2003) "Effect of sensory feedback on immediate object imitation in children with autism." *Journal of Autism and Developmental Disorders 33,* 6, 673–683.

Ingersoll B., Screibman L. and Whalen, C. (2006) "The collateral effects of joint attention training on social initiations, positive affect, imitation, and spontaneous speech for young children with autism." *Journal of Autism and Developmental Disorders 36,* 5, 655–664.

Jennings, S. (1978) *Remedial Drama.* London: Pitman Publishing

Jennings, S. (1994) *The Handbook of Dramatherapy.* London: Routledge

Johnson, D. (1982) "Developmental approaches in drama therapy." *The Arts in Psychotherapy 9,* 183–189.

Just, M. (2004) "Cortical activation and synchronization during sentence comprehension in high-functioning autism: Evidence of underconnectivity." *Brain 127,* 8, 1811–1821.

Kaufman, B. (1995) *Son-Rise: The Miracle Continues.* Tiburon, CA: HJ Kramer.

Kristof, N. (2010) "Do toxins cause autism?" *New York Times,* February 24, 2010.

Landy, R. (1986) *Drama Therapy Concepts, and Practices* (1st edition). Springfield, IL: Charles C. Thomas.

Landy, R. (1993) *Persona and Performance: The Meaning of Role in Drama, Therapy, and Everyday Life.* New York, NY: The Guilford Press.

Landy, R. (1994) *Drama Therapy Concepts, Theories and Practices* (2nd edition). Springfield, IL: Charles C. Thomas.

Landy, R.J. (2008) *The Couch and the Stage.* Lanham, MD: Jason Aronson.

The Medical News (2009) "The Center for Modeling Optimal Outcomes discovers causal path of autism." Available at www.news-medical.net/news/20091118/The-Center-for-Modeling-Optimal-Outcomes-discovers-causal-path-of-autism.aspx, accessed on March 17, 2003.

Medical News Today (2006) "Autism: Carnegie Mellon researchers discover key deficiencies in brains of autistics." Available at www.medicalnewstoday.com/articles/47180.php, accessed on March 17, 2010.

Medscape (1997) "Sexual differences in pervasive developmental disorders: How girls differ from boys with PDD." *Psychiatry and Mental Health eJournal 2,* 3. Available at www.medscape.com/viewarticle/431135_4, accessed on March 17, 2010 [fee to access].

Millon, T. (2004) *Personality Disorders in Modern Life.* Hoboken, NJ: John Wiley & Sons.

Moreno, J. (1978) *Who Shall Survive?* New York, NY: Beacon House.

Moreno J. (1994) *Psychodrama and Group Psychotherapy.* McLean, VA: American Society of Group Psychotherapy and Psychodrama.

National Association for Drama Therapy (undated) "Frequently asked questions about drama therapy." Available at www.nadt.org/faqs.htm, accessed on April 12, 2010.

National Public Television (2009) "The New Science of Learning: Brain Fitness for Kids." Producer: A. Tiano; broadcast June 3, 2009 on New York PBS station WLIW.

Oberman L. and Ramachandran, V. (2006) "Broken mirrors." *Scientific American 17*, 20–29.

Oberman, L. and Ramachandran, V.S. (2007) "The simulating social mind: The role of simulation in the social and communicative deficits of autism spectrum disorders." *Psychological Bulletin 133*, 2, 310–327.

Obradovic, J. (2010) "Autism, vaccines, thermerosal: Further study needed." *Age of Autism.* Available at www.ageofautism.com/2010/03/autism-vaccines-thimerosal-further-study-needed.html, accessed on April 23, 2010.

Piaget, J. (1951) *Play, Dreams and Imitation in Childhood.* London: William Heinemann.

Pineda, J. (2008) "Sensorimotor cortex as a critical component of an 'extended' mirror neuron system: Does it solve the development, correspondence and control problems in mirroring?" *Behavioral and Brain Functions.* Available at www.behavioralandbrainfunctions.com/content/4/1/47, accessed on May 2, 2010.

Salovey, P. and Sluyter, D. (eds) (1997) *Emotional Development and Emotional Intelligence: Educational Implications.* New York, NY: Basic Books.

Scheff, T. (1979) *Catharsis in Ritual, Healing and Drama.* Los Angeles, CA: University of California Press.

Shakespeare, W. (1975) *The Complete Works of William Shakespeare.* New York, NY: Avenel Books.

Shaw, G. (1921) *Back to Methuselah.* London: Constable and Company.

Silberman, S. (2001) "Geek Syndrome." Available at www.wired.com/wired/archive/9.12/aspergers.html, accessed on February 17, 2010.

Skinner, B.F. (1948) *Walden Two.* Indianapolis, IN: Hackett.

Slade, P. (1954) *Child Drama.* London: University of London Press.

Toman, B. (2010) "Celiac Disease: On the rise." Available at http://discoverysedge.mayo.edu/celiac-disease, accessed on March 6, 2010.

Tough, P. (2009) "The Make-Believe Solution: Can imaginary play teach children to control their impulses—and be better students?" *New York Times Magazine,* September 2009, 31–35.

Trowbridge, C. and Hoenk, M. (1983) "Film's fallout: A solemn plea for peace." *Lawrence Journal-World,* November 1983.

Uddin, L.Q., Iacoboni, M., Lange, C. and Keenan, J.P. (2007) "The self and social cognition: The role of cortical midline structures and mirror neurons." *Trends in Cognitive Science 11*, 4, 153–157.

Warner, J. (2010) "Oxytocin hormone may treat autism." Available at www.webmd.com/brain/autism/news/20100212/oxcytocin-hormone-may-treat-autism, accessed on April 26, 2010.

Way, B. (1967) *Development through Drama.* Atlantic Highlands, NJ: Humanities Press.

Yalom, I. (2005) *The Theory and Practice of Group Psychotherapy.* New York, NY: Basic Books.

Yavorcik, C. (2009) "National Children's Health Survey report finds autism prevalence now 1 in 91." Available at www.autism-society.org/site/News2?page=NewsArticle&id=15065&news_iv_ctrl=1882, accessed on April 2, 2010.

Subject Index

action 83–4
activities and games
  board games 232–3
  Calling all Friends! 233–7
  charades 182–3, 186
  Connect the Names 137–8
  Correct the Leader 145–6, 199–200
  Director's Chair 36–7, 96–7, 101, 204–11
  Disappearing Child 154
  Find the Leader 153–4
  Found a Match! 162–3, 164, 180
  Hot Toast 91–2
  How to Be a Real Winner 228–33
  Make One Thing Together 168–70
  My Story 226–8
  Name Hopping 135
  Name Tag 131–2, 136–7, 138
  Out to Lunch 237–40
  People Bingo 163–4
  picture cards 195–6
  On the Right Track 187–92
  Ring that Bell! 225–30
  Roll with It 240–3
  Simon Says 186
  What Were They Thinking? 184–5
  Your Name in Lights 129–32, 179
  see also Power Lines; video modeling, activities
amygdala (of brain) 49–50, 98
anger 53–4, 117
Applied Behavioral Analysis (ABA) 48
Aristotle 65, 123–5
Asperger's Syndrome 18, 43
  as illustrated by David 38–9
  as illustrated by James 35–7
  as illustrated by Janet 39–41
Autism Spectrum Disorders (ASD) see Pervasive Developmental Disorder (PDD)

Autistic Disorder 43
  as illustrated by Jason 29–33
  as illustrated by Kenny 33–5
automatic transmission 60–1
Avatar 260

Back to Methuselah 66
behavior management 53–6, 112–15
board games 232–3
body language 182–7
boundaries 54
bowling alley simulation 240–3
brain 49–50, 59–61, 75–6, 98

calcium bentonite 46
Cameron, James 260
catharsis 67, 89–90
  Aristotelian 65
  emotional 73–4
  and group process 120
celebration, tools for 253–7
celiac disease 47
Center for Modeling Optimal Outcomes 44
Centers for Disease Control and Prevention (CDC) 43–4
challenging social situations
  improving responses to 245–51
  language-based responses 202–11
charades 182–3, 186
chelation 46
cognition and emotion 74–5
comedy, use of 213–16
communication skills 89, 98–9, 122
  conversation building 187–92
  nonverbal expression 182–7
  see also telephone, use of
compliance to program 113–14
conceptual intelligence 72
connecting with self and others 157, 159–61, 162–5
  see also reunion and reconnection
consideration of others 226–8

consolidation of skills 170–4, 216–19
convergence zone (of brain) 75–6
corrective recapitulation 119
costumes 28–9, 107, 152–3, 154–5
Couch and the Stage, The 66

Defeat Autism Now (DAN!) 46
Development, Individual Difference, Relationship-based (DIR) Floortime 48–9
Diagnostic and Statistical Manual of Mental Disorders (DSM) 12, 27–8, 29, 35, 43, 83
diction 88, 124
difficult social situations
  see challenging social situations
Director's Chair 36–7, 96–7, 101, 204–11
drama therapy
  benefits of 41, 99–100, 260–1
  and mirror-neuron system 64–70
  and PDD children 97–102
  Process Reflective Enactment approach 70, 77–97, 101–2, 261–3
  therapeutic function 66–70
dramatic action 83–4
dramatic enactment 69, 70–4, 87
dressing up 28–9, 107, 152–3, 154–5

echolalia 30, 33, 78–9, 98–9, 205
emotion
  and cognition 74–5
  identifying and expressing 147–8, 149–51, 180, 184, 186, 204–5
  role of puppets in expressing 74
emotional catharsis theory 73–4
emotional intelligence 50–1, 89

empowerment 81–4
enactment 69, 70–4, 87
encounters, social 116–18
    simulating 232–43
engagement
    cooperative 168–70
    social 118–20
ensemble 80–1, 120
    building activities 150,
        220–1
environmental toxicity 44–5,
    46–7
envisioning 85–7
equipment 106–8
experience sharing 157–8,
    159–61
eye contact 140–1

facial expression 182–7
facilitator vs. program 259–63
Film Festival 40
finding one's self 147–51
fish oils 46
food and diets 46–7
friend, being a good 231–3
fun, role of 21–2

games *see* activities and games
"Geek Syndrome" 45
genetic predisposition 45
glycine 44
greeting skills
    greeting others 138–42
    responding to greetings
        142–6
group cohesiveness 80–1, 120
    activities for strengthening
        150, 220–1
group leadership 108–10
group protocols 110–15
guided play 95

Hamlet 64
hope, "installation of" 117
hyperbaric oxygen therapy
    (HBOT) 46

I Have Feelings. How About You? 149
imagination 75–6, 85
imitation 58–9, 71–2, 76, 77,
    84, 120
immunization 44
improvisation 96
    activities 135, 137, 160–1,
        168–9, 184–5, 195
individualized socialization
    plans 111–12
interpersonal learning 120

joining in 197–201
joke-telling 213–14, 215–16

Kennedy, John F. 11
Kid Esteem 14, 17, 86, 106–8,
    238

language skills
    in challenging social
        situations 202–11
    expressive 147–8, 149–51
    interactive 193–7
    nonverbal 182–7
leadership role 108–10
learning 99
    interpersonal 120
    role of drama 115–16
    social 121–3
locogram sociometry 95
    activities 149–50, 180,
        204–5, 225–6, 231–2
    sociometric mapping 164

MAPS (Memory, Attention,
    Processing, Sequencing)
    99
masks 95, 139–40, 149, 183–4
matching activities 162–4,
    180, 182
materials 106–8
measles, mumps, rubella (MMR)
    vaccine 44
mechanical activities, attraction
    to 45, 51, 98
medication 46
memory 99
    sharing 256–7
mirror, children's reaction to
    18–19
mirror imagery 14–15, 64, 263
mirror-neuron system 14,
    57–61, 259–61
    and drama 64–70
movie-making 31–2, 40–1, 96,
    172–4, 217–19
movie day 174–6, 219–21

Nambudripad Allergy
    Elimination Techniques
    (NAET) 46
name activities 131–8
napkins analogy 48
Narcissus 67
narration 96
    activities 160–1, 199–200,
        226–8, 247–51,
        253–4

National Children's Health
    Survey Report 44
Na'vi race 260
neurological imitation 58
neuroplasticity 49–50, 53, 61,
    122
*New Science of Learning: Brain
    Fitness for Kids, The* 98–9
noise 148, 168
nonverbal expression 182–7
noticing others 152–5

Omega 3 fatty acids 46
open play periods
    progression in 198–9
    purpose and structure
        111–12, 133
    on return to program 178,
        224–5
    towards program end 246
orientation, program 127–32
oxytocin 46

parental input
    behavior management
        process 114–15
    challenging social situations
        202–3, 240–1, 245
    communication skills 188,
        193–4, 234
    connecting with self and
        others 157–8, 161
    consolidation of skills 171,
        174
    emotional intelligence
        147–8, 177–8
    greeting skills 138, 143
    nonverbal expression 182–3
    noticing and observing 152
    perspectives, broadening
        213–14
    reinforcement of skills
        223–4, 228–9
    remembering names 133
    social rejection 197–8
    working with others 167–8
party room 105–6
personality traits 52
perspective shifts 49–51, 72–3,
    261
    activities 160–1, 187–92,
        232–3, 240–3
    use of puppets 74
perspectives, broadening 213,
    215–16

Pervasive Developmental
    Disorder Not Otherwise
    Specified (PDD-NOS)
    18, 43
  as illustrated by Janet 39–41
  as illustrated by Matthew
    27–9
Pervasive Developmental
    Disorder (PDD) 18, 43
  children with, and drama
    97–102
  developmental considerations
    49–53
  diagnoses 43–4, 53
  positive intervention 53–6
  possible causes 44–5
  treatment approaches 45–9
  see also Asperger's
    Syndrome; Autistic
    Disorder; Pervasive
    Developmental
    Disorder Not
    Otherwise Specified
    (PDD-NOS)
picture cards activity 195–6
play 21–2, 70–1, 73, 95
  interactive 167–70, 226–8
  see also open play periods
plot 87–8
  activities 173–4, 217–18
  components of 123, 124–5
polarized contexts, movement
    between 50, 65, 69–73,
    74, 85
Power Lines
  poster 37, 106, 149, 183,
    204, 248
  scripting 96
  themed hopscotch 108
  words and phrases 37, 113,
    147–8, 202–3, 206,
    210–11
Power Videos 245–51
prizes 55, 112, 114–15, 135
process-oriented social skills
    115–23
Process Reflective Enactment
    70, 77–97, 101–2,
    261–3
program orientation 127–32
program vs. facilitator 259–63
protocols and compliance
    110–15
psycho-stimulants 46
psychodrama 68–9
psychotherapy, impact of drama
    67–77

puppets, use of 34–5, 74,
    135–6, 150–1, 163, 181
Rank, O. 67
real-life events, responses to
    202–11, 245–51
reasoning 88, 124
  and emotion 74–5
recognition 88, 123
reflection, tools for 253–7
rehearsal 90–1, 172–3, 210
reinforcement of skills 174–6,
    219–21
  parental input 223–4, 228–9
Relationship Development
    Intervention (RDI) 48–9
restaurant simulation 237–40
reunion and reconnection
    177–82, 223–8
reversal 124–5
reversibility 50, 72–3
rewards 55, 112, 114–15, 135
ritual 79–80
role-play 96, 97
  activities 39, 173, 186,
    199–201, 218–19

savant characteristics 38
scripting Power Lines 96
self-awareness activities 147–51
sensory overload 40, 132
sensory stimuli 59–60, 77–8
set construction 59–60, 95,
    198–9
Silicon Valley 45
simulation 96
  bowling alley 240–3
  going out to lunch 237–40
  using telephone 233–7
social and emotional
    development theory 73
social skills
  consolidation 170–4,
    216–19
  process-oriented 115–23
  reinforcement 174–6, 219–
    20, 223–4, 228–9
  see also specific skills, e.g.
    greeting skills
sociometry *see* locogram
    sociometry
Son-Rise Program 48–9
space 105–8
special education 11–12
spectacle 77–8, 130, 135
spontaneity 78–9
stage 106–7
story-making 226–8

storytelling 96, 186–7, 253–6
symbolic representation 84–5
  in activities 159–60, 168–9,
    187–92, 195–6
Systematic Social Skills program
    20, 22
  Billy's experience 22–3

taking turns 31–2
telephone, use of 233–4, 235–7
"television talk" 30, 33, 78–9,
    98–9, 205
The Day After 64–5
"theory theory" 57
thimerosal 44
toxins, environmental 44–5,
    46–7
train activity 187–92
transformation 91–2, 101

unity 88, 116–17, 124
  finding myself 147–51
  noticing others 152–5
"universality" 88, 117

vaccines 44
video modeling 97
  activities 31–2, 40, 140–2,
    174–6, 219–21,
    245–51
visual aspects of stage *see*
    spectacle
visualization 86–7

"winner," being a 228–33
working with others 167–70

yearbooks 125, 253–6

Author Index

Akshoomoff, N. 50
Altschuler, E. 61
American Psychiatric
    Association 12, 27, 43
Aristotle 65, 77, 87–88, 123

Baker, J. 115
Belli, B. 45
Bettleheim, B. 12–13
Boal, A. 66
Bolton, G. 71
Bradstreet, J. 44
Brecht, B. 65–66
Breur, J. 67

Carper, R. 50
Celan, P. 13
Centers for Disease Control and
    Prevention 43–44
Chasen, L. 50, 69, 77, 80–81,
    82, 83, 85, 89, 149, 259
Chiu, P. 60, 61, 86
Cody-Hazlett, H. 50
Courchesne, E. 50
Courtney, R. 67, 70–71, 75,
    76, 91

Damasio, A. 13–14, 50–51, 69,
    74–75
Dapretto, M. 59
Dawson, G. 49
Dintino, C. 77
Duffy, T. 72

Emunah, R. 75, 79
Erikson, E. 50, 73

Fernald, M. 49
Food and Drug Administration
    46
Fox, J. 96
Freud, S. 67

Gallese, V. 14, 60, 81, 84, 89,
    94, 97
Galway, K. 91
Goleman, D. 116, 122
Greenspan, S. 48
Gutstein, S. 48

Hadjikhani, N. 60
Healing Thresholds 48
Helliker, K. 64
Herbert, M. 50
Hoenk, M. 64
Horvath, K. 47
Hurd, K. 91

Iacoboni, M. 57–58, 59, 60,
    67, 76, 77, 83, 84, 87,
    90, 108–109, 121
Ingersoll, B. 78

Jennings, S. 75
Johnson, D. 75, 91
Jonassen, D. 72
Just, M. 50

Kaufman, B. 48–49
Keysers, C. 14, 84
Kristof, N. 44–45

Landy, R.J. 66, 67, 68–69, 70,
    75, 78, 79–80, 83, 85,
    89–90, 93, 94, 113

Medical News, The 44
Medical News Today 86
Medscape 51
Millon, T. 67
Moreno, J. 68, 78, 82–83, 95,
    116, 119, 121
Moreno, Z. 66

National Association for Drama
    Therapy 68
National Public Television
    98–99

Oberman, L. 58, 60–61, 84,
    116
Obradovic, J. 44

Piaget, J. 50, 71–72
Pineda, J. 60–61

Ramachandran, V.S. 58, 60–61,
    84, 116
Rizzolatti, R. 14, 84
Rossingol, D. 44

Salovey, P. 151
Scheff, T. 73–74, 89
Screibman, L. 78
Shakespeare, W. 64, 65
Shaw, G.B. 66
Silberman, S. 45
Skinner, B.F. 11
Slade, P. 75
Sluyter, D. 151

Toman, B. 47
Tough, P. 99
Tran, Q. 78
Trowbridge, C. 64

Uddin, L.Q. 59, 75–76, 85

Warner, J. 46
Way, B. 75, 76
Whalen, C. 78
Wieder, S. 48

Yalom, I. 116, 117–118, 120
Yavorcik, C. 44